Representation
and
the Imagination

Representation and the Imagination

Beckett, Kafka, Nabokov, and Schoenberg

Daniel Albright

The University of Chicago Press
Chicago and London

THE UNIVERSITY OF CHICAGO PRESS, CHICAGO 60637
THE UNIVERSITY OF CHICAGO PRESS, LTD., LONDON
© 1981 by The University of Chicago
All rights reserved. Published 1981
Printed in the United States of America
85 84 83 82 81   5 4 3 2 1

DANIEL ALBRIGHT is associate professor of
English at the University of Virginia.

Library of Congress Cataloging in Publication Data

Albright, Daniel, 1945–
   Representation and the imagination.

   Includes bibliographical references and index.
   1. Aesthetics. 2. Art—Philosophy. 3. Representation (Philosophy) 4. Imagination. I. Title.
BH39.A48   700′.1   80–26976
ISBN 0–226–01252–2

1-28-82   KM

Contents

Acknowledgments   vii
Introduction   1

1 Schoenberg 11

2 Nabokov 52

3 Kafka 95

4 Beckett 150

Bibliographical Notes   209
Index   215

acknowledgments

I thank the John Simon Guggenheim Foundation, whose support enabled me to write the first part of this book in the academic year 1976–77.

Books of criticism usually begin with a page of acknowledgments, in which gratitude constructs a little Eden preparatory to the fallen world of the text proper. There is good reason behind this pleasant custom, for not the slightest book could appear without the benevolence and cooperation of multitudes, extending beyond the limits of the author's acquaintance to publishers and heads of state. Among the most notable of these good spirits have been some colleagues of mine from the University of Virginia, Irvin Ehrenpreis, V. A. Kolve, Cecil Lang, Robert Langbaum, J. C. Levenson, and Anthony Winner, whose intellectual companionship has sustained me; and my research assistants, Douglas Herman, Clover Carroll, Michele Totah, Sidney Burris,

ACKNOWLEDGMENTS

and Patricia Emlet. The angel of this walled garden, who has defended my solitude, our community, from mad dogs and policemen, is Karin Larson.

Introduction

This study, like many of the works it treats, is a kind of commentary on Balzac's *Le chef-d'oeuvre inconnu*. In that philosophical tale the young Nicolas Poussin meets a mysterious master, Frenhofer, who has advanced the art of representation further than any other painter of his time; the accuracy and vivacity of his pictures are celebrated everywhere, but he will show no one his masterpiece, the perfected image of a woman, a woman who, though made of oils, *lives*—a new Eve. Poussin is helpless with awe as the master improves another painter's work with a few touches of light; the young man submits utterly to Frenhofer, will even dishonor his mistress by coaxing her to pose nude for the old master. In return Poussin is allowed to see the unknown masterpiece; but the canvas has been so painted, repainted, painted over again, that it is a mere jumble of pigment. In the passionate mess Poussin can recover no intelligible form except in one corner, less tortured than the rest, where he can discern, underneath the "wall of painting," a single foot—but a foot of such magnificence, such attained realization, that no one has ever before seen the like.

The moral of this peculiar tale, in which are blended the stories of Pygmalion and Faust, is that knowledge, like ignorance, can lead to negation; and that the sheer effort of representation may obscure what it tries to represent. The unknown masterpiece is a damned image, an image blasted for striving to supersede the condition of an image.

Frenhofer's itch is one of the first stirrings of a characteristic urge of modern art: to create a work just as potent, just as real as a thing in the world of experience; the artist, not content with copying, would prefer to be a god. W. B. Yeats, struggling to describe the aesthetic of Pound's *Cantos*, found the ambition of Balzac's artist similar to Pound's:

> He has tried to produce that picture Porteous com-
> mended to Nicholas Poussin in *Le chef d'oeuvre inconnu*
> where everything rounds or thrusts itself without edges,
> without contours—conventions of the intellect—from a
> splash of tints and shades; to achieve a work as charac-
> teristic of the art of our time as the paintings of Cézanne,
> avowedly suggested by Porteous, as *Ulysses* and its
> dream association of words and images, a poem in which
> there is nothing that can be taken out and reasoned over,
> nothing that is not a part of the poem itself. [*A Vision*,
> p. 4]

Porteous seems to have wandered in from Scott's *Heart of Midlothian*, but Yeats means Frenhofer. Yeats discovered in the *Cantos* no plot, no chronicle of events, nothing in the text that could be abstracted from the text. The *Odyssey, Paradise Lost* are about something, are contingent on stories or events outside themselves, whereas the *Cantos* are self-sustaining, no more contingent on the external than is Frenhofer's imaginary painting—as detailed, rounded, subtle, glittering, as human flesh. Instead of imposed and conventional artifice, the beginning, middle, and end of a proper fable, Pound offers, according to Yeats, a superior sense of the realness of what he treats, as if he embodies in his text the indeterminacy, the shifting boundaries, the sudden sharpness, the mysterious design of the world as we feel it. Yeats's description of the *Cantos* was written in 1928, and one year later Samuel Beckett was to pay a similar compliment to Joyce's *Work in Progress* in a phrase to be remembered in a thousand discussions of the modern sensibility: "His writing is not *about* something; *it is that something itself*." One sees the common thrust of Frenhofer's, Pound's, and Joyce's aspirations: if art can throw off outmoded techniques, loose the shackles of grammar, solid outline, the well-made plot, it may attempt not to imitate but to *be*. Art would abolish the rules of art and embrace instead the laws of physics, the principles that govern the diffusion of light over a translucent surface, the statistical probabilities of the recurrence of events in a closed system. Yet the catastrophe of Frenhofer's transgression lingers over his distinguished successors: just as Poussin found the unknown masterpiece a chaos of paint, so the *Cantos, Finnegans Wake,* and *A Vision* itself have been condemned as a chaos of words, though many readers cherish a favorite line, a favorite foot.

Many of the most talented artists of this century have been tempted to this heresy, have tried to make works of art that hoist themselves from artifice to reality, as if a book or painting could be as necessary, as welcome, as well connected in the world's economy as a lump of copper or a human soul. One artist who has resisted this temptation is Jorge Luis Borges; and a great many of his stories and essays testify to the uselessness of the artist's desire to become a competing demiurge. In "Tlön, Uqbar, Orbis Tertius" (1940, 1947), an immense secret organization devotes itself to inventing an encyclopedia for an imaginary world; their writings capture the public's fancy, to the point that all nations become wholly engrossed in the study of a nonexistent planet; but it is attractive only because of its orderliness, because it constitutes a tidy refuge from the divine, inhuman, and incomprehensible aspect of the world of experience. A fantasy proliferates until it tries to replace the world; but the more it distends, the thinner it becomes, the more fragile, the more ostensibly fantastic, like the one-to-one scale map of "On Rigor in Science" (1946), a sheet of paper placed over every square foot of an empire, upon which the empire is translated to a decoration, at last eaten away by wind and rain until only a few pieces remain in the desert.

Borges is also sensitive to the more local and limited vanities of artists: in the satirical *Chronicles of Bustos Domecq* (1967), written in collaboration with Adolfo Bioy-Casares, there appears a demented novelist, Ramon Bonavena, who has written an extremely long book describing the contents of his desk-top:

> You're talking about the second and third chapters, where we learn all about the ashtray—the various shades of the copper, its specific gravity, its diameter, the exact distances and angles between the ashtray, the pencil, and the edge of the table, and then the workmanship of the twin china sheepdogs, and what they cost wholesale and retail, and so many other facts no less scrupulous than to the point. And as for the pencil—an Eagle, an Eagle

> Chemi-Sealed No. 2B!—what can I say? You got it down
> so perfectly and, thanks to your genius for compression,
> into only twenty-nine pages—pages that leave nothing to
> be desired by even the most insatiable appetite. [p. 29]

This kind of caricature of the modern novel is not unusual; in Nabokov's *Invitation to a Beheading* there is described a three-thousand-page novel, *Quercus,* which tells everything tellable about a single oak tree. The novelist who cannot substitute a fictitious world for our world can at least hope to raise one verbal artifact to genuine entity, a written pencil condign to an actual one. In the end Bonavena is forced to destroy everything he described:

> "The sacrifice was necessary," he explained. "The
> work, like the child who comes of age, must stand on its
> own feet. To have preserved the source material might
> have exposed it to irrelevant confrontations. Criticism
> might have fallen into the snare of judging it in terms of its
> more or less fidelity. In that way we would have lapsed
> into mere scientism. You are aware, of course, that I deny
> my work any scientific value."
> Trying to console him, I said, "Of course, of course.
> *North-Northeast* is a work of art—"
> "That's another mistake," pronounced Bonavena. "I
> deny my work any artistic value. It occupies, so to speak,
> a plane of its own. The emotions awakened by it, the
> tears, the acclaim, the grimaces, leave me quite in-
> different. It has not been my intention to instruct, to uplift,
> to entertain, to gladden, or to move. My work is beyond
> that. It aspires to the humblest and highest of all aims—
> a place in the universe." [pp. 31–32]

Here is the hope of Frenhofer, outfitted in its proper metaphysic, reduced to its absurdity: in the hope of elevating the description of a pencil to a higher level in the universe than a pencil itself, the real pencil is annihilated; but the fire that consumes the pencil will consume whatever that pencil can write. Frenhofer, Bonavena, perhaps the historical Joyce as well, are trying to violate a kind of law of aesthetic gravitation: no image can lift itself above, usurp, that which it is an image of.

Bonavena is a fool and Frenhofer is a failure; and it is likely that most artists who dabble in this kind of magic will frequently be disappointed. It is a short step from despair about the imagination's ability to make a self-sufficient and authentic image to the desire for a kind of art entirely liberated from images—what is called "abstract" art. The imagination is an obliging servant and, when called upon to provide an absolute reality, or an absolute unreality, will always offer something, though never exactly what is wanted. My thesis here is that hyperrealism and abstraction, the will to perfect images and the will to dispense with them, proceed from the same urge to transgress the limitations of art; they are related strategies for improving the status of the artwork, for enhancing its dignity, its self-reliance. Art cannot be mocked for aping nature if it can be made either equivalent to nature or, on the other hand, unnatural. It is remarkable how a work can be praised simultaneously as too real and too unreal. Joyce's *Work in Progress*, according to Beckett's essay, is at once the most abstract, mythy, artificial novel ever written and a magical seizure of reality; and Pound's *Cantos*, according to Yeats, manifest a deep truth undistorted by the intellect's categories, yet have the musical structure of a "Bach fugue," as if the poem were an abstract permutation of neutral elements:

> There will be no plot, no chronicle of events, no logic of discourse, but two themes, the Descent into Hades from Homer, a Metamorphosis from Ovid, and, mixed with these, medieval or modern historical characters.... He has scribbled on the back of an envelope certain sets of letters that represent emotions or archetypal events—I cannot find any adequate definition—A B C D and then J K L M, and then each set of letters repeated, and then A B C D inverted and this repeated, and then a new element X Y Z, then certain letters that never recur, and then all sorts of combinations of X Y Z and J K L M and A B C D and D C B A, and all set whirling together. [pp. 4–5]

Randall Jarrell, in an essay on William Carlos Williams, has said that nothing is so abstract as the purely concrete; and this convergence of the overrealized image with imagelessness, a convergence for which Frenhofer's unintelligible painting is the emblem, is a common phenomenon in modern art. The way up and the way down are one and the same.

Samuel Beckett and Arnold Schoenberg are the purest examples I know of this odd meeting of opposites: both men, at the beginning of their careers, seem to be digging tunnels into the depths, trying to embody profound shocks, naked cries, the self-torments of an isolated mind; yet both arrive eventually at a condition of extreme elevation, disengagement, elation, ether. One presses his fingers into the dirt to grasp the thing in all its heaviness, its abrasiveness; one finds a stone, several stones, there they are, *there*, now what is to be done, one counts the stones, plays with them, rearranges them, imagines the full array of combinations. What begins as a scream or a stone ends as a game, as music. In an interview with John Gruen, Beckett compared his art with Schoenberg's:

> I think perhaps I have freed myself from certain formal concepts. Perhaps, like the composer Schoenberg or the painter Kandinsky, I have turned toward an abstract language. Unlike them, however, I have tried not to concretize the abstraction—not to give it yet another formal context. [*Vogue*, December 1969, p. 210]

Schoenberg's system of twelve-tone composition, in which the notes of the chromatic scale are given a rigid order throughout a piece, or Kandinsky's tables of the emotional effects of colors, must have seemed to Beckett to compromise the freedom, the inconsequentiality of a truly abstract art, an art as eager to violate its own rules as to violate the canons of traditional art—the narrator of *Malone Dies* tells us the subjects and the sequence of the little stories he wishes to relate, and then does something different from the announced program. I am not sure, however, that Beckett appreciated the full complexity of his, and Schoenberg's, difficulties in these matters. The artist who strives for unthinkable concreteness finds his art growing abstract, disembodied, just as Frenhofer wanted to be Pygmalion and ended as Cézanne or Kandinsky. Similarly, the artist who strives for abstraction will discover solid objects precipitating everywhere from his worldless skies. Schoenberg's *Moses und Aron* (1930–32) is the fullest statement ever made of the impossibility of allowing abstractions to remain abstract: Moses cannot avoid seeing idols; his God effortlessly takes shape, concretizes himself at every turn, although God and Moses seem equally to abominate these images. Beckett too, in his later, avowedly abstract, deadhead works, cannot help making solid models of rotundas, underground plumbing, arenas; these "abstract" pieces, far from being thingless and irrelevant, posit a large array of precise objects. The pursuit of imagelessness only mires the artist more deeply in images.

Beckett and Schoenberg seem disgusted with images because images cannot be more than images; what Schoenberg calls God, what Beckett calls the "ideal real," cannot be attained through the mediation of art, at least not through *their* art. Kafka and, in places, Nabokov are concerned with more pervasive diseases of the imagination. To them, it is not only the transgression of art into magic that is futile or vain; every act of imagining is tainted, delusory, a contamination of the unreal.

Nabokov, alone of the four men treated here, believed that the goals of traditional fiction were neither trivial nor impossible, and he left portraits of vigorous, sane, and successful artists, ambitious but not overreaching—notably Shade in *Pale Fire* and Fyodor in *The Gift*. But many of his most probing and memorable studies concern men who live in falsely invented worlds, atrocities extorted from nightmares.

It may be true that the imagination plays a part in every faculty of the mind: visual recognition, speech, memory, even those acts of reasoning that depend on such prior logical forms as the syllogism, all require the help of images, even if only dim, stark, shriveled, momentary images. The corruption of the imagination, therefore, can debilitate every aspect of the human. The ages of sensibility and romanticism worried that Reason had seized control of the human mind; in this age there is some fear that Imagination may have swollen, grown autonomous, a conqueror, that Los may have grown as despotic as the Urizen he deposed. We have seen that modern art has yearned for an absolute image, a self-validating, self-signifying, independent image. The natural concomitant of the absolute image is the absolute imagination, a pullulating, astonishingly rich phantasmagoria unchecked by any standard of veracity, in which all possible worlds are equally valid, equally enticing—a nightmare would not terrify if it were not gratifyingly interesting—equally chimerical.

The second commandment forbids the worship of images; but there is another, subtler idolatry that it does not mention, the worship of the imagination. The attempt to make a work of art that possesses Being, an absolute image, is a clear transgression of the law; but much of abstract art seems to venerate an imagination so engrossed in the potency and rapidity of its own operations that it refuses to descend into any finite image. When I read Kandinsky or the other apologists of abstract art who praise the superior spirituality of nonrepresentational painting, I seem to hear the voice of pride, the implicit suggestion that no mere image could be worthy of their genius. Similarly, in literature we find novels in which the storytelling process expands giddily but in which no story is told—Beckett's *The Unnamable* approaches this delirium of contentlessness—and we also find novels in which the protagonist is a man so imaginative that his imagination strikes him dead, blind, and paralyzed—Kinbote in Nabokov's *Pale Fire* is such a monster of invention. If the imagination is god, why should not its images cringe before it? Why must images exist at all?

It is not surprising, then, that a certain fear of or distaste for the imagination should be felt, especially by the best, most imaginative artists: the imagination itself threatens the artist's handiwork. Kafka

7

and Beckett both plead at times to be rid of this compulsion, this fury of image-making that chases them day and night. Here is a passage from Kafka's diary for 27 December 1911:

> My feeling when I write something that is wrong might be depicted as follows: In front of two holes in the ground a man is waiting for something to appear that can rise up only out of the hole on his right. But while this hole remains covered over by a dimly visible lid, one thing after another rises up out of the hole on his left, keeps trying to attract his attention, and in the end succeeds in doing this without any difficulty because of its swelling size, which much as the man may try to prevent it, finally covers up even the right hole. But the man—he does not want to leave this place, and indeed refuses to at any price—has nothing but these appearances, and although—fleeting as they are, their strength is used up by their merely appearing—they cannot satisfy him, he still strives, whenever out of weakness they are arrested in their rising up, to drive them up and scatter them into the air if only he can thus bring up others; for the permanent sight of one is unbearable, and moreover he continues to hope that after the false appearances have been exhausted, the true will finally appear.
>
> How weak this picture is. An incoherent assumption is thrust like a board between the actual feeling and the metaphor of the description. [*Diaries I*, pp. 200–201]

This continual upsurge of false images is motivated by the very falseness of the images; if the true image were found it would stay still, shapely and satisfying, but in its absence the imagination exercises itself, helpless, spastic, in a vain attempt to provide a whole cornucopia of shadows when a single solid thing would suffice. This little parable is a kind of abstract of any Kafka story or novel, for the plot of *The Trial* or *The Castle* concerns simply a seeker after truth who beholds a constant agitation of false images, rising from a bottomless barrel, dispersing themselves as they grow hideous with their own unreality. It is noteworthy that this parable, at its end, pronounces itself to be another false image, both a declaration of the imagination's feverish weakness and a model of it. All figures of speech speak wrongly, usurp the correct feeling; Kafka's fictions also pronounce themselves to be surrogates, lies, evasions.

Is it possible to know what the true image is, behind such false images as *The Metamorphosis, The Trial?* I am not sure, but I have a suspicion: it is the face of Franz Kafka:

the best things I have written have their basis in this capacity of mine to meet death with contentment. All these fine and very convincing passages always deal with the fact that someone is dying, that it is hard for him to do, that it seems unjust to him, or at least harsh, and the reader is moved by this, or at least he should be. But for me, who believe that I shall be able to lie contentedly on my deathbed, such scenes are secretly a game; indeed, in the death enacted I rejoice in my own death, hence calculatingly exploit the attention that the reader concentrates on death, have a much clearer understanding of it than he, of whom I suppose that he will loudly lament on his deathbed, and for these reasons my lament is as perfect as can be, nor does it suddenly break off, as is likely to be the case with a real lament, but dies beautifully and purely away. It is the same thing as my perpetual lamenting to my mother over pains that were not nearly so great as my laments would lead one to believe. With my mother, of course, I did not need to make so great a display of art as with the reader. [*Diaries II*, p. 102]

All the histrionic horror of Gregor Samsa, of Joseph K., is mere exaggeration, artifice, a deliberately false effect designed to heighten the beauty of the dying echo, the vanishing away, the passage into oblivion in which the expression on the dead man's face becomes the true image of its author's calm; the real title of Kafka's *Amerika* is *Der Verschollene—The Man Who Was Never Heard from Again*—the proper title of all of Kafka's fictions.

It is as if the imagination were a faculty given to mankind to assuage the pain of being unable to know who we are, as if all novels or paintings spring from our incapacity for real autobiography, real self-portraiture. Narcissus, like Wilde's Caliban, rages because he cannot see any image on his film of water except that of his own face, a face that is not quite his own. Beckett seems to agree with Kafka: his Malone tells himself stories both to distract himself from his own dying and, in some oblique manner, to express it. As Malone finishes the stories of Macmann and Lemuel and the rest of his characters, he says, speaking of the personages in his exercise book: "For I want to put down in it, for the last time, those I have called to my help, but ill, so that they did not understand, so that they may cease with me. Now rest" (p. 274). Malone botches his narration so that he and his images, all random and dissimilar, will grow congruent in death.

This calculated dispelling of images is the last device in the modern artist's repertoire for producing the impression of reality. The artist who cannot name or paint a pencil into being may produce a pseudopencil, a deliberate unreality, designed to grow incredible, to vanish, but to define by its silhouette some of the properties a real pencil would have if it happened to exist there. If the thud, the shock of palpable reality cannot be manufactured, it can be alluded to, witnessed by its absence. Several examples of this conjurer's trick will appear in the chapters that follow, including the two most splendid fictive pencils I know, that of Hugh Person in Nabokov's *Transparent Things* and that of Malone in *Malone Dies*. Each is worthy of Borges's Bonavena. Such a dispelled image is the negative equivalent of an absolute image, an *imago abscondita,* as if nothing were more real than something.

It is perhaps possible, though, that this strategy for giving to fiction body, weight, the sting of truth, will begin to seem oversubtle, disingenuous, a feat of weak magic. The calm and inevitable line that ends the finest of Beckett's recent works, "Lessness" (1970), seems to deny that any act of the imagination can escape from its own imaginariness: "Figment dawn dispeller of figments and the other called dusk." The dawn that dispells figments, the dream images of the night, is itself only a figment, a dream; dusk is also a figment and dispeller of figments. Merleau-Ponty has alleged that underneath all appearances there are only more appearances; and similarly every image is only a brief state in its own dispersal, its becoming some other image, an endless flux of hallucination with no accession into reality. Images simplify, crumble, flatten, but only into other images. In this manner the making and the unmaking of images are seen as identical acts; the rubble that remains when a building is destroyed is considered to be another building, equal in dignity to the original. I am not sure whether this is a last dismissal of art or the final apotheosis of the imagination, gladly freed from all the vanity of representation.

1|schoenberg

ACHIOR. I must admit, I cannot free myself
from these traps in which your words
have caught me; but I am not convinced
by this. I yield to your art,
not to your reason. And I do not wish
to desert the gods
I worship and can see
for a God whom I cannot even imagine.
OZÌA. If we could imagine Him,
He would not be God.
Who can envisage Him? He does not consist
of parts, like the body; He is not distinct
in concept, like our souls;
He is not subject to form, like all creation;
and if you assign parts, concepts, form to Him,
you circumscribe Him,
you mar His perfection.

Metastasio, *La Betulia Liberata*
(Mozart, K. 118)

Representation can always improve, but it can never be exact. The only perfect act of representation would be a duplicate, a pointless copy; and, as Kant has told us, the idea of perfection is inadmissible in a discussion of art. At the beginning of the twentieth century it seemed that representation in art was evolving beyond all limits: Richard Strauss would soon be able to differentiate teaspoons from tablespoons by purely orchestral means; painters would make more subtly precise imitations of vision than any camera; and literary men would enact the most delicate tracery of electricity though the nerves, display the passage of ideas within the brain itself, thought anterior to speech, the Stream of Consciousness. And yet, side by side with this impatient elaboration of images, there arose an art that is skeptical of mimesis, that insists on the gulf between representation and the thing represented, that denies the referentiality of image and symbol. These two

11

themes, mimesis and antimimesis, develop together and often entwine in the work of a single artist, for illusion and disillusion constitute a single enchantment.

The violent quest for verisimilitude at the beginning of the century, the frenzy to uncover the thing beneath the semblance of the thing, may seem somewhat archaic to us, perhaps even a violation of the rules of art; but it is an endearing aspect of art, though an embarrassment to it, that great art may arise out of the most wrongheaded aesthetic theory, that the theme of the most beautiful song may be the singer's inability to sing. When representation is forced to its limits, when the artist taxes his ingenuity not merely to simulate his object but to capture it, embody it, a violent strain is placed on the whole apparatus of his technique; what he will present to his audience is precisely that strain, that tension of reaching, since what he seeks forever eludes his grasp; but this agony of representation may be as conducive to fine art as the more usual tensions, the psychic and emotional stresses with which art has always dealt. It may be stated as a rough law that the urge to do away with convention and technique, the urge to seize and display something real beyond artifice, will lead to increasing preoccupation with the purely conventional and technical aspects of art; and, conversely, that the antimimetic artist who wishes to separate the aesthetic from the real, and to abjure the latter, will discover that his audience finds his work disturbingly representative, in fact can see a whole world in his worldless art. I will call this aesthetic seesaw the paradox of mimesis; and it is the purpose of this essay to investigate, in some of the music and literature of the twentieth century, the operation of this principle—the odd difficulties that beset the artist who aspires to push representation to the point of identity and the even odder difficulties that beset the artist who tries to illustrate the discrepancy between art and reality.

The paradox of mimesis can be seen most easily in the case of painting. There is a school of painting called hyperrealism, which aims for preternatural clarity in its presentation of the visual field: the straightedge of a more naive art is replaced by a microtome, a simple street scene, the facade of a crumbling building, is displayed with no depth of field, with no distortion of air or eye, as if it were erected in total vacuum on a moon of Jupiter and studied through a telescope. The spectator sees the building itself, ponderable to Locke in heaven; all that is subjective has been refined away into solid slabs of light. And yet he marvels not at what is depicted—he has seen it himself a thousand times—but at this immense technical ingenuity, the finesse of brushstroke, the sheer knowledgeability of the artist who knows the exact outline of each piece of fruit half-hidden behind the casual shadows of wooden crates. Indeed, the artist seems to invite this admiration of artifice by his choice of such a banal subject. In theory the object is supreme and the medium has vanished into transparency; but in fact we are so enamored of the cleanness, the invisibility, of the pane of glass that we forget to look through it. The very stylelessness is an affectation of style, just as the attempt of Seurat in an earlier generation to imitate the retina's cones and rods by resolving solid color into points of pigmentation—another plausible discovery of the ultimate truth of vision—became a cliché of illustration.

Similarly, it has proved difficult to develop a wholly abstract style of painting. For several generations painters exercised every conceivable means of ridding art of representation, but for many critics representation has stubbornly inhered. When Lévi-Strauss claims (*The Savage Mind,* pp. 29–30) that abstract painters are not abstract at all, that they seem only to paint imaginary objects, one knows what he means: three blobs of paint on a fuzzy field are effortlessly interpreted by the eye according to past visual experience and become buoys floating on the ocean, balloons at sunset, mushrooms in a meadow. No pattern is ever so far removed from the visible world that philistine reminiscence cannot reduce it to something known from a life rich in bread mold, oil slicks, coral, ice needles, plumes of rust.

Kandinsky—who, despite his celebrated loosening of the strictures of representation, claims that a wholly abstract design is beneath art and would be fit only for a necktie—writes that the painting of the future will repudiate the flatness of Cézanne and return to the presentation of three-dimensional space; and in fact many of Kandinsky's canvases show lattices or arrows ranged in orderly space, spheres swimming before and behind, obedient to the old laws of perspective; sometimes one could even build a mobile of these lucid imaginary objects that, from a certain point of view, would yield exactly the scene Kandinsky has painted. It is an art remote from nature, perhaps, but not remote from representation. The paintings of Jackson Pollock, with their tight networks of spatters that seem to display no fixed pattern of shape and color but the vehemence, the effort that forces the paint into its arbitrary configuration, seem as far from representation as painting can get. Yet the expressiveness that abstract expressionism claims for itself suggests not that representation is repudiated, but that something deeper, more point-blank than the mere forms of the visible world is being represented: interior tension, the dynamics of the brain. Anger is a striated track of paint that the sweeping fist leaves on the canvas; resignation is a slow dripping. The Pollock who says "I *am* nature" (*New Yorker,* 6 May 1967, p. 162) is an artist searching for the magical seizure of reality, the collapse of the analogy that representation offers into identity—the same heresy that beguiles so many other artists of this century.

Indeed, for an artist who is genuinely antimimetic, skeptical of the value of representation, we must look to the school of trompe l'oeil, to such draftsmen as M. C. Escher, who seem to deny that mimesis is the goal of art by elegant subversions of it, in which no single frame of reference will make sense, in which space itself has grown twi-formed, monstrous. If mimesis cannot be slain, perhaps it can be tricked into committing suicide. Yet, as the paradox of mimesis suggests, it is Pollock who is still caviar to the general, whose attempts at electric immediacy appeal chiefly to the lovers of technical innovation, art historians, connoisseurs; whereas Escher's drawings adorn, or did adorn ten years ago, the walls of every college dormitory in America, have attracted a public who enjoy the simple pleasure of looking at impossible staircases, architectural Möbius strips, these teasing constructions of visual nonsense. In painting it is very difficult to show the artificiality of art, the gap between what is on the canvas and the world of representable objects to which the image points. Merely to make a poor representation does not prove that all representation is necessarily poor; and to incorporate bits of real objects into painting or sculpture is only to extend the notion of the artist's materials, not to demonstrate that a painted stamp is incompatible with a genuine stamp—I am alluding to a real painting, J. D. Chalfant's "Which Is Which?" (ca. 1890), in which a postage stamp is pasted next to its exact image. The challenge of the title is easily met now and doubtless was in 1890 too; but the stamp and its counterfeit, both of which are images, concord well together, gesture together towards a well-known world in which real envelopes can be mailed if certain decorations appear on one corner. Every heightening of the spectator's sense of the artificiality of art only stresses, so to speak, the customariness, the propriety, the naturalness of artifice; nothing is so brittle, so outrageous, that it does not belong, that we cannot clasp it to us. T. S. Eliot argues in his dissertation that the term "a round square" is not ideal nonsense, a purely verbal formula, but a naming of an object, however chimerical, in the real world. It is similar with representations in painting: whatever is on the canvas may be construed as a representation of something, however bizarre or implausible or self-contradictory, in the world of visual experience. The mere appearance of the painting itself extends the world of visual experience to include what it depicts. Reference is unavoidable. The one thing no artist can paint is paint.

The history of music, much more than the history of painting, is dominated by the notion of progressive mastery of the representation of affect. In painting, the immediate representation of emotion—

Pollock's abstract expressionism—is a recent sophistication; but in music the dangerous affiliation of mood with melody has been recognized since ancient Greece. Monteverdi, at the beginning of the seventeenth century, wrote in the preface to his eighth book of madrigals that music can depict three principal passions, *concitato* (excited), *molle* (sweet), and *temperato* (restrained). The last two he found everywhere in the music of contemporaries; but he had never heard the proper equivalent for the *concitato,* the music appropriate for a brave warrior in battle. Despite this omission, Monteverdi thought he could deduce or reinvent from meditation on the pyrrhic meter and Plato's writings exactly the right *stile concitato,* which turns out to be repeated staccato sixteenth notes. Thus, at the beginning of modern music, the extension of emotional representation becomes a principal justfication for musical novelty; and many subsequent innovations in harmony and structure will be defended on the grounds not of irresistible musical logic, but of passion. Much of what is known of early secular music is written for dancing; and music seems to evolve through the elaboration of biological rhythms, from the beat of medieval dance, the heart's iambs, to complexities of ensemble that require metronome or conductor to keep proper time, an eighteenth-century delicacy of nerves. The temple-throbbings of Beethoven seem to put more pressure of blood into music than ever before; and from Wagner onward no stricture of meter will be allowed to interfere with the representation of a tumultuous mind and body. To my ears Wagner's music is, above all else, slow; even when it is frenzied, agitated, full of sixteenth notes, there is rarely the clear underlying beat that alone can make music seem rapid. Motifs that are pronouncedly rhythmic—such as, in the *Ring des Nibelungen,* the motifs Ernest Newman calls Annihilation, Nibelungs, Hunding, or Giants—tend to represent evil, as if rhythm were the antagonist Wagner must destroy. The passionate, lovely Wagnerian motifs are typically a long, free swelling and detumescence. In the next generation Richard Strauss attempts, in the prelude to *Der Rosenkavalier* and in the *Symphonia Domestica,* a conscious representation of orgasm. The last organ that music must include for its body to be complete is the brain; and perhaps one can see, in a recent piece such as Györgi Ligeti's *Clocks and Clouds,* with its references to the philosophy of Sir Karl Popper, an imitation of the brain's humming rhythmlessness.

This little critical myth of the evolution of music as a kind of physiological extension is only a prelude to a discussion of Arnold Schoenberg, who seems to me the supreme figure in art of the twentieth century. Schoenberg's career as a composer extends from the 1890s until

1951; and the development of his musical thought will provide the best possible example of the modern artist's confrontation with the problem of interior representation. I think no artist ever lived with a fiercer desire to abolish all that is mediate, obstructive, stale, merely "musical," all that stands in the way of the emotion itself; expression in Schoenberg's early works is wrought to new intensity, new incisiveness, is given a clearer voice, a more fully articulated "body."

Sympathetic critics have always praised Schoenberg for being closer to reality, the Freudian id, than any of his predecessors; here is Theodor Adorno in *Philosophy of Modern Music,* from an essay written in 1941:

> The first atonal works are case studies in the sense of psychoanalytical dream case studies. In the very first publication on Schoenberg, Vassily Kandinsky called the composer's paintings "acts of the mind." The scars of this revolution of expression, however, are the blotches which have become fixed in his music as well as in his pictures, as the heralds of the id against the compositional will. They destroy the surface and are as little to be removed by subsequent correction as are the traces of blood in a fairy tale. [p. 39]

This striking passage was remembered thirty years later by the composer Alexander Goehr, who describes the practice of the early Schoenberg as follows:

> This way of writing resulted from the need to express new things. These long leaps, exaggerated rhythms and complex figurations are not a substitute manner of creating more conventional objects. These are, as Kandinsky named them, *Gehirnakte* (actions of brain). They are explicitly related to the protocols of Freudian psychoanalytical experiment. Th. W. Adorno says they are not the artistic expression of emotions (sorrow, joy, anguish) in the Romantic manner but the actual notations of symptoms of unconscious forces, shocks and traumata. Quoting the mysterious *tremoli,* unresolved arpeggiations of pieces like the *Little Piano Pieces Op. 19* or *Erwartung,* he sees: "bloodstains as in a fairytale." [*The London Sinfonietta: The Complete Instrumental and Chamber Music of Arnold Schoenberg and Roberto Gerhard,* p. 42]

To Adorno and Goehr, music until Schoenberg had created for itself a fairy-tale world, in which suffering and joy alike are transformed into effortless, pure song; but in Schoenberg's work the blood beneath has spilled through, an aspersion and reproach to the world of illusion, to old tales and songs in which nothing important can happen. A comparison of the mad scene of Donizetti's *Lucia di Lammermoor* (1835) with Schoenberg's monodrama *Erwartung* (*Expectation,* 1909) will show what is meant. The former is the kind of operatic agony for which the myth of Philomel is the proper description: the unhealthiness, the intolerable violation, suddenly resolves into gorgeous raving, dizzy falls of melody, voice and flute twined into a single acanthus; while in the latter it is not the soprano but the madness itself that sings. A single woman is the only character on the stage; there is a dark wood, a clearing, a path to a house; the words she sings—the text was by Marie Pappenheim, evidently written in close collaboration with the composer—are disconnected phrases, an unmistakable imitation of a patient's speech to his psychoanalyst. In the deep shadows, images slip and slide and will not stay still: a tree trunk seems like a dead body; when the woman thinks she has found a bench on which to rest, it turns out to be a man, her lover; but she cannot at first tell whether he is alive or dead. What she sees and feels, what we in the audience hear, is only the bristling of her dementia, a prolonged moonstruckness; and the music does indeed sound like "actual notations of symptoms of unconscious forces, shocks, and traumata"—one hears her feathery pulse, the ringing in her ears, the eccentric trilling of something loose and about to fall, the chirps of crickety things, the low gurgling, the leaking of sweet blood from an artery in the brain. The woman is in such ecstasy that she is disconnected from the world; her ceaseless caressing of the corpse is nearly a metaphor for her mind's desire to play upon, stimulate every physiological process, extract from the body every nuance of feeling; and the atonality, pantonality, the remoteness of the music from any conventional harmony is a reflex of the mind's self-preoccupation, its loss of society, its intense concentration upon its own processes. The woman, if she has murdered her lover, has gone mad from guilt; but her madness is not an escape into the unreal loveliness of the mad Lucia di Lammermoor, but a hellish isolation, a self-excoriation.

The audience of Schoenberg's time, like the audience of today, was scarcely prepared for the strangled clarinet, the glissant violins, the sounds of the brain entertaining itself with its own amplified noises; it seemed that madness, not content to suffer in silence, had to inflict its suffering on concertgoers as well. Schoenberg seems to satirize his own public image in an essay of 1924:

> But it should not be forgotten that the only man able to make himself noticed here will be the one found interesting by the fashion of the moment. And that varies too much to be able in itself to become the standard. Don't forget: if, for example, at present it is the one who knows

> how to scream loudest, or softest, most interestingly or
> most atmospherically as each pain jars him, before long it
> could again be the one who under no circumstance moves
> even a muscle. [*Style and Idea*, p. 254]

This connoisseur of screaming is a caricature of the expressionist composer; but in what respect is it not accurate, if the resources of voice
and orchestra are so bent, banged, twisted into the semblance of
screams? There must be some principle, some musical law underlying
the music of *Erwartung* and its relatives if they are not to be heaps of
shrieks, with only such consequence as an electroencephalogram can
provide.

One of Schoenberg's purposes in writing his *Harmonielehre* (*Theory
of Harmony*, 1911) was to investigate the practice of his own "atonal"
works; but he did not ever feel that he had adequately described the
aesthetic satisfaction that such intuitive works as *Erwartung* provided
for him and a few friends. In 1975 Charles Rosen, in his book *Arnold
Schoenberg*, proposed an ingenious explanation for the harmonic
structure of *Erwartung*, which I will oversimplify. Mr. Rosen distills
chords containing six notes each from the agglomerations of notes in
the printed score and notices that these chords tend to alternate in a
peculiar manner: chord B, immediately following chord A, will tend to
contain exactly those six notes that are not in chord A; that is, chords
A and B are complements of each other and together add up to the
twelve notes of the chromatic scale. Mr. Rosen sees in these
progressions—he calls it the theory of *chromatic saturation*—a new
definition of consonance; the ear takes a certain satisfaction in the
filling-out, the movement of sounds in the direction of a chromatic blur,
all the twelve notes played at once, the musical analogue of white light.
The end of *Erwartung* provides a perfect, perhaps a suspiciously perfect, example of what Mr. Rosen means: there is an extremely quiet,
extremely rapid smear of strings up and down the chromatic scale in
which different sets of instruments move at different speeds. This is
Robert Craft's description of its effect:

> The phrase "Ich suchte" trails off unresolved, and so
> afterwards does the music, a bar and a half of musical
> gooseflesh, an orchestral shiver that seems not to stop
> but to vanish, the listener knows not when or how. It is
> the most extraordinary ending I know of and, to my
> mind, it gives a new interpretation to the work and suc-
> ceeds in lifting it to a higher plane. [Notes to Columbia
> Record M2S 679]

Other ears besides Mr. Rosen's testify to a sense of gratification or fulfillment at hearing progressions of chords that move toward chromatic saturation: Adorno mentions it in the "Harmony" section of his "Schoenberg and Progress"; and many composers reserve for moments of special intensity the use of the blur, the playing of all twelve notes simultaneously—for example, Schoenberg's pupil Alban Berg directs a pianist, at the end of the prologue of his opera *Lulu,* to smash the keys of the piano with his forearms so that all tones sound at once. This plenum of sound, then, is the first and finest representation of the scream in twentieth-century music, the aural equivalent of Munch's famous woodcut; it is magically identical to the condition of the brain in which all synapses are firing at once, the cerebral orgasm, the oceanic experience described by Freud.

> No, it is bad to speak of it, it lies aside from and outside of speech, language has naught to do with and no connection with it, wherefore she knows not rightly what time-form to apply to it and helps herself perforce with the future tense, even as it is written: "There shall be wailing and gnashing of teeth." Good; these are a few word-sounds, chosen out of a rather extreme sphere of language, yet but weak symbols and without proper reference to what "shall be" there, unrecorded, unreckoned, between thick walls. True it is that inside these echoless walls it gets right loud, measureless loud, and by much overfilling the ear with screeching and beseeching, gurgling and groaning, with yauling and bauling and caterwauling, with horrid winding and grinding and racking ecstasies of anguish no man can hear his own tune, for that it smothers in the general, in the thick-clotted diapason of trills and chirps lured from this everlasting dispensation of the unbelievable combined with the irresponsible. [*Dr. Faustus,* p. 245]

This is a passage from Thomas Mann's *Dr. Faustus,* an imaginary biography of one Adrian Leverkühn, the inventor of the method of composing music in twelve tones. Mann was a neighbor of Theodor Adorno (and of Schoenberg) in southern California as he wrote the novel, and the figure Leverkühn is to a large extent an idealized and stylish version of Schoenberg as one might infer or deduce him from Adorno's theories about his music. We see how resonant in the modern imagination the idea of chromatic blur, the "thick-clotted diapason," has remained: it is the ultimate, beyond language, beyond representation. It is hell.

Earlier in the same chapter of *Dr. Faustus* the devil explains to Leverkühn the nature of inspiration: if it is from God it is simply a germ, the trace of an idea with which the composer must struggle, labor through many patient drafts in order to bring to fruition; but if the inspiration is from the devil it is an instantaneous presentation of the whole, a thunderclap, a fit of epilepsy in Leverkühn's syphilis-sharpened brain. No biographer has recorded any pact between the devil and the historical Arnold Schoenberg, but Schoenberg has left us a remarkable record of a similar paroxysm in his music drama *Die Glückliche Hand* (*The Gifted Touch*, 1913), in which the Man, a baritone representative of the modern artist and the only soloist in the piece, creates with a single casual blow of his hammer the diadem that the menacing, envious, astonished workmen could not manufacture with much hard labor. Creation therefore is a swift and decisive flight of genius, and in fact Schoenberg had written the whole of *Erwartung,* for example, in seventeen days. But just after the Man, laughing, lightly tosses the diadem into the gaggle of workmen—Siegfried contemptuous of the sword that Mime with all his cunning could not forge—he is struck by a windstorm, a storm of colors, a light-crescendo extending from dull red to dirty green to dark blue-gray to violet to an intense dark red, as the spectrum intensifies through a full gamut. At last a blood red is mixed more and more with orange until a climax occurs on a shade of glaring yellow, which inundates the Man's grotto from all sides at once:

> During this crescendo of light and storm, the Man reacts as though both emanated from him. He looks first at his hand (the red light); it sinks, completely exhausted; slowly, his eyes grow excited (dirty green). His excitement increases; his limbs stiffen convulsively, trembling, he stretches both arms out (blood red); his eyes start from his head and he opens his mouth in horror. When the yellow light appears, his head seems as though it is about to burst.

This is what Leverkühn would call demonic inspiration; and Schoenberg seems to have deployed every resource of music and lighting in a sensory assault, eye and ear alike engrossed by chromatic saturation. The music for the strings insists on chord after chord distilled to maximum dissonance; and from this harmonic pressure numerous unclear motifs for trumpet, celesta, and woodwind are continually extorted, an image in sound and light of the iridescence of glaucoma, the nimbus of migraine, brain swelling, convulsion.

This moment is, I take it, the end point of expressionism. Expression is in danger of becoming literal ex-pression, extrusion of brain tissue; the barriers between inside and outside, the skull and the impermeable meninges, are about to break from too much pressure; art is frustrated that it cannot go beyond the conditions of art, into the annihilation of sensuous intermediaries, into the direct insertion of electrodes, exencephaly. In *Die Glückliche Hand,* this scene of revelation yields to the Man no accomplishment or joy, only a nagging despair; the Woman, who seems ambiguously to represent visionary beauty eluding his pursuit or a public hostile to his person, at last deserts him for good; and the drama ends, as it began, with a tableau of the Man eaten alive by a fantastic animal, a hyena-bat, and mocked by a chorus that reviles him for trying to find worldly fulfillment of his unworldly vision, for not contenting himself with what he can grasp, his own body, his own physical and mental pain: "Do you not feel what you touch, the wounds first in your flesh, the pain first in your body, the joy that is absent from your soul?"

The happiest hand is the hand most content to explore immediate sensation, the environment nearby; and *Die Glückliche Hand* is a fine parable of the artist of the early twentieth century, who espouses an aesthetic of simple expressionism, the depiction of common pain and joy, but whose imagination leads him onward to impossible or divine expression, regions of lightning and howling, storm and stress, which can never find satisfactory representation in art, in which the depiction of catastrophe itself becomes catastrophic. The Schoenberg who limits himself to the good advice of his chorus, the openhanded, finely delineating, accessible Schoenberg of *Verklärte Nacht,* the first and fourth string quartets, the *Book of the Hanging Gardens,* or the piano suite, is a great and attractive composer. But it is the Schoenberg of the wilderness that is the concern of this essay, the Schoenberg of the *Gurre-Lieder,* the second string quartet, *Erwartung, Moses und Aron*— irrational, lavish, unbalanced works, pieces that assault the limit of expression and venture into rapture, unreliability, the unintelligibleness of God.

What gives Schoenberg's experimental pieces their peculiar savor is his intelligent recognition of the impossibility of what he attempts. It is characteristic of Schoenberg that in *Die Glückliche Hand* a choral commentary is appended to the sudden kindling of the artist's inspiration, his shivering into light, in order to deride the artist for attempting to convey the unconveyable not five minutes after it is conveyed. It is an unwieldy solution for the problem that Schoenberg also will set himself in his masterpiece, *Moses und Aron* (1932): how to try a feat of magic, the representation of what can never be brought to earth, and yet simultaneously show that the trick has failed, illustrate the distance between the sensuous image presented in music and that which it can never actually be the image of. Schoenberg remains obsessed by the art of interior verisimilitude, the art of the blast or short circuit, direct connection of brain to brain, throughout his career; but, except in *Erwartung*, there is typically some retreat from ambition or confession of failure whenever he attempts it. In *Die Glückliche Hand* it is the debunking chorus. In *Pierrot Lunaire* (1912) there is a song called "Vulgarity" in which Pierrot drills a hole into the bald skull of his fellow clown Cassander; he plugs tobacco into the hole, screws in a pipestem, and smokes comfortably as Cassander "rends the air with screaming." One can see the same preoccupation with opening up the brain to immediate experience, expression, as in the bursting head of *Die Glückliche Hand*. As Kafka says, "A segment has been cut out of the back of his head. The sun, and the whole world with it, peep in" (*Diaries II*, p. 192). But this is a minor, deformed, ironic analogue of immediate experience, the screaming of Cassander depicted only by the tiny monotone of a piccolo note. Schoenberg ridicules the notion of high expressionism here; it has sophisticated into a puppet show, and no spots of blood can intrude sinisterly into the fairy tale when all the characters are made of wood. Schoenberg's last experiment with trephination is the third string quartet (1927), although there is a programmatic description of a doctor's hypodermic needle entering his heart, after a nearly fatal attack, in the string trio (1946) (Willi Reich, *Schoenberg: A Critical Biography*, p. 219). Of the third quartet's first movement Schoenberg wrote:

> As a little boy I was tormented by a picture of a scene of a fairytale "Das Gespensterschiff," (The Ghostship) whose captain had been nailed through the head to the topmast by his rebellious crew. I am sure that this was not the "program" of the first movement of the third string quartet. But it might have been, subconsciously, a very gruesome premonition which caused me to write this work, because as often as I thought about this movement, that picture came to my mind. I am afraid a psychologist might use this story as a stepping-stone for premature conclusions. Being only an illustration of the emotional background of this movement, it will not furnish enlightenment of the structure. [*Schoenberg Berg Webern: The String Quartets: A Documentary Study*, ed. Ursula v. Rauchhaupt, DG 2720 029, p. 52]

Despite Schoenberg's discouragement, I am tempted to hear in the movement's first theme—a chattering melody in accented eighth notes—a representation of the light, incessant strokes of the crew's hammer; and in the second theme, a woeful falling motif in sustained notes, a representation of the captain's wailing, the slow liquidation of his pain. But in any case Schoenberg has used this grisly picture only as a stimulus to his imagination; the movement obeys the strict formality of the sonata, and no untoward event, no cerebral accident, disrupts the neat flow of the music.

In fact, the reader of Schoenberg's essays would scarcely suspect that Schoenberg the musician ever attempted any sort of violence or electrical discharge or experimentation with the dangerously vivid. But this is perhaps not odd, for Schoenberg was accused in public of such musical insanity that it is to be expected that he would display himself as a sober, conservative, unsparing yet benign man. And yet one can find a few passages in Schoenberg's prose in which the usual self-publicity, the caution, the sarcasm disappear and Schoenberg reveals the composer struck dumb before the inexpressible revelation—the same picture as that of *Die Glückliche Hand:*

> In Divine Creation there were no details to be carried out later; "There was Light" at once and in its ultimate perfection.
>
> Alas, human creators, if they be granted a vision, must travel the long path between vision and accomplishment; a hard road where, driven out of Paradise, even geniuses must reap their harvest in the sweat of their brows.
>
> Alas, it is one thing to envision in a creative instant of inspiration and it is another thing to materialize one's vision by painstakingly connecting details until they fuse into a kind of organism.
>
> Alas, suppose it becomes an organism, a homunculus or a robot, and possesses some of the spontaneity of a vision; it remains yet another thing to organize this form so that it becomes a comprehensible message "to whom it may concern." [*Style and Idea,* p. 215]

This system of metaphors governs much of Schoenberg's thinking: musical structure, the succession of notes in time, is a physical body, intricate, fascinating, but ultimately of no value except insofar as it can point beyond itself to something psychic, immaterial, instantaneous, all white light. What Schoenberg wishes to convey is not the clever articulation of his golem, its obliging eagerness to haul water or dance, but instead the divine breath that animates it, as if the subject of a musical composition were neither its themes nor its development, but Inspiration itself.

In an early aphorism Schoenberg says that "the work of art is a labyrinth, at every point of which the initiate knows the entrance and the exit" (Adorno, p. 114), in which even false paths and digressions lead toward the proper goal. Again we see the same emphasis on indications, pointing, an apparent multiplicity of arrows and cues that in fact leads to some single indefinable goal. There is something gnostic in these doctrines, and, though Schoenberg is properly known as the keenest investigator of harmony, technique, and sound color of his era, one must not forget that to his ear even the most delicate, subtle, uncanny combination of sound is still somewhat heavy, lumpish; he musters every technique known and invents what was not employed before, only that he may pass beyond technique, rid himself of all baggage. Schoenberg even has a certain contempt for the purely aural aspects of music—timbre, instrumentation, the blandishments of sound:

> I am much less irritated than amused by the critical re-
> mark of one Dr. X, who says that I do not care for
> "sound."
> "Sound," once a dignified quality of higher music, has
> deteriorated in significance since skilful workmen—
> orchestrators—have taken it in hand with the definite and
> undisguised intention of using it as a screen behind which
> the absence of ideas will not be noticeable. Formerly,
> sound had been the radiation of an intrinsic quality of
> ideas, powerful enough to penetrate the hull of the form.
> Nothing could radiate which was not light itself; and here
> only ideas are light. [*Style and Idea*, p. 240]

Here it seems that music and those notes that alone can convey music can be nearly antithetical. If the composer lacks the single-minded vision of some exterior goal toward which all the players' gestures point, then the audience hears only noise, a dead husk; the "robot" is only a heap of tin after all, unless a spark of inspiration can animate him.

Schoenberg's habitual violations and supersessions of the received rules of the art, in order to surpass "music" entirely in favor of something more electrical, are attempts to realize a music in which the audience's primary experience is not of sound but of light; all is pointless and trivial that does not resemble solar radiation. No wonder such a composer would include a color organ in the score of *Die Glückliche Hand* or would, in his 1938 setting of the *Kol Nidre*, require a narrator to shout the words "Let there be light!" above a single trill of such volume and intensity that the auditor might imagine a whirligig inside his head, eating his eyes away.

> Let there be light! Out of space a flame burst forth. God
> crushed that light to atoms. Myriads of sparks are hidden
> in our world, but not all of us behold them.

It is the task of the composer to seek out these sparks, engage and enfold them in the case of musical form for public display, for the enlightenment of the unrepentant.

The sound and the substance do not matter. Another who agreed with Schoenberg's philosophy was Wassily Kandinsky; and their mutual admiration, mutual fructification, at a critical moment in both their careers, 1912, is one of the remarkable events in the history of modern art. Kandinsky thought that Schoenberg's music bore the closest analogy to his own aesthetic goals; as he says in *Concerning the Spiritual in Art,* Schoenberg "leads us into a realm where musical experience is a matter not of the ear but of the soul alone" (p. 17):

> To those who are not accustomed to it the inner beauty appears as ugliness because humanity in general inclines to the outer and knows nothing of the inner. Almost alone in severing himself from conventional beauty is the Austrian composer, Arnold Schoenberg. He says in his *Harmonielehre:* "Every combination of notes, every advance is possible, but I am beginning to feel that there are also definite rules and conditions which incline me to the use of this or that dissonance." [pp. 16–17]

Schoenberg's music records the very motions of the spirit, untrammeled by the usual apparatus of form and harmony; and, like Goehr and Adorno after him—Adorno's favorite description of Schoenberg is "seismographic," suggesting a vibrating needle, intense sensitivity to the depths of being—Kandinsky feels that a certain superficial ugliness results from extreme psychic delicacy, unconventional self-expression. In this way much of the oddity of twentieth-century art results from the horror the artist feels at contaminating his vision with paintbrush or instrumental sound; and ugliness, external ugliness, becomes a proof of honesty, a kind of badge that proves to the world the artist's contempt for his material medium.

What Schoenberg learned from Kandinsky is more complicated; indeed, *Concerning the Spiritual in Art* is a book sufficiently ambiguous to justify many different aesthetic stances. Schoenberg's chief response to Kandinsky was the essay "The Relationship to the Text," published in 1912 in a publication Kandinsky supported, *Der Blaue Reiter:*

> Thence it became clear to me that the work of art is like every other complete organism. It is so homogeneous in its composition that in every little detail it reveals its truest, inmost essence. When one cuts into any part of the human body, the same thing always comes out—

blood. When one hears a verse of a poem, a measure of a composition, one is in a position to comprehend the whole. Even so, a word, a glance, a gesture, the gait, even the colour of the hair, are sufficient to reveal the personality of a human being. So I had completely understood the Schubert songs, together with their poems, from the music alone, and the poems of Stefan George from their sound alone, with a perfection that by analysis and synthesis could hardly have been attained, but certainly not surpassed. However, such impressions usually address themselves to the intellect later on, and demand that it prepare them for general applicability, that it dissect and sort them, that it measure and test them, and resolve into details what we possess as a whole. And even artistic creation often goes this roundabout way before it arrives at the real conception. When Karl Kraus calls language the mother of thought, and Wassily Kandinsky and Oskar Kokoschka paint pictures the objective theme of which is hardly more than an excuse to improvise in colours and forms and to express themselves as only the musician expressed himself until now, these are symptoms of a gradually expanding knowledge of the true nature of art. And with great joy I read Kandinsky's book *On the Spiritual in Art,* in which the road for painting is pointed out and the hope is aroused that those who ask about the text, about the subject-matter, will soon ask no more. [*Style and Idea,* p. 144]

Kandinsky here is called upon to support the theory that, when a composer sets a poem to music, or a painter paints a portrait, it is not the lyric or the sitter that is illustrated, given an image, but the composer or painter who illustrates himself by means of this oblique vehicle. (This theory is to some extent a misreading of *Concerning the Spiritual in Art,* for Kandinsky does not regard self-expression as the highest goal of art. Although he despises whatever impedes the artist's free expression and uses this as a ground on which to attack the constraints imposed by the old obligation to imitate nature, he nevertheless also is certain that the expression of the artist's personality is unimportant compared with the artist's obligation to something in art that is so worldless and pure that it transcends nation, epoch, and personality alike—see Kandinsky, pp. 34–35.) Schubert's songs, according to this theory, express first Schubert, and only secondarily Goethe. Schoenberg goes so far as to allege, at the end of his essay, that the relation of Stefan George's poems to Schoenberg's song-settings of them is that of carbon to albumen. Again we see the hatred of the material; the artist is the alchemist who takes charcoal—dirt—and refines it, quickens it, transforms it into egg white, whips it into a froth, resolves it into a luminous medium for self-presentation, a kind of ectoplasm. What Schoenberg chiefly learns from Kandinsky is that the multifarious forms of the natural world constitute a heavy chaos until the artist abstracts them, sublimes them, raises himself by means of these airy vehicles toward the single apex of spirit, the One, a pyramid surmounted by a solitary gleaming eye.

Yet this early essay does not provide a solution to the problem of expression wholly satisfactory to Schoenberg. Near the end of his life he repudiated the doctrine that a song's only obligation is to express its composer, not its text, in a note to bad modern composers called "This Is My Fault." Here he acknowledged that certain of his early writings might be misinterpreted to mean that a composer was allowed to write music "in a strict aversion against all that his text presented" (*Style and Idea,* p. 146). What was in 1912 a manifesto, an unshackling of creativity, has become by 1949 an invitation to licentiousness; and Schoenberg ridicules music that is incongruous to its text: "Why not play a boogie-woogie when Wotan walks across a rainbow in Valhalla?" (p. 146).

In 1912 Schoenberg argued, almost paraphrasing a passage of Kandinsky's (*Concerning the Spiritual in Art,* p. 51), that apparent divergences between music and text "were necessary because of a higher parallelism" (*Style and Idea,* p. 145); but Schoenberg's greater tact in 1949 clearly required that lower parallelism be observed as well. One is tempted to believe that Schoenberg has retreated from his earlier notion of the primacy of self-expression, but he has not; the bad composer who would conceive of asking Wotan to jitterbug is not asserting that the composer's self-expression takes precedence over the expression of his text, he is instead blaspheming against self-expression:

> In the near future there will be machines like the lie-detector, and the craft of the graphologists will be developed and supported by similar devices and gadgets. They will accurately reveal what you hide and tell what you expressed—your bluff will then be called. [*Style and Idea,* p. 147]

What Schoenberg is attacking, then, is the attempt by recent composers to justify dishonesty, deliberate self-concealment in parody or chosen banality, by his own theory of radical self-expression. Concealment is impossible; by their music ye shall know them. This, then, is the attitude of Schoenberg's maturity toward self-expression: it is inevitable, and therefore not a goal toward which music strives but a condition of its being. It is in light of this attitude that one should understand Schoenberg's reevaluation in 1926 of his essay of 1912:

> This is the point to mention that the appeal to the "text" in operas, songs and symphonic poems must be regarded as one attempt at producing cohesion among the heterogeneous elements, and to recall that in my essay, "The Relationship to the Text," in *Der Blaue Reiter*, 1912, I was perhaps the first to turn away from expressive music—theoretically, for the time being—very soon after my first steps in a new territory where I had still been using expression to the fullest extent, even if unconsciously. [*Style and Idea*, p. 260]

This is, I believe, another version of the paradox of mimesis. The more expressive a work of art becomes, the more the very effort of that expressiveness complicates the single-minded effect for which the artist strives. The greater the strain of every technical resource grows in the struggle to achieve breakthrough and revelation, the more the massiveness of the technique calls attention to its artificiality. The more one insists that expression is the only aim of art, the more befuddled the audience grows about just what it is that is expressed.

One of Schoenberg's other occupations in 1912 was the writing of *Die Glückliche Hand,* with its artillery, battering rams, and flamethrowers all directed at self-projection, self-expression; and its inevitable concomitant is a turning away from self-expression to some other aesthetic. One reaches a wall, and then further pounding is in vain. It is odd that Schoenberg in 1926 conceived his *Der Blaue Reiter* essay of 1912 as a turning away from expressive music, when it only asserted that there was a higher expressiveness beyond the mere supplying of decorative effects suggested by the imagery of poems; but indeed Schoenberg was evolving in the critical years after World War I a new kind of music, in which his earlier explorations of self-expression were abandoned. The atonal style of composition was discarded, with its reliance on intuition, the unconscious, free association; and what replaced that style is perhaps the most peculiar discipline an artist ever imposed upon himself, the method of composition with twelve tones, in which expression seems, on the face of it, impossible.

But before we discuss the nature of self-representation in twelve-tone music we must investigate another aspect of Schoenberg's thought. I have said that the metaphor of a physical body behind which lies something else, an implicit governing idea, is one of Schoenberg's most frequent analogies for the relation of the sequential, discursive pattern of sounds to the particular inspiration of a piece, its entelechy; and in the passage from the essay of 1912 cited above, Schoenberg refers to the central idea of a composition as something homogeneous, circulating like blood through every member of the musical organism. This image is refined in 1931, in a discussion of the nature of repetition in music:

> Whereas in the poem the strophes, the non-repeated parts, test the meaning of the refrain, in the musical rondo there is a different point to those sections which are seldom or never repeated. They are subsidiary and incidental ideas, whose point and purpose is digression, linking, introduction, transition, preparation, interruption, etc.—and contrast, which banishes the danger of monotony arising from so much repetition. The point of all these is purely functional and promotes the aims of the principal theme. That is their importance, and the degree of need to repeat them is in keeping with it, as also with their development. They serve their purpose at once, on the spot. And just as in our body blood is present throughout, whereas eyes, arms, legs, etc., occur merely twice, so here, too, the subordinate status of the merely auxiliary organs is expressed in the form of less prolific repetition. [*Style and Idea*, p. 266]

A rondo is an episodic form in which the main melody frequently recurs in the midst of a symmetrical pattern of digressions, such a form as ABACABA; it is a pleasing articulation, a labyrinth designed not to confuse but to indicate its entrance and exit in every passage. No theme can fully embody the idea behind the work, that "soul" that surpasses any realization in sound; but, in a composition containing several themes, the most repeated, the most insisted-upon theme is closest to the abstract idea, the statement of which is the goal of the work. As Kandinsky says, frequent repetition of a word "will not only tend to intensify the inner harmony but also bring to light unsuspected spiritual properties of the word itself" (p. 15). If the composer is to cut to the quick, the blood must take precedence over the arms and legs, the mere structural members, the digressions.

If one regards Schoenberg's earliest atonal compositions according to this corporeal metaphor, they are all body. What makes them hard to listen to—and they are still difficult to hear, seventy years after they were written—is precisely that nothing is repeated. Schoenberg's ear became bored more easily than any before him. What most angers him about Debussy, about Wagner, about any composer, is excessive repetition; and in his own works from 1908 until World War I he composes music of endless melody, endlessly shifting harmony, in which no note can be felt as a consequence of the notes before it according to the usual principle. Therefore every bar is a new event or bears only the traces of its evolution within itself. When Mann's Leverkühn invents the aphorism—it was actually invented by Adorno—that art would like to stop being pretense and play and instead become knowledge, it is a motto appropriate to Schoenberg's atonal works, which suppress any feeling of play by the sheer novelty of gesture, perfect irregularity of form. What has no discernible rules cannot be a game. This unpredictability is also responsible for the nervous quality of the music; what Schoenberg represents in the "body" of such a composition as *Erwartung* is chiefly a web of nerves, responding to a near-random succession of shocks and cries, which may be self-induced or may be inflicted from without, though one cannot know, since there is only the inconsequent flayed skin. Thus Adorno speaks justly of the new "reality" in Schoenberg's work, the fairy tale disfigured by something welling from beneath. Schoenberg seems to cut beneath illusion, to approach his goal, his central idea, not by means of some carefully articulated structure of repetition and digression, but by some higher nakedness, some higher immediacy; *Erwartung* does not point to something beyond itself, it *is* that thing. The chromatic smear at its conclusion, the "bit of musical gooseflesh," is a declaration of some greater existential fullness than was previously available to art. If all notes are played at once, all cries cried out in perfect choiceless unrestraint, then one has gone as far as possible toward making art *be*. The labyrinth is razed, exploded; one need not search for the thread that displays entrance and exit, for one is already outside, in the blank air.

Erwartung may succeed as a drama, but as magic it fails; the barrier between the artist and audience remains, and we know that the gooseflesh is on someone's skin but only vicariously on our own. Adorno has a shrewd critique of the aesthetic by which art attempts to be more real than reality: "Since the work, after all, cannot be reality, the elimination of all illusory features accentuates all the more glaringly the illusory character of its existence" (p. 70). If a demented biologist were to sew bat's wings and a goat's head onto a lizard, teach the poor creature to flap and yowl, the chimera would not become less chimerical for being real; art cannot grow so substantial, so insistent, so identical to body or mind that it can become objective in the way that natural things are objective, self-reliant, uncomplicit with illusion. Art's claim to uncontingent reality cannot be admitted; but Schoenberg's lifelong quest for the real, the setting-out in music of the most authentic cry, the decisive spasm of light, is no less moving for that necessary unfulfillment.

After *Erwartung* and its contemporary works Schoenberg seems to have grown tired of the nervousness, the corporeality; and a certain revulsion against the music of the body occurs. What he had hoped would be the eidolon of a human physique becomes first a homunculus, then a robot. In a little essay of 1923, "New Music," Schoenberg denounces a group of young composers for writing "psychological music":

> I hear that the young call their music "psychological" music. This supposedly means its effect is to be purely on the nerves. But the only changes needed for that would not be in the music, but in the nerves. One cuts them off from the rest of the personality, and henceforth the oldest and newest music alike will merely tinkle in the ears— nobody will have to think about an artist any more. That is easy enough, but I find it correspondingly difficult to think how to produce the necessary music. Imagine the X-rays it will need to use, if its own effect is to be limited to the lower half of the mind. Or, since the complete personality turns away these rays, are they supposed to stop short in monstrous disorder? What sort of parts must one write to achieve this? [*Style and Idea*, p. 138]

A snide comment at the beginning of this piece makes it clear that the composers to whom this is addressed are the followers of Richard Strauss; but he has forgotten for a moment that he, Arnold Schoenberg, is the most distinguished of that crew. Indeed, the final scene of Strauss's *Salome* is one of the principal antecedents of *Erwartung*— there is perhaps a subtle allusion to *Salome* when the woman sings, "now I kiss myself to death upon you," as she embraces her lover's corpse, over a melody similar to that over which Salome sings of biting the mouth of the dead Jokanaan as one bites into ripe fruit. In many of Schoenberg's earlier works horror is evoked by Straussian means— *col legno* violins, grisly string harmonics designed to raise the hair on one's body with the impact of chalk scraping on a blackboard. That Schoenberg is speaking in this essay of tendencies in his own music is shown by a passage in which he tells these deluded youths that he himself has had to overcome the same temptations.

Schoenberg is, in effect, announcing the end of his own attempts at psychic verisimilitude, the style of *Erwartung* and *Die Glückliche*

Hand. It is interesting to note here the intimacy music can have with the physical body—it is an X ray penetrating body and brain, and a direct electrical stimulus to the nerves as well:

> To say it without more ado: if I understand aright, the young demand that their listeners are no longer to take a musical impression for anything more than it is. They want the sound that goes in at one ear to do nothing, before it goes out at the other, but stimulate the brain or spinal cord at a more or less definite point. (I trust I reproduce this in its full severity.) And it is of their listeners (I repeat) that they demand this—for only the latter are in a position to localize the impression, and even that only if they succeed in making themselves into a body which is, up to a point, non-conductive for music. This is certainly not impossible; joking apart (if without charity), it is not impossible, as one sees from the popular saying that certain dance music goes where it belongs—to the feet. [*Style and Idea,* pp. 138–39]

Schoenberg derides the lavish attention to sound quality, musical color, the notion that the acoustic response to music should be like the response of Volta's dead frogs to electrical current; but his derision is clearly directed against a caricature of aspects of his own earlier music. He is trying to extricate music from the organism, from psychology, from the "lower half of the mind"; he wishes now to write a kind of music that is not the magical image of a perceiving human body, of the sensory network, but is instead something higher, the music of the soul. First Schoenberg attempted to capture inspiration, the soul's trembling, by a complicated simulation of physical reflexes, nervous tremors; but by 1923 he has seen that to dwell on such sensation too minutely may tend to isolate the body from the soul, so involve the body in the delicacy of its own responses that it leads downward into the fallen world, not upward into the spirit.

Madness is an attractive subject for writers and composers insofar as the representation of pure psyche, the mind wholly subjective and involute, can be accomplished only when the mind it depicts is cut off from any sane relation to an external world. A work like *Erwartung* can arise only from a composer of extraordinary purity of intention, who wishes to record and capture the mind in itself, uncontaminated by any soddenness or grossness of matter, who wishes to display only the nervous system in its quickest, most enraptured, most elevated state. But such intensity of subjectivity is itself a corruption of the mental faculties; and in any case, though the tension of the music can be heightened and heightened and heightened by harmonic means, eventually the discord begins to rest more easily on the ear, the music starts to slacken, to lose the illusion that it is representing a mind screwed to the breaking point by terror. This is the phenomenon Schoenberg called "the emancipation of the dissonance," the ear's acclimatization to minor seconds, major sevenths, augmented fourths, the classical discords. The *diabolus in musica,* when confronted headlong, begins to smile, his horns shorten, his face grows less red, he begins a little shuffle and song. Every resource of dissonance is deployed to evoke the physical edge of horror on the audience, the slow bristling, the sudden start; yet after a while the audience begins to hear the music not as the representation of a crazy mind, but as music again, intelligible though strange sounds, descant and melody. The artifice of art, musicality of music, according to the paradox of mimesis, will reassert itself most strongly when most distorted to representation. *Erwartung,* when stripped of its aesthetic, its rationale, relapses at last into the *lyrical;* it converges with that to which it seemed so fundamentally opposed, the mad scene of *Lucia.* Both are really unreal, unreally real.

One of Schoenberg's first desires after composing *Erwartung* was to justify it as pure music, in his *Harmonielehre* (1911); and the principal movement of his imagination for the next ten years is to turn away from psychological representation to other tactics for embodying the unnamable, the inspiration, the idea. One celebrated trial was the *Six Little Piano Pieces,* opus 19 (1911), each of which lasts about one minute; this extreme brevity shows the composer's unwillingness to tamper with, extend, play upon, or in any way develop the austere impulse behind the composition, its idea. In the case of Schoenberg's great pupil Anton Webern this utter concision of gesture became the predominant feature of his career; but in Schoenberg's case this miniaturism was quickly abandoned. The music of the next decade of his career is, with the great exception of the *Four Orchestral Songs* (1916), less decisive and accomplished than the style of the "atonal" period, 1908–12; the period is dominated by the unfinished Swedenborgian oratorio *Die Jacobsleiter* (*Jacob's Ladder*), by the interruption of World War I, by religious and artistic meditation, by performance and pedagogy.

The breakthrough, the discovery of the method of composing in twelve tones, occurred in the summer of 1921. A piece of music should be governed in every detail, except perhaps rhythm, by a single sequence of the twelve notes of the chromatic scale, the so-called tone row; and no note may recur until the row has completed itself. The row may be segmented and arrayed into any pattern of chords, two chords of six notes each, or three of four notes each, and so forth, but the principle of plenitude takes precedence over any principle of hierarchy, of tonic governance; chromatic saturation has been promoted from intuition into law. Melodies may be generated from any segment of the row, or by playing the row backward, or by inverting the row, or by playing backward the inversion of the row; thereby a tone row is four-fold, a magic square like the arithmetical squares that so bemused the young Leverkühn in Mann's *Dr. Faustus*.

This system of composition, so indifferent to any given tonality, so mathematically defensible, so equanimous, held many kinds of fascinations for Schoenberg. It offered a technique by which music could be left available to extension in time, investigation of melodic possibility, exploration at leisure of the tensions inherent in the design of intervals in the row, yet a technique that in no way distorted or compromised its *donnée*, its idea, in which superfluity vanishes because every bar can be justified as a permutation of the basic row. Indeed, part of the danger of the system is that one can hardly see how a strict practitioner can write bad music; it offers a magical combination of effortless economy and effortless elaboration; and so Schoenberg repeatedly insisted that the usual virtues of imagination, clarity, tact, and structural acumen were as necessary in twelve-tone as in traditional music.

The peril that the *Six Little Piano Pieces* seemed to suggest, the fear that the quest for spiritual realism, the most severe possible presentation of the idea, would demand such brevity that music would exhaust itself in a single telling instant, contract to zero, is thus avoided by a clever tactic. Music may expand itself—Schoenberg disliked the word "develop," which evidently suggests a condition in which the goal of the music is not inherent within it but imposed by force, by the composer's trickery—for minutes, hours, in which the composer's invention, as long as it obeys the one law, is free to play to the heart's content, to make every alteration and extravagance. Even the smallest units of a given composition contain, then, an entire realization of the composition's idea; and this omnipresence of fulfillment satisfies Schoenberg's profound desire for spiritual justification, a music earthless, without tonic gravity, a long unfolding in outer space of something simple and supreme.

In his important essay "Composition with Twelve Tones" (1941), Schoenberg makes clear the superior claim to reality of serial music:

> the unity of musical space demands an absolute and unitary perception. In this space, as in Swedenborg's heaven (described in Balzac's *Seraphita*) there is no absolute down, no right or left, forward or backward. Every musical configuration, every movement of tones has to be comprehended primarily as a mutual relation of sounds,

of oscillatory vibrations, appearing at different places and times. To the imaginative and creative faculty, relations in the material sphere are as independent from directions or planes as material objects are, in their sphere, to our perceptive faculties. Just as our mind always recognizes, for instance, a knife, a bottle or a watch, regardless of its position, and can reproduce it in the imagination in every possible position, even so a musical creator's mind can operate subconsciously with a row of tones, regardless of their direction, regardless of the way in which a mirror might show the mutual relations, which remain a given quality. [*Style and Idea,* p. 223]

Just as an object in three-dimensional space is independent of the coordinate system by which alone it can be apprehended—a bottle is still a bottle whether upside down or right side up, in Charlottesville or Vladivostok or in orbit around the earth—so the tone row is independent of and inherent in its incarnations, whether its statement is straight or in its inversion or in its retrograde or in its retrograde inversion; in fact, there is no good reason for denominating any one of the four as the "straight" or "prime" version; all possible formulations and aspects of a given row are equally just, equally valid. As Adorno says, deprecating the monotony, the "magnificent failure" of the twelve-tone style, "Each form of the row is 'the' row with the same validity as the previous row, no row is more and no row is less" (Adorno, p. 99).

But Adorno does not seem to understand that this evenness, this blandness of texture, is part of the explicit aesthetic of such "spiritual" music. The "body" of the music, its realization in instrumental or vocal sounds, has dwindled to transparency; since every four or six bars brings a new restatement of the row, the music simply presents an ever-changing succession of new avatars, each as important as the last, each as unimportant as the last, and the listener is moved to contemplate no single acoustic representation but the underlying idea, everywhere immanent, subsistent, inviolate. Twelve-tone music, therefore, is an attempt to reach the condition of light, to demonstrate the triviality of everything that is not idea. The strictness of method belies the contempt it expresses for methodology; one might say that Schoenberg deifies technique in order to abolish it.

In music of this degree of purity, of formlessness, in which all form is simply an accretion of replication, in which it is almost fair to say that all pieces of music based on the same row are the same piece of music, independent of style, seemingly independent of the composer himself, how is it possible to speak of self-expression? Webern exclaimed in 1932 over the method of composition with twelve tones, "there will no

longer be any possible distinction between science and inspired creation. The further one presses forward, the greater becomes the identity
of everything, and finally we have the impression of being faced by a
work not of man but of Nature'' (Willi Reich, *Schoenberg: A Critical
Biography,* p. 135). One remembers Jackson Pollock's I *am* nature. But
if the spheres of the heavens have been given a singing voice, if Newton's laws have been trained to speak, is not individual emotion,
human declamation, necessarily excluded?

> If you count the syllables, there are twelve, and all twelve
> notes of the chromatic scale are set to it. . . . It is the basis
> of all the music . . . a formal treatment strict to the last
> degree, which no longer knows anything unthematic, in
> which the order of the basic material becomes total, and
> within which the idea of a fugue rather declines into an
> absurdity, just because there is no longer any free note.
> But it serves now a higher purpose; for—oh, marvel, oh,
> deep diabolic jest!— just by virtue of the absoluteness of
> the form the music is, as language, freed. In a more con-
> crete and physical sense the work is done, indeed, before
> the composition even begins, and this can now go on
> wholly unrestrained; that is, it can give itself over to ex-
> pression, which, thus lifted beyond the structural element,
> or within its uttermost severity, is won back again. The
> creator . . . can, in the previously organized material, un-
> hampered, untroubled by the already given structure,
> yield himself to subjectivity; and so this, his technically
> most rigid work, a work of extreme calculation, is at the
> same time purely expressive. The return to Monteverdi
> and the style of his time is what I meant by ''the re-
> construction of expressiveness,'' of expressiveness in its
> first and original manifestation, expressiveness as la-
> ment.
> Here marshalled and employed are all the means of
> expression of that emancipatory epoch of which I have
> already mentioned the echo-effect—especially suitable
> for a work wholly based on the variation-principle, and
> thus to some extent static, in which every transformation
> is itself already the echo of the previous one.
> . . . Here is the deep-drawn sigh . . . the recurrent sus-
> pensions, even though only as rhythmical device, the
> chromatic melody, the awful collective silence before the
> beginning of a phrase, repetitions such as in that *''Las-
> ciatemi,''* the lingering-out of syllables, falling intervals,
> dying-away declamations. [*Dr. Faustus,* pp. 487–89]

But this is nothing of Schoenberg, this is Adrian Leverkühn's final masterpiece, the Faustus oratorio, from Mann's novel. This is indeed a way by which the rigidities of twelve-tone music could turn supple, rhetorical, expressive; but it is not Schoenberg's way. The melting, the madrigal passions of Monteverdi—the sighs, the suspensions, the *stile concitato,* while technically feasible, would work against the disembodied quality, the calm luminosity, that the serial style was manufactured to convey. Behind Leverkühn's oratorio, as so often in *Dr. Faustus,* one hears the nostalgia of Mann's mentor Adorno for a less barbaric and artificial century, a music that would naturally evolve back to nature; but for Schoenberg the natural, the physiologically expressive, is depraved unless it is a realization of the supernatural. Some of Mann's description of these stylized moans, heavy breathing, might apply to such a piece as *Erwartung,* written in the psychologically engorged style of 1908–12; but twelve-tone style is largely a renunciation of psychology.

And yet Schoenberg insists, both early and late in his career, that self-expression is the primary purpose of art; as he says in his long essay of 1948 on Mahler, the first draft of which was written in 1912, "In reality, there is only one greatest goal towards which the artist strives: *to express himself.*" But it is hard to see how Schoenberg plans to achieve this goal, in the face of the increasingly antipsychological tendency of his music; if the acoustic vehicle of the idea does not matter very much, and the idea is only an abstract redistribution of the chromatic scale, then how is the self of Arnold Schoenberg to leak into his compositions?

One perhaps unsatisfactory solution was the composition of an opera, *Von Heute auf Morgen* (*From Today to Tomorrow,* 1928), which tells a recognizable anecdote from Schoenberg's marriage; in fact, the libretto to this little comedy of flirtation was written by Schoenberg's wife. It bears an odd similarity of intent to Richard Strauss's domestic opera *Intermezzo,* in which the lead singer was given a mask of Strauss's face to wear onstage.

But the most ambitious solution to the problem of self-expression in the twelve-tone style is found in Schoenberg's masterpiece, *Moses und Aron* (1930–32): Moses, the major role in the opera, is a speaking voice, while all the other roles are sung. Instead of the method of Leverkühn's Faustus oratorio, in which the expressiveness is made integral with the music, Schoenberg relegates his protagonist to a separate kingdom, in perpetual anguish at his own incompetence of expression, while the music goes its own way, fluent, dramatic, sensuous, vivid. In the speech of Moses—it is carefully notated *Sprechstimme,* half-sung in an imitation of a rising and falling voice, but never lyrical—we hear the usual declamatory devices of classical rhetoric, expostulation, sighing, cries of anger, sometimes uttered clearly and impressively but often thrown away in a stuttering, mumbled undertone beneath the long melodies that ignore him, rapt in their own beauty. The effect of this disjunction is like no previous effect in musical drama; it is nothing at all like the melodrama of earlier composers, Gomatz's entrance in Mozart's *Zaïde* or the Leonora-Rocco duet in act 2 of *Fidelio,* in which the orchestra intensifies the emotion of the spoken line it so tactfully interrupts. Instead the music proceeds in deliberate irresponse to Moses' plaints and summonses, while it swells and heightens the feelings of Aron, the high priest, the Israelite orgiasts, everyone else in the opera.

Expression, then, works in two distinct ways in *Moses und Aron:* according to the traditional operatic means, by which all affect veers into beauty, such as in the florid coloratura of Aron, a true Donizetti tenor; and according to the outrageous grumbling of Moses, whose expression chiefly disparages the whole notion of expression, complains at the defectiveness of his own mouth and of human speech in general. It is true that Moses is permitted once in the opera to sing; but what he sings—"Purify your thinking. Free it from worthless things. Consecrate it with truth"—could be paraphrased to mean, in context, Shut up. Aron is appointed to be Moses' mouth; but Moses is so appalled by what he hears this mouth sing that he is continually waging war against it, simultaneously working to utter God's will and to retract it as soon as it is uttered, to sing and to abolish song. We are all familiar with the artist who offers as one of his characters a little simulacrum of the author, invested with full authority in all that he says; but here we have, in the figure of Moses, a representation not of the Author but of the Critic, always carping at the whole apparatus of operatic expression, its intricate gorgeousness. As George Steiner says, in a fine essay in *Language and Silence,* it is an opera about opera, an opera that calls opera into question. By his insistence on speech Moses calls attention to the artifice, the threadbareness, the conventionality of song; it is as if he were pushing over the cardboard palm tree, denying the virtue of theater, of music, of representation. This is a method by which an artist can obtain a sudden effect of the accession of reality: to incorporate into his art a built-in disillusionment, to erect a structure of artifice only so that the audience may marvel at its collapse.

No reteller of the story of Moses could dramatize Moses' reluctance more effectively than Schoenberg. The opera opens with Moses crying out to the burning bush, "Single, eternal, omnipresent, invisible, and unrepresentable God!"; and it would be difficult to be less eager than Moses to be the representative of the unrepresentable God. The Voice of the Burning Bush—which Schoenberg represents by six singers and six speaking voices, intoning, sounding and resounding in a delirium of awe, an effect of sober eeriness designed to suggest by the overlapping of speech and song a condition beyond either, an inexpressible Godhead—instructs Moses to free his people, to be a model to them; but Moses' feeling of laborious inadequacy makes painful inter-ruptions: "I am old, let me graze my sheep in peace . . . my tongue is stiff: I can think, but not speak." The central problem of the opera is simple: the divine idea seems to demand expression, fulfillment, the righteous man as a model to his people; but that expression, when it takes place, is always partial, tainted, oversimplified, corrupt.

This is why the opera makes such a rigorous separation of Moses and Aron; Schoenberg must somehow show the discrepancy between thought and expression, dramatize the inadequacy of the dramatic method, have his music and abolish it. Moses is given a commandment he cannot obey; and, though Schoenberg insisted that the subject of his opera was religious philosophy, not an allegory of the artist (*Letters,* p. 288), the artist is nevertheless in an analogous position according to Schoenberg: he is commanded to convey his inspiration, but he cannot obey the command without falsifying his idea.

Schoenberg's career is a continual tension between the construction of elaborate musical devices designed to point to the idea beyond, labyrinths that indicate entrance and exit, and an impatient desire to supersede all artifice and mediation, to burst forth in flame with the in-spiration in itself; between the slow assembly of glass and tungsten into a light bulb and the direct utterance of *fiat lux;* between Aron and Moses. According to Moses, Aron made a great error when struck the rock with his rod instead of simply commanding the rock to give forth water (act 3, scene 1); to Moses, the use of physical mediation is a betrayal of the stark communion of man and God, the rapture of trance.

Despite his pragmatism, his demagoguery, his facility, Aron is still a figure of power; I do not think Schoenberg intends all virtue to be on Moses' side. Aron represents the principle of the validity of analogies, representations, images; his arias overflow with metaphors and orna-ments, just as their musical content is a tissue of continual restatement, transposition by mirror and crab, of the basic row of the opera; in fact, the first four lines he sings are, respectively, the row, its inversion, its retrograde, and its retrograde inversion. Moses says at the end, when Aron is a prisoner, that, although words and images have run away from Aron, he nonetheless remains, living in his images (3.1); and apart from this dwelling-in-images, this pictorial quality, Aron is nothing. Indeed, Aron dies when Moses tells the soldiers to release him—"Set him free, and if he can he shall live"—because an image cannot survive without something to be an image of; no image can be self-sufficient. Yet while he was Moses' mouth he was impressive in his ceaseless outpouring of representations; the celebrated miracles of the story, all of which are performed by Aron in Schoenberg's version, are simply stiff, overliteral enactments of metaphors. When Aron turns Moses' rod into a snake (1.4), it is a rhetorical device to illustrate a point and strike the gullible with awe: "In Moses' hand a rigid rod: the law; in my hand the supple serpent: discretion." The inconceivable God of Moses, who does not answer prayer or reward devotion or acknowledge offerings, is rejected by the Israelites; the plastic, discreet, responsive deity presented by Aron is more acceptable to them. Aron is a master of conjuror's tricks, of theater; but to Moses all this suppleness, this transformation, this instability, this metamorphosis is mere illusion, deceitful charm. Behind Aron's slick metaphors, the law—like Moses' rod, like the twelve tones of the row—was never altered in the first place, eternally defined beyond alteration. In the second of the *Six Pieces for Male Chorus* (1930), written at the same time he was working on *Moses und Aron,* Schoenberg has this to say about the relation between law and miracle:

> When things go as always they have gone,
> All's in order; we can understand.
> But when things are diff'rent, it is "a wonder"!
>
> And yet, that every day
> Follows still the same course,
> Is not that the wonder,
> That should seem beyond your understanding?
> That there should be one law
> And all things on earth obey it,
> As thou dost thy Lord?

This is exactly the Mosaic position: that we derive sustenance, comfort, from the cosmic rigidity of the law; the miraculous is an intolerable violation.

Yet the brilliant play and the specious analogies of Aron are necessary in the scheme of the opera. If the twelve-tone series—the abstract series prior to any sensuous realization in voice or orchestra—is like God, as David Levin and others have suggested, then the opera itself is like the golden calf.

> ARON. O shape of highest fantasy, how it thanks you that you charm it into an image!
> MOSES. No image can give you an image of the unimaginable. [1.2]

To a certain extent both statements can be true at once. If the primary impulse of the opera is iconoclastic, then one needs to construct the image before one can smash it. The image may be fleeting, unstable, provisional, a parody, but an artist has no other recourse; without images there can be no opera, no music, only private uncommunicable meditation. Moses' chastity of intellect is only meaningless taciturnity without the contrast of Aron's too-easy expressiveness. Though Aron compromises, takes satisfaction in half-truths and temporizing, he nevertheless is the avatar of imagination, of brotherly affection, of human fellow feeling. Moses, despite his hatred of the partial, is himself only a part of an ideal whole that comprises both Moses and Aron, like the quasi-Zionist Max Aruns (Moses-Aron) of Schoenberg's play *Der Biblische Weg* (*The Biblical Way*, 1926), who dies trying to establish a Jewish homeland in Africa but who nevertheless is simultaneously a visionary and a political organizer, the prophet and the voice. In a letter of 25 March 1933 to Walter Eidlitz (*Letters*, p. 172), Schoenberg says, "My Moses more resembles—of course only in outward aspect—Michelangelo's. He is not human at all." Much that is valuable to Schoenberg is lacking in this horned, inhuman Moses, his stone shoulders poised to shatter from stress.

> Thy birth with care is tended,
>> *Blessings on thee!*
> A grave is dug for thee,
>> *Rest in peace!*
> Thy wounds are nursed in the hospital,
>> *Quick recov'ry!*
> Quenched thy fires, thyself saved from drowning,
>> *Have no fear.*
> Thou, thy self, hast compassion for others,
>> *Help is near, thou art not alone!*

This is the last of the *Six Pieces for Male Chorus*, one of the loveliest works Schoenberg ever wrote; and its humane gentleness shows the Aaronic side of the composer, his not unworthy concern for public welfare. Moses is opposed to human feeling; but a more balanced view might permit men to feel yet nevertheless make strenuous objection to the deification of feeling.

When the dejected Israelites lose faith that Moses will return from the mountain, and cry out for the slaughter of the priesthood, Aron agrees to build an idol, and they rejoice: "Rejoice Israel! Gods, images to our eye, gods, lords of our senses!... The contents of your gift to your gods are your innermost feelings" (2.2). This is an intolerable mixing of the sensuous with the divine, a confusion that reaches its height when the Seventy Elders shout "Spirit is sense" (2.3); and Aron carries his ingenuity of metaphor to the point of blasphemy when he declares of the golden calf, "This image witnesses that a god lives in all things that exist. Unchangeable, like a law, is the material, the gold that you have given . . . the shape is secondary," a simile that turns the spiritual upside down and equates it with malleable gold.

The orgy that follows looses all restraint on feelings, looses a wilderness of music, the diversity and power of which make one feel again how implicated music must be with the low, the carnal; the row becomes unintelligible in the incessant tumult of tiny fragments broken from it. Butchers dance with knives and toss out chunks of raw meat; rivers of wine are poured, everyone fornicates, but while the revelers exult, others simply commit suicide in a rapture of self-sacrifice. "Powerful human virtues are reawakened: seriousness and joy, moderation and immoderation, good cheer, happiness and yearning, energy and rest, temperance, lust, abstention, greed, squandering and envy, everything beautiful, good, ugly, evil, everything that can be witnessed, perceived, felt. Sense first gives sense to spirit. Spirit is sense" (2.3).

This is the affective equivalent of chromatic saturation, a rainbow of emotion; every human desire is put into play at once. Aron had hoped that feeling, affection could somehow elevate itself to God: "The almighty transforms sand into fruit, fruit into gold, gold into joy, joy into spirit" (1.4); this is the God of Aron, himself a magician, who vouchsafes the efficacy of the expression of idea and the reality of miracles. In a way Aron is right, though the golden chain by which the Almighty hauls human feeling into heaven works more complexly than he supposes.

The orgy does not intensify into revelation; it simply exhausts itself, falls into stupor. This is how self-expression, the loosing of emotion, must necessarily operate, for priest, orgiast, and artist alike: the expression exhausts what it expresses, and leaves a condition of peace. In the list of "powerful virtues" cited above, a certain self-canceling effect is evident; and in the free expression of lust and temperance, greed and happy satisfaction, each virtue embraces its antonym, making a double annihilation, a calm neutrality. Aron's upward aspirations collapse in utter defeat; and Moses returns from the mountain, gesticulates, and destroys the golden calf with a great shout: "Begone, you image of your own powerlessness to capture the Boundless in an image!" (2.4). It is my belief that this is the proper formula for the opera itself: *Moses und Aron* is an image of imagelessness.

When the golden calf is made to disappear, the opera is almost ready to end. In the last scene of act 2 Aron and Moses comment upon what has happened, already somewhat removed from action, abstracted into recitative; and Aron, in his finest moment, uses Moses' own principles to refute him, leaving him powerless to defend himself:

> MOSES. Your image faded at my word!
> ARON. But your word renounced image and miracle,
> which you detested. And yet, when your word destroyed
> my image, that miracle was itself only an image. [2.5]

Moses, the purifier, cannot justify the purity of his conduct; by taking an action, by destroying the golden calf, he has rendered himself complicit with gesture, miracle, image. The abolishing of a symbol is a form of symbolic action, a piece of self-conscious theater. But a darker tangle awaits him. Aron proves that the Ten Commandments, fashioned by God on Mount Sinai, are only an image; and Moses in despair shatters the tables of the law. Moses had not understood until this moment how extensive was the collusion between God and image; and it is with something akin to horror that he looks up and sees the Israelites, singing joyfully, marching in a parade toward the Promised Land, led by a pillar of cloud by day, a pillar of fire by night, themselves images, always images.

Schoenberg wrote a brief third act, a single scene showing the triumph of Moses and the death of Aron, but he could not manage to set it to music, although he attempted it sporadically for twenty years; and it is perhaps as well that the opera ends where it does, with Moses' hopes collapsing soon after Aron's, the balance of power between the major characters intact:

> MOSES. Thus I have myself made an image, false, as an
> image must be! Thus I am defeated. Thus everything that
> I had thought was madness, and cannot, must not, be
> spoken. O Word, thou Word, that I lack! [2.5]

These phrases, the last phrases of the opera, are declaimed against unison violins, playing with utmost urgency first the row, then the retrograde of the row, as the row seems to fold itself up again after its prolonged involvement with the human world, its teasing and shattering into musical expression, and retreat like the law back into heaven, lingering for a final moment on its first note as Moses contemplates the silence he has uttered.

Here everything leaves off. All strategies by which one tried to grasp the inconceivable have failed, the idol is properly destroyed, and yet stray images keep proliferating, as if by their own power, more rapidly than one can abolish them. The opera ends with a paradox, a sense of profusion and inadequacy, of revelation everywhere that does not quite add up to the Revelation. It is impossible to know what to do; the commandment against graven images was itself a graven image and has annulled itself. The mechanism of the drama can be compared to that wind-up toy, a black box out of which, when one turns the switch on, a small hand reaches to turn the switch off; Schoenberg has made a gesture that is accomplished only for the sake of its own termination, has designed a song that intensifies silence, that dramatizes its own poverty of expression. It is still a kind of self-expression, but a kind peculiar to the modern sensibility.

In the same essay in which Schoenberg says that self-expression is the one greatest goal for any artist, he refines the concept of self-expression in an unusual manner: "There is only one content, which all men wish to express: the longing of mankind for its future form, for an immortal soul, for dissolution into the universe—the longing of this soul for its God" (*Style and Idea,* p. 464); and later in the essay he applauds Mahler for the nigh spirits of his First Symphony, the resignation of his Sixth Symphony, the glorification of the joys of a world already nearly abandoned expressed by his Eighth Symphony, the pure impersonality of his Ninth Symphony, its "objective, almost passionless statement of a beauty which becomes perceptible only to one who can dispense with animal warmth and feels at home in spiritual coolness" (p. 470).

This is self-expression: one delivers oneself of all feeling, expends oneself like the orgiasts before the golden calf, exhausts oneself of all that one is. Self-expression is self-sacrifice. The ensuing silence needs no appeal to the mystical limitedness, restrictedness of language of Wittgenstein, or even to Keats's celebration of the sweetness of unheard melodies; language and song admirably acquit themselves precisely because they can utter the utterable and then have done with it, leaving the auditor receptive to what can only be pointed to, gestured at. It is the final trick of art to be so complacent, so openhanded about its own illusions, the limitations and failures of representation, that the spectator believes that what art hints at is more real than what it palpably depicts. In this way art can try to create out of its own wreck the thing it contemplates.

I believe that in all art self-expression and self-evasion constitute a single act; but only in recent times have artists consciously employed this double nature for complicated effects. Several of Schoenberg's essays—such as the Mahler essay and "Opinion or Insight?"—suggest that Schoenberg deliberately intended self-expression for the sake of self-surpassing, a self-expression that is conscious atonement, a preliminary to prayer. Mann and Adorno also agree that when subjectivity is raised beyond a certain level, it becomes objective; as Beethoven expanded and defined his personality through his middle period, it at last elaborated into a transpersonal myth—an "exhaustiveness, an abandonment of self—a new relationship, conditioned by death" (*Dr. Faustus,* p. 53). I doubt whether Beethoven would have agreed that this was his intention, but it is clearly the intention of Adrian Leverkühn, the Schoenberg surrogate of Mann's novel, whose last composition passes beyond the expressiveness of madrigal to an impersonal, inhuman despair:

> Here, towards the end, I find that the uttermost accents of mourning are reached, the final despair achieves a voice, and—I will not say it, it would mean to disparage the uncompromising character of the work, its irremediable anguish to say that it affords, down to its very last note, any other consolation than what lies in voicing it, in simply giving sorrow words; in the fact, that is, that a voice is given the creature for its woe. No, this dark tone-poem permits up to the very end no consolation, appeasement, transfiguration. But take our artist paradox: grant that expressiveness—expression as lament—is the issue of the whole construction: then may we not parallel with it another, a religious one, and say too (though only in the lowest whisper) that out of the sheerly irremediable hope might germinate? It would be but a hope beyond hopelessness, the transcendence of despair—not betrayal to her, but the miracle that passes belief. For listen to the end, listen with me: one group of instruments after another retires, and what remains, as the work fades on the air, is the high G of a cello, the last word, the last fainting sound, slowly dying in a pianissimo fermata. Then nothing more: silence, and night. But that tone which vibrates in the silence, which is no longer there, to which only the spirit hearkens, and which was the voice of mourning, is so no more. It changes its meaning; it abides as a light in the night. [*Dr. Faustus,* p. 491]

It is similar to the end of *Moses und Aron*—it is only the difference between a cello's high G and a violin's low F-sharp—and something of this "transcendence of despair," this oddly affirmative sense of absence, silence, night, is indeed present in Schoenberg's work. What this sort of art can do is to make absence explicit, manifest; to show the gap between what has been done and what is not doable; to illustrate the defectiveness of our state, our knowledge of what we lack: grace.

The great discouragement to nineteenth-century art was its distrust of the intellect; the great discouragement to twentieth-century art is its distrust of art. To Schoenberg, the composer was a conscious trafficker in idols, and much of the oddity, the strain of his development, arises from his need to criticize his music in the very act of writing it, to attempt by *coup de théâtre* to elevate music from idolatry to prayer. The Christian artist can also be led to similar conclusions. The motto of T. S. Eliot in *East Coker,* "The poetry does not matter," is amplified in his *Little Gidding:*

> You are here to kneel
> Where prayer has been valid. And prayer is more
> Than an order of words, the conscious occupation
> Of the praying mind, or the sound of the voice praying.
> And what the dead had no speech for, when living,
> They can tell you, being dead: the communication
> Of the dead is tongued with fire beyond the language
> of the living.

This admiration for the speech of the dead, who live in a perpetual Pentecost, for a speech flaming and telepathic, instantaneous, can only result in contempt for poetry, for merely human art.

But Schoenberg is not as certain as Eliot of the incompatibility of art and prayer. In several of the works that follow *Moses und Aron* he employs its basic combination of voices, namely a speaking voice, a chorus, and an orchestra. In two of these works, *Kol Nidre* (1938) and *A Survivor from Warsaw* (1947), the sufferings of humanity—in the case of the latter, Nazi persecution—resolve at the end into a choral setting of actual Hebrew liturgy; abjection, misery, feeling heighten themselves into the traditional and impersonal consolation of prayer. To this extent Moses' inhumanness—his Michelangelesque largeness, loftiness—is not dogmatism or apathy but transpersonalness, the state of having perfected and surpassed the sensuous, the human. He does not repudiate affection, he is in the process of going beyond it. The golden calf is destroyed to remind Aron that the phenomenal world is not everything; and divinity makes itself apparent in tablet and pillar to remind Moses that the phenomenal world is not nothing.

In Schoenberg's last work, the *Modern Psalm* (1950), he seems to find a reconciliation of these warring opposites, a manner of prayer that is faithful to both human finitude and divine starkness:

> O, my Lord, everyone praises you and assures you of his
> devotion. But of what significance is it to you whether or

not I do also? Who am I to believe that my prayer is a
necessity? If I say "God," do I know that I am therewith
speaking of the only, eternal, omnipotent, omniscient and
unimaginable, of whom I neither can, nor should, create
an image? To whom I neither dare, nor am able, to utter a
demand, who will not notice or fulfill my warmest
prayer? Yet, nevertheless I pray, as all the living pray; in
spite of this I beg for favors and miracles, fulfillment.
Nevertheless I pray, for I don't want to lose the blissful
feeling of unity in the union with you. Oh, my Lord, your
grace left us prayer as a bond, a blissful bond with you.
As a rapture that gives us more than any fulfillment.

This piece, unlike any other in Schoenberg's canon, has the sound of
the opening of *Moses und Aron:* a baritone speaker solemnly intones in
the foreground, while a chorus makes complicated interweavings in the
dark depths; in fact, the text with its "only, eternal, omnipotent, omniscient and unimaginable" God is a close echo of what Moses says at
the beginning of the opera. God is no nearer to the speaker of the psalm
than he was to Moses; God still pays no attention to man, does not
fulfill prayer, remains arbitrary and inconceivable. But all has changed.
Moses had asked God to relieve him of responsibility, had interrupted,
objected to the divine will; but here what the speaker says is identical
to what the chorus sings in the background. It is as if Moses' speaking
voice had joined in perfect distinctness, perfect unanimity into the six
speakers and six singers who had represented the Voice of the Burning
Bush; this device is a musical representation of the unity, the communion with God, which gives more than any fulfillment. Tacit Moses
has found his voice, can declaim with his old vigor; but the message he
speaks is the news of his own dissolution into the Godhead. With his
free will he abandons his old recalcitrance, chooses to obey, to find his
peace in the divine will. Like the rabbi in a story of Isaac Bashevis
Singer who decides to live in unceasing fasting, atonement, flagellation,
a perpetual Yom Kippur, and who justifies his behavior by calling it
sheer selfishness and self-indulgence in what gives him pleasure, so
Schoenberg seems to find all human feeling subordinate to the pleasure
of orthodoxy of devotion; his aesthetic of self-expression demands the
expression of this high selfishness.

Yet one cannot say that the *Modern Psalm* is a full, harmonious
solution to the aesthetic problems of Schoenberg's career: he never
completed the music, which breaks off at the second appearance in the
text of "Nevertheless I pray," as if a conclusive choral allegation of
actual, available fulfillment would violate a certain tact, would make

the prayer too confident of its own successfulness in binding man to God. Schoenberg, in the remaining months of his life, wrote words to several more psalms, one of which even speaks of his admiration for Jesus, but he attempted no more musical settings. Schoenberg, in his youth an agnostic Jew, had been baptized a Protestant in 1898, then returned to formal Judaism in 1933, *after* the composition of *Moses und Aron;* but despite the flux of religion the essential religiousness of his art remained the same from beginning to end.

To the critic of art all religions are one religion, and the mark of religious art is the same in the work of Jew, Christian, or atheist: it is the antimimetic theme, the concentration on the disparity between the image and what it is image of. In art, the divine is most aptly suggested by the inadequacy, the incompleteness of the work of art. We are used to thinking of the artist who renounces imitation not as an orthodox believer, but as an aesthete or symbolist, who is the priest exclusively of art; but art cannot distinguish the worshiper of art from the worshiper of another god. It is not fortuitous that the most formidable aesthete of English letters, Oscar Wilde, became a Roman Catholic on his deathbed, for art can only express the condition of devotedness, not the transcendental object of devotion; and Christ was in no way incompatible with the aesthetic religion, whose preoccupation with style always suggests a certain contentlessness, an arbitrariness of subject or theme. Auden has put it this way:

> Poems, like many of Donne's and Hopkins', which express a poet's personal feelings of religious devotion or penitence, make me uneasy. It is quite in order that a poet should write a sonnet expressing his devotion to Miss Smith because the poet, Miss Smith, and all his readers know perfectly well that, had he chanced to fall in love with Miss Jones instead, his feelings would be exactly the same. But if he writes a sonnet expressing his devotion to Christ, the important point, surely, is that his devotion is felt for Christ and not for, say, Buddha or Mahomet, and this point cannot be made in poetry; the Proper Name proves nothing. [*The Dyer's Hand*, p. 458]

The work of art is Christian, then, not in its overt subject, but in such oblique matters as form, style, concinnity; as Auden says in a notable maxim, "Every beautiful poem presents an analogy to the forgiveness of sins" (*The Dyer's Hand*, p. 71).

This doctrine—and I believe it is the proper doctrine for religious art—leaves the religious artist in an odd relation to his ostensible content; there is continual embellishment of ancillary matters, the edges and corners of the frame, but at the center something is missing. What Lévi-Strauss has observed about nonrepresentational art becomes the explicit condition of the religious artist's labor: "It is a school of academic painting in which each artist strives to represent the manner in which he would execute his pictures if by chance he were to paint any" (*The Savage Mind,* p. 30). The antimimetic artist, even if his aims have nothing to do with religion, even if he only wishes to illustrate the uncapturability of the real, to suggest the poverty of representation, finds himself converging with a peculiarly religious approach to art. In this way "modern" art, art that despairs of its own achievement, finds satisfactions, kinship with the religious art of previous centuries—Dante, Bach, the self-consciously sublime, George Herbert, who calls attention to his metaphors that he may say farewell to them—while the vigorous, secular, representational art of the nineteenth century, satisfied with the accuracy of its modeling, falls into disfavor.

The artist who has striven for perfection of verisimilitude discovers that reality eludes him, transcends his art; and this knowledge of transcendence puts him in the position in which the religious artist has found himself all along. Maturity comes when the conditions of transcendence are accepted, deployed, made ingenious. Auden, in his masterpiece *The Sea and the Mirror*, has Caliban speculate on the extreme difficulty of Christian art:

> Having learnt his language, I begin to feel something of the serio-comic embarrassment of the dedicated dramatist, who, in representing to you your condition of estrangement from the truth, is doomed to fail the more he succeeds, for the more truthfully he paints the condition, the less clearly can he indicate the truth from which it is estranged, the brighter his revelation of the truth in its order, its justice, its joy, the fainter shows his picture of your actual condition in all its drabness and sham, and, worse still, the more sharply he defines the estrangement itself—and, ultimately, what other aim and justification has he, what else exactly *is* the artistic gift which he is forbidden to hide, if not to make you unforgettably conscious of the ungarnished offended gap between what you so questionably are and what you are commanded without any question to become, of the unqualified No that opposes your every step in any direction?—the more he must strengthen your delusion that an awareness of the gap is in itself a bridge, your interest in your imprisonment a release, so that, far from your being led by him to contrition and surrender, the regarding of your defects in

> his mirror, your dialogue, using his words, with yourself
> about yourself, becomes the one activity which never,
> like devouring or collecting or spending, lets you down,
> the one game which can be guaranteed, whatever the
> company, to catch on, a madness of which you can only
> be cured by some shock quite outside his control, an
> unpredictable misting over of his glass or an absurd mis-
> print in his text. [*Collected Longer Poems*, pp. 247–48]

The religious artist must hope that his art, along with the mimetic joy of
an audience that delights in seeing itself represented, will somehow
sabotage itself, leading to ruin and disappointment, awareness of the
awful gulf between ourselves and the authentic revelation. The image
that occurs to Caliban best to express this condition is "the greatest
grandest opera rendered by a very provincial touring company":

> Our performance—for Ariel and I are, you know this
> now, just as deeply involved as any of you—which we
> were obliged, all of us, to go on with and sit through right
> to the final dissonant chord, has been so indescribably
> inexcusably awful. Sweating and shivering in our moth-
> eaten ill-fitting stock costumes which with only a change
> of hat and rearrangement of safety-pins, had to do for the
> *landsknecht* and the Parisian art-student, bumping into,
> now a rippling palace, now a primeval forest full of holes,
> at cross purposes with the scraping bleating orchestra we
> could scarcely hear, for half the instruments were missing
> and the cottage piano which was filling-out must have
> stood for too many years in some damp parlour, we
> floundered on from fiasco to fiasco, the schmalz tenor
> never quite able at his big moments to get right up nor the
> ham bass right down, the stud contralto gargling through
> her maternal grief, the ravished coloratura trilling madly
> off-key and the reunited lovers half a bar apart, the knock-
> kneed armies shuffling limply through their bloody battles,
> the unearthly harvesters hysterically entangled in their
> honest fugato.
>
> Now it is over. No, we have not dreamt it. Here we
> really stand, down stage with red faces and no applause;
> no effect, however simple, no piece of business, however
> unimportant, came off; there was not a single aspect of
> our production, not even the huge stuffed bird of happi-
> ness, for which a kind word could, however patronizingly,
> be said. [*Collected Longer Poems*, pp. 248–49]

Yet it is at this instant, pressed by every burden of inadequacy, after
the collapse of illusion into derision, that "for the first time in our lives

we hear . . . the real Word.'' The only genuine tool of religious art is this heady disillusionment. *Moses und Aron,* with its clumsy Moses, his plain speaking voice annulling all the artifice of song, is an opera just like the subverted Donizetti of Caliban's fantasy. I know of no art before the twentieth century that makes of its own self-destruction such a calculated, impressive effect, an effect that corresponds to sublimity as implosion does to explosion.

2|Nabokov

One would like to study the art of representation by comparing the image with what it represents. A visit to Rouen will present the critic with the same cathedral face whose disclosure of light so beguiled Monet; and the cuckoo's song that Pasquini, Mahler, and Messiaen have elaborated is still to be heard in the forests of Europe. But verbal representation does not allow us such comparisons as these. A guidebook to Stonehenge may specify the number of megaliths present and the height and weight of each; but this is a mathematical, not a verbal representation. If we bring with us to Stonehenge a description of the place and compare it with the actual spectacle before us, we may readily assent to the mathematical tabulations—though counting itself is a difficult art—but it is improbable that we will be satisfied that the author's *verbal* images of what he has seen correspond well to our own. I am not speaking of the clearly fanciful and impressionistic descriptions common in tourists' handbooks—the Druid sacrifices, the too-vivid prehistoric sunrise—but of sober, objective presentations of what is there. When the simplest experience is plucked, trussed, cooked into a verbal representation, it is forever excluded from the world of things that are seen and heard and felt; it finds itself in the kingdom of words, where relationships between things are phonic, grammatical, literary—where the gropings of the verb toward the object replace the delicate taxis of the heliotrope toward the sun, the stone's devolution toward the center of the earth. Any honest representation of the world of experience is everywhere defeated by the richness-in-relation of a text to the body of similar texts, by the inferiority, the poverty-in-relation of that text to the sensuous world. When Thoth lived on earth and writing was new, a declarative sentence must have seemed more nearly a magical aperture into what it described; those endless inventories of wine jars and consignments of grain that constitute nearly the whole of what is known of Sumerian or of Cretan Linear B may for all I know have been as exciting as poems; but the sheer weight of accumulated texts over the millennia has overwhelmed our poor combinations of words in verbal relationships, smothered them in their own verbality.

Let us return to Stonehenge once more, though it is already dark and the tourists have long been restless; this time we shall take along the celebrated description by Defoe. In the massive blocks of these sentences, so craftily balanced on each other, we shall find a representation of the old ruin if representation can be discovered at all.

> I shall suppose it, as the majority of all writers do, to be a monument for the dead, and the rather, because men's bones have been frequently dug up in the ground near them. The common opinion that no man could ever count them, that a baker carry'd a basket of bread, and laid a loaf upon every stone, and yet could never make out the same number twice; This, I take, as a meer country fiction, and a ridiculous one too; the reason why they cannot easily be told, is, that many of them lye half, or part buryed in the ground, and a peice here, and a peice there, only appearing above the grass, it cannot be known easily, which belong to one stone, and which to another, or which are separate stones, and which are joyned under ground to another; otherwise, as to those which appear, they are easie to be told, and I have seen them told four times after one another, beginning every time at a different place, and every time they amounted to 72 in all; but then this was counting every peice of a stone of bulk, which appear'd at above the surface of the earth, and was not evidently part

of, and adjoyning to another, to be a distinct and separate body, or stone by it self.

The form of this monument is not only describ'd but delineated in most authors, and indeed 'tis hard to know the first, but by the last; the figure was at first circular, and there were at least four rows or circles, within one another; the main stones were placed upright, and they were joyn'd on the top by cross stones, laid from one to another, and fastn'd with vast mortices and tenants: Length of time has so decay'd them, that not only most of the cross stones which lay on the top are fallen down, but many of the upright also, notwithstanding the weight of them is so prodigious great: How they came thither, or from whence, no stones of that kind being now to be found in any part of England near it, is still the mistery, for they are of such immense bulk that no engines, or carriages which we have in use in this age could stir them. [*Defoe's Tour*, 1:197]

But something is wrong. The stones before us do not stand in the configuration Defoe alleges; there are not seventy-two stones to be found; no one could have seen four concentric circles. The author has been careless; or he has never been to Stonehenge and has relied on the reports of others; or he has lied. Defoe has punctured the "meer country fiction" of the baker's loaf-numbering only to substitute a more durable, definite, and specious fiction of his own. I take this as a parable of the nature of representation: standing before the world's ruins, we offer our still more ruined images of them. What had seemed a representation of a monument has turned into an episode in the history of travel writing, into a pretext for speculating about Defoe's literary psychology; and if a description of Stonehenge must endure this resorption into the verbal, how much more tenuous must be the connection of most writing to its ostensible referent in the physical world. When we turn, for example, to the nineteenth-century novel and ask ourselves, What has the novelist represented? we find almost nothing, except for a few London streetscapes, now much altered by time, to which we could journey for purposes of comparison. The objective referent is contingent, hovering, imaginary, to be found only in the confines of the novel; yet it is a critical error to say, as some students have done, that the representation and what is represented are identical. Of course we know nothing of the municipal organization of Middlemarch besides what Eliot tells us, and Bleak House is not one whit more or less bleak than Dickens says it is; but the reader will go astray who confuses the words on the page with that wholly imaginary but three-dimensional, consistently described, lovingly ornamented, slowly altering place that the words of the novel shadow forth. This place—the "what is represented" of the nineteenth-century novel—is one of the most fascinating achievements of the century's intellect, and its topography and ethnology have been exhaustively described by Henry James, E. M. Forster, John Updike, and many others, most of whom have stressed the quaintness of its customs (such unceasing banquets, such blushes, such biceps) and its heightening of effect, its parodic relation to the world of experience, the blunter world in which gravity is a constant and most days are neither particularly rainy nor particularly sunny. It is true that the buildings, the denizens, the forests, the skies depicted in the novel seem stylized and distorted when compared with our own. But what is more difficult to appreciate is the great effort it took, from the birth of the novel to the end of the nineteenth century, not only to adjust the focus, the width of aperture, but also to imagine a commodious and representable kingdom that neither strains too much toward an exact likeness of the world of experience nor thins out into bald fantasy. The novel can pride itself on its verisimilitude because it attempts to describe an imaginary place whose contours have been artfully shaped to maximize representability, whose planes and angles are all open to inspection. If George Eliot is omniscient it is because what she is representing is an extensive realm without shadow or secret, aggressively overt in its depths as well as its surfaces, a great delitescencelessness. Indeed, the author's knowledgeability seems less remarkable to me than her invention of a world so knowable. *Ulysses* still seems in many ways the end of the traditional novel; and in *Ulysses* the world of knowable representation has proliferated to such an extent that it seems to encroach upon, usurp, the genuinely unknowable world of experience. It is a disturbing book, not least because it offers the possibility that the comforting wall that insulates fiction from fact may break down. But we know better.

What does the reader want the novelist to provide? In a sense, he wishes every novel to be an escape. But the serious novel differs from the detective story or the thriller in that it offers the reader an escape into the place where he already is; it is as if a prisoner dug a tunnel from the exercise yard back into his own cell. There are three elements to this peculiar maneuver: (1) the words on the pages, which are ideal and substantial and intend a world that is *like* the world of experience; (2) the world intended by the words, which is the imaginary subject hypothesized by the novel—the "what is represented"—and turns out not to be much like the world of experience at all; and (3) the world of experience, into which the intended world of the novel is designed to collapse and which is a predator only too happy to swallow it. It is a little ballet in which the real and the unreal clasp hands, lift each other into the air, and dance; and the word "fiction" properly denotes this state of suspended realities, grounded unrealities, Antaeus on the trapeze, the chimera flightless, helpless and flapping, its legs turned to stone. *Ulysses,* by making the unreal seem too real, tends to confuse or short-circuit the process—although the Homeric parallels do tend to reassert the antique fictiveness, the impossible sailor's yarn, the necessary imaginariness of the text. In reading a novel, then, we begin and end in the room where we sit, the room of which the novelist has offered a preposterous guided tour; and much of the task of criticism is to describe as exactly as possible the charlatan's trick by which a mediate, hybrid, and lucid locus, at once a representation of our dwelling place and a deliberate unrepresentation, is smuggled into our obdurate and inspissated world so that its deflation will give us the impression of enlightenment. As Borges has said, the "imminence of a revelation which does not occur is, perhaps, the aesthetic phenomenon" (*Labyrinths,* p. 188).

It is very difficult to make a verbal representation of a thing, though it is easy to give an impression of the shadowy trace, the track of a particle through a cloud chamber, that a thing leaves in its passage through the world. What would constitute an ideally representative verbal act? We have never encountered such a thing in traditional fictions, but when it is approached—as in the celebrated descriptions of hats in *Tristram Shandy* and *Madame Bovary*—it appears suspiciously like a stunt or interruption. It calls attention to itself; it seems to hinder rather than to further the evolution of the novel. Indeed, the classic defenses of realism, such as the seventeenth chapter of *Adam Bede,* not only insist on the extraordinary difficulty of showing something as it is, but even make it seem that art itself facilitates the fantastic and unreal:

> Falsehood is so easy, truth so difficult. The pencil is conscious of a delightful facility in drawing a griffin—the longer the claws, and the larger the wings, the better; but that marvellous facility which we mistook for genius is apt to forsake us when we want to draw a real unexaggerated lion. Examine your words well, and you will find that even when you have no motive to be false, it is a very hard thing to say the exact truth, even about your own immediate feelings—much harder than to say something fine about them which is *not* the exact truth. [*Adam Bede,* p. 176]

Verisimilitude is a struggle; the realist goes against the grain of her medium, tries to impose a rectitude of line while her pencil wishes to elaborate, to gaud. George Eliot goes on to compare the art of her novels to Dutch genre painting:

> I turn to that village wedding, kept between four brown walls, where an awkward bridegroom opens the dance with a high-shouldered, broad-faced bride, while elderly and middle-aged friends look on, with very irregular noses and lips, and probably with quart-pots in their hands, but with an expression of unmistakable content-ment and goodwill. "Foh!" says my idealistic friend, "what vulgar details! What good is there in taking all these pains to give an exact likeness of old women and clowns? What a low phase of life! What clumsy, ugly people!"
>
> But bless us, things may be lovable that are not altogether handsome, I hope? . . . I believe there have been plenty of young heroes, of middle stature and feeble beards, who have felt quite sure they could never love anything more insignificant than a Diana, and yet have found themselves in middle life happily settled with a wife who waddles. Yes! Thank God; human feeling is like the mighty rivers that bless the earth: it does not wait for beauty—it flows with resistless force and brings beauty with it. [*Adam Bede*, pp. 176–77]

She congratulates herself for her "exact likeness," yet it is clear that what she is representing is not an objective world—on the previous page she has railed against the "harder, colder eye" of the dis-passionate onlooker—but is instead the field on which her sympathy operates, the mighty river of human feeling. The world of her expres-sion is effusive, tender, shaped by the pressure of the heart; the work-rooms of the carpenter, so solid-seeming, hammered together and planed so vigorously that sawdust and wood shavings are strewn about the floor, are, like the honest face of the carpenter himself, only the momentary forms borne up by the current of human love, soon to disperse. In this manner the usual nineteenth-century novel becomes as insubstantial, as phantasmagorical, as those Italian Renaissance paintings of "prophets, sibyls, and heroic warriors" it deprecates; by changing the locus of representation from the objective to the subject-ive, the thing-as-it-is-felt rather than the thing-as-it-is-seen, the aesthe-tic of verisimilitude introduces something indeterminate, intangible, and begins to collaborate with deliberate falsification, the same desire to depict "higher truth" that inspired Leonardo to draw his angels. It is perhaps true that every goal other than representation for which the novelist may strive—beauty of syle, clarity of structure, the in-telligibility of description, possibly even grammar itself—will tend to defeat representation. All artists claim to be realists, as Robbe-Grillet says while gracefully laughing at his own pretensions to realism, but all artists prefer to abandon realism rather than to pay what its severity demands, for it costs everything.

In the twentieth century, in general, the desire for exact verbal representation has grown more acute, while the doubt of its achievement has grown greater. Modern novels explore both the limits of representation and the limits of the possibilities for repudiating it. The modern writer is conscious of the conditions by which his art operates and is often eager to claim, in the manner of Flaubert and Robbe-Grillet—"I do not transcribe, I construct"—that the world of his fiction is independent of the world of experience, uncontingent and self-sustaining. This attitude may lead him either to dismiss the similarities between the two worlds as trivial coincidence or to feel a certain guilt that he has appropriated something into his fiction and thereby diminished the world of experience, as if representation were theft. In Nabokov's *The Gift,* the artist-hero Fyodor, rereading a poem about a visit to the dentist, wonders:

> What, then, compels me to compose poems about my childhood if in spite of everything, my words go wide of the mark, or else slay both the pard and the hart with the exploding bullet of an "accurate" epithet? [*The Gift,* pp. 30–31]

Here it seems that representation may be murder; the powerful operations of the imagination reduce to dust, annihilate, the material on which they act. Yet I believe the writer who holds the simplest object before his face will usually worry, not whether his paragraph of description will turn it to rubble, but whether he will be able to say anything meaningful about it, be able to represent it at all.

The problem of representation is complicated by this discrepancy of perspective. The critic has two choices: he may either study the object and imagine what kinds of verbal representations of it are possible, or he may look at the text of a description and imagine what sort of object it represents. It is difficult to make these two perspectives converge, even in a gross manner. From the point of view of the world of experience, every screwdriver or bowling ball is a black hole, a hunger, a maw that eats up every representation, every attempt to come to *terms* with it, just as the corpses of stars are so heavy that they absorb light; the dimmest candle can outshine the word *sun.* The very syntax of language emphasizes the futility of representation, for one can name the subject—shoelace, leaf, box—and then all the rest is predicate, accident, superficies—thirty-six inches, lobed and veined, cardboard—and not even ten thousand pages of adduced description will ever add up to the beating essence, the thinghood of the thing. From the other side, the kingdom of words, the view is entirely different. Here every verbal act—"the sky is blue"—erects a calm and appealing little field of awareness—the blue is the color of a child's crayon, the sky is the part just above the fovea centralis of the eye—that rigorously resists any intrusion from the world of things, the asperities of the real, its cold winds. Indeed, the typical epithets of the sky—depthless or deep, oblivious, vaultlike, immense—are only conventional attempts to restore to the word some of the shockingness of the thing itself, the thrill of confrontation. Here truth is only a matter of internal consistency, never of congruence. At the beginning of Virginia Woolf's *Orlando* the young artist-hero is having trouble writing a poem:

> At last, however, he came to a halt. He was describing, as all young poets are for ever describing, nature, and in order to match the shade of green precisely he looked (and here he showed more audacity than most) at the thing itself, which happened to be a laurel bush growing beneath the window. After that, of course, he could write no more. Green in nature is one thing, green in literature another. Nature and letters seem to have a natural antipathy; bring them together and they tear each other to pieces. The shade of green Orlando now saw spoilt his rhyme and split his metre. [*Orlando*, pp. 16–17]

At the end of the novel a reconciliation takes place as Orlando, now a woman, starts to bury her poem "The Oak Tree" under an oak tree, but this seems a fantastic allegation of concord rather than a genuine embrace, an intertwining, of word and thing. When Beckett's Molloy declares, "there could be no things but nameless things, no names but thingless names" (*Molloy*, p. 31), he is scarcely exaggerating the incommensurability of the verbal and the actual that many writers have discovered, a loss of relations that becomes a pretext for irony, playfulness, humility, pride, despair. To speak is to falsify: the sky is not blue, the blue is only a chromatic aberration; even to declare that the sky is sky-colored is perhaps venturesome.

In modern painting as well as modern literature it is a common trick to juxtapose a representation of a thing with the thing itself, often in order to be explicit about the illusoriness of illusions. A painting that incorporates bits of seashell glued onto a background of painted shells demands at once that the viewer admire the ease of transition, the guileful likeness, and also that he confront the impossibility, the silliness, of pigment trying to hump itself, exfoliate into calcium carbonate.

An author is not permitted by his publisher to include an actual object bound into the pages of his book, but if he is determined to represent he can usually find something so familiar that every reader can find it on his desk, nearly identical to that original thing the author endeavors to show:

It was not a hexagonal beauty of Virginia juniper or African cedar, with the maker's name imprinted in silver foil, but a very plain, round, technically faceless old pencil of cheap pine, dyed a dingy lilac. It had been mislaid ten years ago by a carpenter who had not finished examining, let alone fixing, the old desk, having gone away for a tool that he never found. Now comes the act of attention.

In his shop, and long before that at the village school, the pencil has been worn down to two-thirds of its original length. The bare wood of its tapered end has darkened to plumbeous plum, thus merging in tint with the blunt tip of graphite whose blind gloss alone distinguishes it from the wood. A knife and a brass sharpener have thoroughly worked upon it and if it were necessary we could trace the complicated fate of the shavings, each mauve on one side and tan on the other when fresh, but now reduced to atoms of dust whose wide, wide dispersal is panic catching its breath but one should be above it, one gets used to it fairly soon (there are worse terrors). On the whole, it whittled sweetly, being of an old-fashioned make. Going back a number of seasons (not as far, though, as Shakespeare's birth year when pencil lead was discovered) and then picking up the thing's story again in the "now" direction, we see graphite, ground very fine, being mixed with moist clay by young girls and old men. This mass, this pressed caviar, is placed in a metal cylinder which has a blue eye, a sapphire with a hole drilled in it, and through this the caviar is forced. It issues in one continuous appetizing rodlet (watch for our little friend!), which looks as if it retained the shape of an earthworm's digestive tract (but watch, watch, do not be deflected!). It is now being cut into the lengths required for these particular pencils (we glimpse the cutter, old Elias Borrowdale, and are about to mouse up his forearm on a side trip of inspection but we stop, stop and recoil, in our haste to identify the individual segment). See it baked, see it boiled in fat (here a shot of the fleecy fat-giver being butchered, a shot of the butcher, a shot of the shepherd, a shot of the shepherd's father, a Mexican) and fitted into the wood.

Now let us not lose our precious bit of lead while we prepare the wood. Here's the tree! *This* particular pine! It is cut down. Only the trunk is used, stripped of its bark. We hear the whine of a newly invented power saw, we see logs being dried and planed. Here's the board that will yield the integument of the pencil in the shallow drawer (still not closed). We recognize its presence in the log as we recognized the log in the tree and the tree in the forest and the forest in the world that Jack built. We recognize that presence by something that is perfectly clear to us but nameless, and as impossible to describe as a smile to somebody who has never seen smiling eyes.

Thus the entire little drama, from crystallized carbon and felled pine to this humble implement, to this transparent thing, unfolds in a twinkle. Alas, the solid pencil itself as fingered briefly by Hugh Person still somehow eludes us! But *he* won't, oh no. [*Transparent Things,* pp. 6–8]

This pencil, the first and probably the finest of several literary pencils we shall enjoy in this essay, is the temporary property of Hugh Person in Nabokov's *Transparent Things*. I own a pencil somewhat similar to it, and I am looking at it. I notice that Nabokov is exact in his description of the discoloration of the wood circumjacent to the graphite, and, further, that the outer paint has soaked into the wood and stained it a color slightly different from the color of the paint; the sharpener has imparted a mossy texture to the conical tip, and left it scored, rayed, peaked with fine intersecting lines. This is the sort of description Nabokov provides at the beginning of the passage, impressions of color and texture—mostly the secondary qualities, to use Locke's term, of the pencil. But when the narrator starts his account of the history of the pencil, I am lost. I am ignorant of the manufacture of pencils; though I could look up pencil-making in an encyclopedia, as I presume Nabokov has done, nothing I could do would ever show me the site of the particular tree cut down for my particular pencil. The more closely I attend to my pencil, the more obscure it grows; if I assigned myself to write a page, a chapter, about my pencil I would increasingly have to lie or plagiarize. Or, if sheer truthfulness were my goal, I would have to write in a more and more attenuated and obtuse manner about my incomprehension and nescience; that is, the more concrete a representation I attempt, the more I am driven to either fantasy or abstraction. These are, I believe inevitably, the two directions to which extreme representation will lead: either to making exact representations of wholly imaginary objects, as Nabokov does in this passage, trying to pretend with a sickly grin that his cylindrical hallucination bears resemblance to an actual pencil; or to making representations of the unrepresentability of real objects, descriptions of their impenetrability, mysteriousness, and opacity. In either case we are led away from the world of experience, just as our hand has made its last effort to grasp it.

In this way my pencil mocks my attempts to represent it, traces idle scrawls when I wish it to write the most devastating word; and it will be extinguished by my sharpener or stolen by a student before I can make it utter itself. But why should I bother to try? This particular pencil means nothing to me; indeed, in my hypothetical representation of the pencil I would be driven to write about my own disinterest, fatigue, and boredom at the necessity of continuing this tedious translation from wood to word. One of the jokes of Nabokov's passage is that the narrator pretends that the pencil, which has no consequence in the plot of the novel and no significance to any of the characters, is so infinitely precious that the very shavings from its point are worthy of study and recovery. Thus the passage is a sophistication, expansion, and burlesque upon the nineteenth-century novel's doting on the homely and beloved minutiae of domesticity. Just as the true subject of George Eliot's representation is the plastic stress of her affection, which alters and infuses things until they are obligingly available for display, so Nabokov has imbued his pencil with a phony glamor and a specious openness, so that the universe of pines and fat sheep that is responsible for its provenance may be educed from the narrator's close attention. The parenthetical interjections, as if the narrator were making a commentary for a child's documentary film about a pencil, heighten the falseness of tone, the falseness of the narrator's stance with respect to the reader. Just as the pencil grows more and more egregious as the description keeps embellishing it, the narrator too grows deformed by the unsavory intensity of his concentration on the pencil; he becomes panicked as he speaks of the atomic dispersal of the pencil shavings, as if the attender saw his own fate in the object of his attention; and when he examines the pencil-cutter, old Elias Borrowdale—it is, after all, a borrowed pencil—he seems to dwindle to a free-floating eyeball, a mouse that can run up Elias's forearm. This is another lesson to be gained from *Transparent Things:* not only does the desire for a too-exact representation lead to an explicit sense of the unreality of the object represented, it also makes the representer himself increasingly unreal, puts him in a false and untenable relation to his object; and in fact in extreme cases the representer may lose his identity and unite himself with what he scrutinizes, dissipate as his pencil slowly disintegrates into wood shavings and dust. It is not surprising that the pencil should be dismissed from the novel with the cry, "Alas, the solid pencil itself . . . still somehow eludes us!" for when it was only a casual pencil in a desk drawer it seemed acceptably real; it is only the extremity of seizing, of reifying, that has made it elusive. The reader finds it easy to credit what is opaque, mute, closed; these transparent things are freaks, disturbing and monstrous, like the transparent fish one sometimes sees in aquariums, fish in which every bone is visible, and a red bladder, and the trembling heart pumping clear ichor through the veins. This disquieting feeling that excursions into transparency do not belong in novels, that fiction is the province of superficies, the deaf and the dumb, is made into a statement of Nabokov's aesthetic in an interview he gave to explain his novel:

> Allow me to quote a passage from my first page which baffled the wise and misled the silly: "When we concentrate on a material object . . . the very act of attention may lead to our involuntarily sinking into the history of that object." A number of such instances of falling through the present's "tension film" are given in the course of the book. There is the personal history of a pencil. There is also, in a later chapter, the past of a shabby room, where, instead of focusing on Person and the prostitute, the spectral observer drifts down into the middle of the previous century and sees a Russian traveler, a minor Dostoevski, occupying that room, between Swiss gambling house and Italy.

> *Another critic has said—*

> Yes, I am coming to that. Reviewers of my little book made the lighthearted mistake of assuming that seeing through things is the professional function of a novelist. Actually, that kind of generalization is not only a dismal commonplace but is specifically untrue. Unlike the mysterious observer or observers in *Transparent Things*, a novelist is, like all mortals, more fully at home on the surface of the present than in the ooze of the past. [*Strong Opinions*, pp. 194–95]

Thus Nabokov warns the novelist to investigate the farther reaches of representation only at his peril, at the peril of getting lost in the pullulating and irrelevant universe that the simplest object can provoke the imagination into loosing, a welter in which the representer and the represented alike founder, drown.

To represent a particular thing, then, requires the novelist to construct a busy little world in which the thing can locate itself in the most flattering manner, the contingent and cradling world where it was manufactured, where it is used, and where it lies about, in which all vectors point toward Hugh's pencil. This worldlet, whose prime minister is Elias Borrowdale and in which Shakespeare exists only as a calendar entry to fix the discovery of pencil lead, is eerily unrelated either to the world of experience or to the world of the action of the novel; it is doubly a sham, a flippant invention developed only to satisfy the needs of representation. I have said that, from the point of view of the world of experience, every object is a black hole that swallows words; and Nabokov speaks somewhat similarly of the unknowability of things:

> *In your new novel,* Pale Fire, *one of the characters says that reality is neither the subject nor the object of real art, which creates its own reality. What is that reality?*
>
> Reality is a very subjective affair. I can only define it as a kind of gradual accumulation of information; and as specialization. If we take a lily, for instance, or any other kind of natural object, a lily is more real to a naturalist than it is to an ordinary person. But it is still more real to a botanist. And yet another stage of reality is reached with that botanist who is a specialist in lilies. You can get nearer and nearer, so to speak, to reality; but you never get near enough because reality is an infinite succession of steps, levels of perception, false bottoms, and hence unquenchable, unattainable. You can know more and more about one thing but you can never know everything about one thing: it's hopeless. So that we live surrounded by more or less ghostly objects—that machine, there, for instance. It's a complete ghost to me—I don't understand a thing about it and, well, it's a mystery to me, as much of a mystery as it would be to Lord Byron. [*Strong Opinions,* pp. 10–11]

The pencil of *Transparent Things,* which at once creates and destroys, devises and eats up the little world of Elias Borrowdale, seems to me one of the greatest expressions of this popular theme of the twentieth century, the unintelligibility of the objective world. Research, attentiveness, anatomy have never gotten to the core of anything; but we may relish the middle of the onion so greatly that we cannot be sad that we never attain to the center. The description of Hugh's pencil is not only a representation of the impossibility of seizing the object, but a representation of the delight, the sheer friskiness of the imagination in its clever evasions of responsibility, its deformities, grotesqueries. We have tried to draw a lion and unfortunately a griffin came out instead; so let us be connoisseurs of griffins in the absence of lions. Nabokov does not suggest that we should abandon the search for the innermost reality we can discover; his perseverance, his eyestrain, as a specialist in butterflies is proof. Indeed, the stress of trying to discover or represent the real is exactly what inspires, gives energy to the imagination in its construction of the fantastic. The best griffins appear for the artist who is trying to draw lions; he who sets out to draw griffins will produce only mangy and tuberous lions.

Despite Nabokov's archness and exaggeration, the description of Hugh's pencil is, at last, a kind of celebration of the real. The mad narrator who flouts and flogs the pencil for three pages only to discover that it was never there in the first place belies another narrative consciousness who goes about the ever-frustrated task of representation with a kind of love; the crazy declarations of the pencil's uniqueness, a haecceitas that makes that pencil visible like Michaelangelo's sculptures in the raw material from which it will be cut, belie a hidden affection for its homely serviceability. To Nabokov the necessary angel of the imagination, reconciling man to the inhuman world, is a flighty and potbellied fellow, sometimes a heroin addict and a sexual pervert like Clare Quilty in *Lolita,* but with many simple tastes as well, never able to succeed long at his job, impotent, deserving murder, but no less necessary or angelic for all that. In a short story written forty-five years before *Transparent Things,* Nabokov describes a museum in the year 2120 in which a writer looks at a Berlin streetcar:

> Everything, every trifle, will be valuable and meaningful: the conductor's purse, the advertisement over the window, that peculiar jolting motion which our great-grandchildren will perhaps imagine—everything will be ennobled and justified by its age.
> I think that here lies the sense of literary creation: to portray ordinary objects as they will be reflected in the kindly mirrors of future times; to find in the objects around us the fragrant tenderness that only posterity will discern and appreciate in the far-off times when every trifle of our plain everyday life will become exquisite and festive in its own right: the times when a man who might put on the most ordinary jacket of today will be dressed up for an elegant masquerade. [*Details of a Sunset,* p. 94]

Here the narrator is not so strained and antic, fatuous, as the narrator of *Transparent Things,* nor is he a lunatic pervert like Clare Quilty, but he has been injured in the war and is so mutilated that people shudder to look at him; again, in these works of art in which Nabokov describes the extreme reaches of the imagination the narrator is often distorted by the intensity of his own imaginative processes. This story, "A Guide to Berlin," ends with the narrator's realization of his own memorability, his knowing that the child who sees his twisted face will never forget him; the narrator is himself an object in his own hall of remembered things, the future museum. The creator and the created alike are cut off from ordinary participation in human life; the artifact and the artificer are each put in a glass display case, isolated from any usual context or relation, until the sheer thingliness becomes a cause of wonder, "exquisite and festive." This aesthetic proposition—it is similar to the hope of Wordsworth and Conrad of discovering what is miraculous in everyday life—suggests how strongly the object represented must be abstracted, removed out of everyday life, placed in an imaginary museum containing only one object, if its miraculousness is to be made manifest. The pencil's private universe in *Transparent Things* is only an inflation of this kind of museum. To represent a particular thing is to lock it up, freeze it; Hugh's pencil is nearly sacred, and to write with it—though we suspect it is the implement with which the novel is written—would be for an ordinary man an act of sacrilege. Instead of George Eliot's impression of a vibrant and interrelated world in which carpenters sing to the rhythm of their hammering, we have now a row of labeled cases: a hammer resting on velvet, with a mirror behind it to show the extractor claw, the nails it will never touch laid out side by side across the room, the mummy of the carpenter nearby. Donald Barthelme's story "At the Tolstoy Museum" perhaps may be read as a description of this victory of analysis, isolation, display, and concentration in modern fiction. What is significant must be stopped, scrutinized, shown from all sides at once; the world in which it and it alone has meaning must be educed. In Nabokov's *The Real Life of Sebastian Knight,* a woman is found who seems to be the ideal mistress for the artist-hero:

> She possessed, too, that real sense of beauty which has
> far less to do with art than with the constant readiness to
> discern the halo round a frying-pan or the likeness be-
> tween a weeping-willow and a Skye terrier. [*The Real
> Life of Sebastian Knight,* p. 83]

Sebastian Knight had won a prize for his book *The Laws of Literary Imagination,* and these seem to be the two central operations of that imagination: (1) verbal representation, the investing of common objects with the nimbus of words, the reverent preservation of the frying pan in the little museum of its own aura; (2) the discovery of occult resemblances in nature, as if metaphors and similes were latent in the world of experience, as if nature, in a recondite manner, obeyed aesthetic, even verbal laws. A mind that beholds the world in such a manner—as a heap of sudden immanences, each precise thing flaunting itself in simple irrelation, and, in the opposite fashion, as a set of tight congruences, transformations, all things intermetamorphosable with each other—sees a nature that is already verging on artifice, a world of experience laid out in novelistic fashion and asking to be written down. Genius, for Nabokov, usually has these two components, on one hand, the faculty of intensely knowing the special object, and on the other the faculty of discovering wild, remote, but intrinsic resemblances:

> What he should be really teaching was that mysterious and refined thing which he alone—out of ten thousand, a hundred thousand, perhaps even a million men—knew how to teach: for example—multi-level thinking: you look at a person and you see him as clearly as if he were fashioned of glass and you were the glass blower, while at the same time without in the least impinging upon that clarity you notice some trifle on the side—such as the similarity of the telephone receiver's shadow to a huge, slightly crushed ant, and (all this simultaneously) the convergence is joined by a third thought—the memory of a sunny evening at a Russian small railway station; i.e., images having no rational connection with the conversation you are carrying on while your mind runs around the outside of your own words and along the inside of those of your interlocutor. [*The Gift*, pp. 175–76]

This is Fyodor in *The Gift*, one of Nabokov's most vivid geniuses, who has X-ray vision into the thing-in-itself, has the creator's absolute knowledge of the inner workings, and who yet has such a motile, acute, and multiplex eye that he sees the crushed ant sleeping in the telephone. The happiest fictions are those in which the two faculties work harmoniously together, in which accurate representation is combined with the melting perspectives, the sleights of hand, the invisible links of the artistic conjurer; in which what one sees looking from the actual to the verbal and what one sees looking back from the verbal to the actual converge, become identical. But they do not readily converge, and *Transparent Things* is a witness to the jarring, the clashing of perspectives; the "transparent things" remain outside the fable, unassimilated, as if the novel could not treat what is too oppressively actual. Hugh's pencil cannot be tamed by witty metaphor; it recalcitrantly resists any attempt to be related to the action of the story. From the perspective of the verbal—and this is true of many writers besides Nabokov—images of things take priority over the things they represent; a description of a tennis match has greater ontological dignity than a real tennis match, which is sweaty, messy, and insufficiently coordinated. The main action of *Transparent Things* emphasizes this primacy of image by an unusual device: images are allowed to become voodoo dolls, controlling and altering the things of which they are representations. For instance, Hugh meets on a train an attractive woman, busy reading an insignificant novel about a little girl who sets her dollhouse on fire, leading to the conflagration of the whole villa. First the toy house burns, then the real one—Hugh himself will die at the end of the novel in a hotel fire, as if the fire in the paperback novel could kindle the wood of an actual hotel. This reverse Platonism, in which the copy is more genuine and potent than the original, is still better exemplified by the Old World novelist Baron R's insistence that no editor be permitted to tinker with his text:

> He went on to explain that if your true artist had cho-
> sen to form a character on the basis of a living individual,
> any rewriting aimed at disguising that character was
> tantamount to destroying the living prototype as would
> driving, you know, a pin through a little doll of clay, and
> the girl next door falls dead. If the composition was artis-
> tic, if it held not only water but wine, then it was in-
> vulnerable in one sense and horribly fragile in another.
> Fragile, because when a timid editor made the artist change
> "slender" to "plump," or "brown" to "blond" he dis-
> figured both the image and the niche where it stood and
> the entire chapel around it; and invulnerable, because no
> matter how drastically you changed the image, its pro-
> totype would remain recognizable by the shape of the
> hole left in the texture of the tale. [*Transparent Things*,
> pp. 69–70]

Auden has explained that art is the mirror of life because they are exact opposites: life is a chaos that works toward a secret order, while art begins in a state of orderly intendedness, its outlines obeying the rule of simple proportions, and elaborates itself toward plenitude, toward the wilderness of the real. In the world of art, causality is therefore re-versed, and images exert influence upon, compel obedience from, the things they are images of. The "transparent things," like the Terra of *Ada,* are attempts to spoil this easy effect, to show the partiality, the inadequacy, of the purely aesthetic perspective. I have alleged that traditional fiction labors toward its own deflation, finally dispels its own illusions in order to leave us with the flavor of the reality of our world. If that reality cannot be seized by representation it can be attained indirectly, by creating an ostensibly fictive world and then puncturing it, leaving us with the happy ending that reminds us—in a manner only slightly less blatant than that of Peachum at the end of *The Three Penny Opera,* who informs us that the king's merciful messenger seldom comes and that in real life the fate of the poor is especially bad—that there are no happy endings. The point of the pencil in *Transparent Things* is the instrument of this puncture; the pencil defies representation, yet its extreme gravity violates, pulls down the fragile, concocted world of the fable. Most of Nabokov's books, especially *Invitation to a Beheading,* end with some sort of disassembly of the novel.

The parable of the failed opera in Auden's *The Sea and the Mirror*—the greatest grandest opera performed by a hooty, off-the-beat provincial touring company, which Auden takes as an image for the forked condition of art, its mission to remind us simultaneously of the truth and of our condition of estrangement from it—suggests that it is the responsibility of every work of art to disenchant by first enchanting, to devise its own sabotage, to be beautiful and to make us uncomfortable at the sight of its beauty. The twentieth century has been particularly inventive in strategies to induce discomfort and giddiness, but the art of every generation has taken the same matters into account. The school of trompe l'oeil painting, which is at least as old as Zeuxis' grapes, has always faced a certain critical disdain, a sense that the artifice that makes through too-perfect representation a fool of the eye is at once labored and meretricious; in this way representation has always been associated with magic, with the evocation of a wonder that verges on queasiness. This affiliation of wonder with a kind of sacred revulsion at the artist who competes with the divine in the potency of his creation—and fails in the comparison—is one example of the intertwining of enchantment and disenchantment; but traditional, non-trompe l'oeil art also has its built-in flaws. Imperfect perspective, stylization, diapered backgrounds, "literary" dialogue, have always seemed a relief from the stridencies of representation. We would rather that some dramatic and irregular gesture, some roughness of outline or looseness of description, some seductive but anatomically impossible pose divert us from the rigor, the banality, the orthodoxy of the world of experience. The art of trompe l'oeil clamors for continual comparison between the image and what it represents; and by asserting its own contingence and dependency it loses our sympathy, our willingness to engage our imaginations with a frankly incorrect, imaginary subject. We like to think, as Browning thought in "Andrea del Sarto," that behind every faultless painting is a faulty and repressed, unimaginative painter. There are few things in art—which, after all, prides itself on mimesis—that are more difficult to account for than this taste for the not-quite-right, the spoiled; but I believe that Auden's explanation is the proper one, that we demand that our artworks illustrate, by internal self-perversion, the unbridgeable gap between art and life. Meat that is slightly gamey has the best flavor; and a certain tinge of rot, of iridescence, will often make representation more palatable. Even the trompe l'oeil painter seems to like best to show the carcasses of hanging partridges or rabbits.

In nineteenth-century fiction there is typically a Providence whose openhearted benignity guides the benighted characters of the novel to a morally satisfactory outcome; and this imposed justice, this wholly imaginary orderliness, is so pervasive in the "realistic" fable that the real and the unreal are inextricable; the representation of a dingy and squamous London is everywhere mitigated by the primacy, the invincibility, of the heart's affection. Auden's Caliban in *The Sea and the Mirror* perhaps does not properly appreciate the efficacy of this sort of mingled art, in which it is difficult to say what is enchantment, what is disenchantment—to Caliban it seems only to offer a lying reconciliation of the aesthetic and the human, a palliative to our plight. It is perhaps generally true that the art of the twentieth century has preferred to keep strictly separate the fabulous and the verisimilar, and yet to illustrate in a single work both worlds and their ironic commentary on each other. Nabokov's *Transparent Things* is just such an example of the unbridgeable gap between the world of art and the world of experience; the fable everywhere stumbles over the transparent things, an incessant clatter of interruptions; but by comprising both the transparent things and the story of Hugh Person's life, the novel attains a kind of wholeness, comprehensiveness, even though the two worlds it depicts are immiscible, hostile. There are many novels in which the sense of the vivacity and immediacy of the real is created negatively, by the laborious building of a purely unreal world, faulty in construction, riddled with holes, but in which the holes and faults are felt as the tangible impressions of our own world of experience, a world that can be shown in fiction only as a kind of palpable absence. Hugh's pencil is one such vivid hole.

To Martin Heidegger this hole outlining a pencil would be a "clearing," through which mankind is reconciled to the earth of his dwelling. Heidegger's "The Origin of the Work of Art" (1950) and Auden's *The Sea and the Mirror* (1947) are the two most profound aesthetic treatises of the twentieth century that I know, and perhaps the two most optimistic as well; they both lie on the interface between philosophy and art, and both are works of the imagination in which the imagination is asked to turn its eyes inward, to become intelligent with self-regard. Heidegger's well-known description of Van Gogh's painting of a pair of peasant shoes would make a novelist blush that a philosopher was capable of such minute and expansive verbal representation:

> A pair of peasant shoes and nothing more. And yet.
>
> From the dark opening of the worn insides of the shoes the toilsome tread of the worker stands forth. In the stiffly solid heaviness of the shoes there is the accumulated tenacity of her slow trudge through the far-spreading and ever-uniform furrows of the field, swept by a raw wind. On the leather there lies the dampness and

saturation of the soil. Under the soles there slides the
loneliness of the field-path as the evening declines. In the
shoes there vibrates the silent call of the earth, its quiet
gift of the ripening corn and its enigmatic self-refusal in
the fallow desolation of the wintry field. This equipment
is pervaded by uncomplaining anxiety about the certainty
of bread, the wordless joy of having once more withstood
want, the trembling before the advent of birth and shivering at the surrounding menace of death. This equipment
belongs to the *earth* and it is protected in the *world* of the
peasant woman. From out of this protected belonging the
equipment itself rises to its resting-in-self. [*Philosophies
of Art and Beauty,* p. 663]

If we compare this to Hugh's pencil in *Transparent Things* we see that
Van Gogh–Heidegger seems to have accomplished the very miracle
that Nabokov's narrator was too fussy, flighty, ironical to perform; the
being of the shoes is seized by the artifice, and along with the shoes the
whole landscape and rustic life of their owner are hauled out into visible
apparition. Hugh's pencil brings forth a little self-contained universe, a
bubble in the text of the novel; but the peasant woman's shoes rest with
their tops gaping wide, almost everted, splayed open, so open that a
kind of volcanic eruption can take place, an ever-growing immanence
in which the peasant's feet and the furrows of her field and the ground
on which Heidegger and you and I all stand will radiate forth. The
image of the peasant shoes is a secular sacrament:

Thus in the work it is truth, not merely something true,
that is at work. The picture that displays the peasant
shoes, the poem that declares the Roman fountain, not
only make manifest what this isolated entity is as such—
if they manifest anything at all—but also they let unconcealment as such happen in regard to what *is* as a
whole. The more simply and essentially the shoes appear
in their essence, the more uncluttered and purely the
fountain appears in its essence, the more directly and
fascinatingly does all that *is* attain to a greater degree of
being along with them. That is how self-concealing being
is illuminated. Light of this kind dispenses its shining into
the work. This shining [*das Scheinen*], fitted into the
work, is the beautiful [*das Schöne*]. *Beauty is one way in
which truth occurs as unconcealment.* [*Philosophies of
Art and Beauty,* pp. 680–81]

Van Gogh, Hölderlin, Ictinus, and the rest are angels whose mediation makes us the concording denizens of the dark earth on which we
walk.

To describe the operations of the artistic process, Heidegger distinguishes between *world* and *earth:* the realm of open display and human history, the kingdom of the intelligible, is *world,* while *earth* is tangible, impenetrably closed, a living concealment.

World is not a mere collection of countable or un-countable, familiar and unfamiliar things that are merely present-at-hand. But also world is not a merely imagined framework added to the sum of such given things. *World worlds [Welt weltet]* and is something that *is* to a greater degree than the tangible and perceptible realm in which we believe ourselves to be at home. World is never an object that stands before us and can be beheld. World is the ever un-objective realm that shelters us as long as the paths of birth and death, blessing and curse keep us ex-posed to being. Wherever the essential decisions of our history are made, are taken up and abandoned by us, mistaken and re-examined, there the world worlds. A stone is worldless. Plant and animal equally have no world; but they belong to the hidden pressure of an envi-ronment within which they fall. On the other hand the peasant woman has a world because she dwells in the openness of that which *is.* In its reliability her equipment gives to this world its own necessity and nearness. In-asmuch as a world opens itself, all things receive their lingering and hastening, their farness and nearness, their scope and limits.

What is the earth that it attains to the unconcealed pre-cisely in such a manner? A stone presses downward and manifests its heaviness. But while this heaviness exerts an opposing pressure it denies to us any penetration into it. If we attempt such penetration by breaking open the rock, it still does not display in its fragments something inward that has been disclosed. The stone has merely withdrawn again into the same dull pressure and bulk of its fragments. If we try to lay hold of this in another way by placing the stone on a balance, we merely bring its heaviness into the form of a calculated weight. This perhaps very precise determination of the stone remains a number but the weight has escaped us. Color shines and wants only to shine. When we analyze it intellectually by measuring its wave-frequencies it disappears. It shows itself only when it remains undisclosed and unexplained. Earth thus sets to nought every attempt to penetrate into it. It causes every merely calculating approach to it to turn into a destruction. This may carry with it the appear-ance of control and of progress in the form of technical-scientific objectification of nature, but this control nevertheless remains an impotence of will. The earth appears openly illuminated as itself only when it is perceived and preserved as that which is essentially undisclosable, that which recedes before every disclosure and constantly keeps itself closed up. [*Philosophies of Art and Beauty*, pp. 671–72, 673]

Heidegger's image of the stone is the exact opposite of his image of the peasant shoes, which, grounded in earth, rise up into the historical and humane world of the peasant woman and set forth, erect, the whole truth of things. Instead of this astonishing forthcomingness, evocation, there is simply the stone's retreat from the light, its mute, passive insistence on its own obscurity; a battery of floodlights, a mass spectrometer, an X-ray machine may all be deployed, may all belabor it, but the stone will remain concealed though it is pummeled to atoms. The stone's recalcitrance is an image of the separation of world and earth, their mutual dependence and mutual exclusivity. To Heidegger world and earth are in a precarious, ever-shifting equilibrium, the opacities and dumbnesses of earth continually heaving themselves up into the worldly light, the comprehended things of world continually subsiding, huddling back into the earthly darkness; and in this treacherous flux of light and dark only the work of art can confidently comprise and manifest both world in its openness and earth in its closedness. The stone may be closed, but Heidegger the artist has managed to represent it in its state of closure, just as he had managed, following Van Gogh, to represent the openness of the peasant shoes. In the perpetual struggle of earth and world there obtains a line of demarcation, a film that separates them, and this line is the proper subject matter for the artist. Indeed, every successful work of art traces the pattern of this bounding line. The German word *Riss*, which means both rift and design, suggests the almost unthinkable manner in which, in the work of art, world and earth converge, draw together, define each other, and yet remain apart and, by remaining opposed to and yet intimate with each other, form a figure that it is the task of art to describe:

But as a world opens itself the earth comes to tower upward. It shows itself as that which bears all, as that which is secure in its law and constantly self-closing. World demands its determination and its measure and lets what *is* attain to the Open of its paths. Earth aspires, bearing-towering, to keep itself closed and to entrust everything to its law. The conflict is not a rift [*Riss*] as the ripping open of a mere cleft; rather, it is the intimacy of opponents that belong to each other. This rift draws [*reisst*]

> the opponents together into the source of their unity
> out of the single ground. It is a ground-plan [*Grundriss*].
> It is an elevation [*Auf-riss*] that draws the basic features
> of the rising up of the lighting of what *is*. This rift does not
> let the opponents break apart; it brings the opposition of
> measure and limit into the single boundary [*Umriss*].
> [*Philosophies of Art and Beauty*, p. 686]

All art, in a sense, is the neat drawing of that S-shaped boundary line
that separates yin from yang, the major polarities of being, so that the
whole circle is divided into two embracing and interconsuming paisley
figures, the dark and the light, each of which regards the other with the
small dot of an eye.

When we look at the actual practice of such great contemporaries of
Heidegger as Auden, Nabokov, and Beckett, we see a somewhat
gloomier and more limited view of the rights and duties of art. Art still
attempts to mediate between intelligible inventions and fables—what
Heidegger would call *world*—and the point-blank and ignorant earth of
our experience; but the artist attempts to pull them together not across
the infinitesimal rift line of Heidegger, but across a vast distance over
which his arms can scarcely reach. To Auden, as we have seen, it is the
artist's responsibility to show that the gap cannot be bridged, to sub-
vert the mediating function of his own art. The description of Hugh's
pencil in *Transparent Things* is interesting in that it seems to begin with
assumptions like those of Heidegger—that art is adequate to embrace
the whole sensuous universe by the exact grasping of one particular—but
it ends with the pencil's escape from the narrator's clutches, an effect
of sabotage akin to that for which Auden calls; instead of an exhilarat-
ing world-disclosure like Van Gogh's shoes, the pencil has turned out
to be as involute and self-concealing as a stone. Instead of Heidegger's
world, the matrix that nourishes us and in which our deeds have
meaning, the modern novelist offers brittle artifices, privately real or
self-consciously unreal; instead of Heidegger's *earth* he offers the
spectacle of a blind and nerveless impingingness, the dim impression of
ponderousness, gravity, in the absence of a representable dwelling
place.

The modern novel is full of characters who are aware that they are
characters in novels—it is a short step from the verbal representation
of a human being to the verbal representation of a representation's
representedness—and frequently these too-knowing characters, caught
up, translated, assumed into a fictive world, are asked to turn their
heads and look down at the worldless earth they have left behind. Like
Lazarus in heaven peering over the edge of a cloud to behold burning
Dives, they often see something puzzling, reproachful, horrified,

quaint, even dreamlike. To a character in a novel, an intelligence grown a little too articulate, verbal, human, whose very body is articulated in sentence form, the terra firma that is outside the boundary of the novel and yet the locus imitated, alluded to by the furniture that surrounds him, must appear as an invisible massiveness, a distant rumor, an inaudibly deep noise, finally a kind of myth of a life elsewhere from which he is, for no good reason, excluded. Both Kingsley Amis and Nabokov have written novels about imaginary places in which our commonplace earth is a science fiction tale dismissed as balderdash by most of the enlightened. The main point is not, I think, that homely earth is every bit as preposterous and invented as the verbal kingdoms erected in the text—though Nabokov says exactly that in *Pale Fire,* canto 2, lines 214–20—but that a kind of shock of disillusion, the sabotage on which Auden dotes, can be made by piling up two self-canceling illusions on each other. We are told, in Nabokov's *Ada,* that the novel takes place on a world called Demonia or Antiterra, in which countries resembling Russia and America coexist amiably on the same continent, in which no major war has occurred in a century, and in which electricity has long been forbidden—a world where the scrambled Russian-American heritage of Nabokov, his memories, prejudices, and dreams, are elevated into a shared, dignified, public realm, the author's human uniqueness turned inside out and made the basis of a world. The inhabitants of Antiterra believe themselves to be dwelling in a disorderly, even hellish place—the Russian word *ada* is the genitive of Hades—but they dream of a vibrant, tumultuous, ideally dramatic, aesthetically pleasing, light-years-distant planet called Terra. By means of the diligent scholarship of the hero, Van Veen, who combs asylums looking for visionary lunatics with news about Terra, this planet elaborates itself from a trite and insipid afterlife, with soulful angels playing harps, into a well-focused world greatly resembling our own, complete with World Wars I and II. It never attains full identity—for instance, the *Führer* is named Athaulf Hindler or Mittler—but it is continually ramifying, devolving, into identity with the reader's known earth. At the end of the novel Van Veen is angry with a director who has made a film of his book about Terra, for the director has employed artistic license and distorted the events to make them more cinematically effective; but the reader sees that every distortion brings Terra closer to historical earth. Near the beginning of the novel Van Veen explains the differences between Antiterra and Terra as follows:

> There were those who maintained that the discrepancies and "false overlappings" between the two

worlds were too numerous, and too deeply woven into the skein of successive events, not to taint with trite fancy the theory of essential sameness; and there were those who retorted that the dissimilarities only confirmed the live organic reality pertaining to the other world; that a perfect likeness would rather suggest a specular, and hence speculatory, phenomenon; and that two chess games with identical openings and identical end moves might ramify in an infinite number of variations, on *one* board and in *two* brains, at any middle stage of their irrevocably converging development. [*Ada*, pp. 18–19]

Antiterra is not a mirror image of Terra but is irresistibly converging with it, and, unknown to Van Veen, both are converging with the reader's earth. At the present instant they are, it seems, identical; it is only in retrospect that private memory and historical truth, the fabulous and the well known or established, the invented and the commonplace, seem to diverge in a great forking-backward into vision and knowledge. As T. S. Eliot says in *Burnt Norton:*

> What might have been is an abstraction
> Remaining a perpetual possibility
> Only in a world of speculation.
> What might have been and what has been
> Point to one end, which is always present.
> Footfalls echo in the memory
> Down the passage which we did not take
> Towards the door we never opened
> Into the rose-garden.

Both *Burnt Norton* and *Ada* are studies in the use of the imagination to point to, indicate, that which can never be directly said or embodied in words, the realness of reality. Nabokov has erected this interlocking folderol, this dance of worlds, to point an outstretched member at that deaf and dumb, unspeakable earth that Terra and Antiterra are competing images of. Terra intricately qualifies, modifies, reshapes Antiterra; because Terra is an invention within an invention, it can revise, reform, correct the built-in errors of the original invention, Antiterra, the inaccuracies of representation inherent in any verbal construct. *Ada* is a machine devised to give off increasingly accurate approximations of reality. All great novels try, in a sense, to sum up and terminate the genre of the novel, but the claims of *Ada* are better than those of many.

But why has Nabokov made the residents of Antiterra—so clearly fabulous and frisky, labile, amenable—consider their home nasty and chaotic, while they regard war-ridden Terra as the seat of art and order, an enchanted Cythera? This is part of the self-corrective strategy. The Antiterran Van Veen, faced with the death of his aunt Marina and with decades of separation from his half-sister and lover Ada, begs for a sign from the world beyond. When it does not come, he wonders "what really kept him alive on terrible Antiterra, with Terra a myth and all art a game" (p. 452); and, when he sees an ominous dead moth on a window ledge, just before he is about to see Ada after their long, long absence, he says, "Thank goodness, symbols did not exist either in dreams or in the life in between" (p. 510). Van insists that Antiterra is deadly, devastatingly real, unprovidenced and unsymbolic, sodden and opaque—in short, not invented by a god or a novelist but a horror in its own right. Ada has the same feeling, and, like Van, whose exploration of Terra is an attempt to overcome this unpleasant knowledge, she does what she can to mitigate despair. Acting in Chekhov's *Four Sisters* (in Antiterra the play contains a supernumerary sister) is one sort of relief from the aleatory: "In 'real' life we are creatures of chance in an absolute void—unless we be artists ourselves, naturally; but in a good play I feel authored" (p. 426). This is a stratagem by which one can obtain the desired sense of design behind life, the thrill of authoredness that the author imparts to his characters only at moments. Sometimes it comes spontaneously, outside the theater, as when the middle-aging lovers begin a series of trysts at a Swiss hotel:

> the alberghian atmosphere of those new trysts added a novelistic touch (Aleksey and Anna may have asterisked here!) which Ada welcomed as a frame, as a form, something supporting and guarding life, otherwise unprovidenced on Desdemonia, where artists are the only gods. [*Ada*, p. 521]

But artists may be divine enough. From the point of view of the reader, the development of the novel is a series of approximations to reality; from the point of view of the characters in the novel, the development is a series of approximations to art. The reader leaves the novel with the image of an almost perfected Terra, while Van and Ada die "*into* the finished book, into Eden or Hades, into the prose of the book or the poetry of its blurb" (p. 587)—and the last page is the construction of a dust jacket, the bright coffin that will enfold and preserve in imperishable art this very verbal couple. Van and Ada complain of the lack of design and symbol in an Antiterra that is to the reader a hall of mirrors, twins, incestuous multiplicities, shimmery reflections on water—indeed, Marina, Aqua, and to an extent Ada herself *are* the running figments of water, as her sister Lucette is a shape beheld in fire. Van and Ada, as the novel unfolds, learn how to see themselves and their

Antiterra, which seemed at times so squalid and disorderly to them, as figured, literary, fabulous, and at last ascend into the elysium of art; while aesthetic Terra impends, swells, gains weight, looms, a great molten drop about to fall. Each readjusts itself, shifts from the inversions of fiction into what it ought to be. Antiterra and Terra, which wore each other's clothes at the beginning of the novel—Antiterra seemed like stable disenchanted ground, while Terra seemed to be the heaven of human invention—at last show themselves as Heidegger's *world* and Heidegger's *earth,* respectively. It is a process of mutual subversion, in which the conventions of fiction unravel, in which, as artifice ceases to pretend to be real, acknowledges its own artificiality, there descends from the sky like some New Year's celebration in Times Square the great gilded ball of earth, the reality that falls effortlessly on the reader as he puts down the novel. This effect of disillusionment, this manner of resolving illusion so satisfactorily that it evaporates before the reader's eye, as I have said, is one of the major purposes of traditional fiction as well; but Nabokov wishes to calculate, to control the effect so precisely that he introduces into *Ada* Terra, a surrogate earth, a kind of tumor of disillusion, a fetus growing in the novel until the dehiscence of the final page.

In a way, not only *world* and *earth* but Heidegger and Auden as well are reconciled by the strategy of *Ada.* Auden's insistence upon the estrangement of art from life, of our invented, intuited paradises from our hideous, fallen earth, finds expression in the antithesis of Terra and Antiterra. In Nabokov's *Pale Fire* there is a fantastic organization of regicidal conspirators, one of whom loses his leg trying to make antimatter; and to an extent the Terra and Antiterra of *Ada,* as they draw close to each other and touch, seem to explode, cancel each other out, dismiss each other as insubstantial wrack, spume. The ruining effect on which Auden dotes could scarcely be improved. And yet in another sense Terra and Antiterra draw upon each other's substance, grow rich and fruitful by the joining together of the fictive and the earthy, the lunatic and the commonsensical, moon and sun and terra firma. Nabokov, though he professed to despise the novel's hero, Van Veen, never wrote a happier book than *Ada,* except perhaps for *Speak, Memory.* In this autobiography Nabokov testifies movingly to the joy of discovering the design, the "intricate watermark" unique to one's own life; and he tells one of his finest parables, Kuropatkin and the Match Theme, in order to show the origin of this knowledge, the engraving of the Nabokov monogram.

One afternoon at the beginning of the same year, in our
St. Petersburg house, I was led down from the nursery

into my father's study to say how-do-you-do to a friend of the family, General Kuropatkin. His thick-set, uniform-encased body creaking slightly, he spread out to amuse me a handful of matches, on the divan where he was sitting, placed ten of them end to end to make a horizontal line, and said, "This is the sea in calm weather." Then he tipped up each pair so as to turn the straight line into a zigzag—and that was "a stormy sea." He scrambled the matches and was about to do, I hoped, a better trick when we were interrupted. His aide-de-camp, was shown in and said something to him. With a Russian, flustered grunt, Kuropatkin heavily rose from his seat, the loose matches jumping up on the divan as his weight left it. That day, he had been ordered to assume supreme command of the Russian Army in the Far East.

This incident had a special sequel fifteen years later, when at a certain point of my father's flight from Bolshevik-held St. Petersburg to southern Russia he was accosted while crossing a bridge, by an old man who looked like a gray-bearded peasant in his sheepskin coat. He asked my father for a light. The next moment each recognized the other. I hope old Kuropatkin, in his rustic disguise, managed to evade Soviet imprisonment, but that is not the point. What pleases me is the evolution of the match theme: those magic ones he had shown me had been trifled with and mislaid, and his armies had also vanished, and everything had fallen through, like my toy trains that, in the winter of 1904–05, in Wiesbaden, I tried to run over the frozen puddles in the ground of the Hotel Oranien. The following of such thematic designs through one's life should be, I think, the true purpose of autobiography. [*Speak, Memory*, p. 19]

The experiment with the toy trains was performed because the five-year-old Nabokov had read how the Japanese hoped that the Russian trains would founder in Lake Baikal if the Russians tried to lay track over the ice. The inherent pattern that Nabokov has found—it is a zigzag, like the "stormy sea" matchsticks of 1904—is a Heideggerian *Riss,* a rift-design at the delicate juncture of *world* and *earth*. In the midst of a universal lapsing, the scattering of matches and the drowning of toy trains and real ones, the artistic imagination has sought out the radiant design, expansive, even hilarious in the heart of ruin. The known tumbles into the unknown and reemerges, stumbles back into the light, disguised, wearing a peasant's sheepskin coat; and the immanence of the rift-design is a kind of theophany, or what takes the place of a theophany in a world where artists are the only gods.

Many modern writers describe what could be called rift-experiences; Joyce's epiphanies, Proust's madeleine are clearly related phenomena, but I would like to use the term rift-experience only for those revelations or illuminations that are accompanied by some sense of the fragility of things, of lapsing or collapsing, of the tenuous changingness of the boundary between the known and the unknown. One might compare the parable of Kuropatkin with this passage from Virginia Woolf's *A Sketch of the Past;* she has spoken of sudden intuitions, of the wholeness of the flower with its roots and earth, of the knowledge of an acquaintance's suicide—and from these "sledgehammer" blows of the real she adduces a kind of philosophy:

> From this I reach what I might call a philosophy; at any rate it is a constant idea of mine; that behind the cotton wool is hidden a pattern; that we—I mean all human beings—are connected with this; that the whole world is a work of art; that we are parts of the work of art. *Hamlet* or a Beethoven quartet is the truth about this vast mass that we call the world. But there is no Shakespeare, there is no Beethoven; certainly and emphatically there is no God; we are the words; we are the music; we are the thing itself. And I see this when I have a shock. [*Moments of Being*, p. 72]

Nabokov was always coy when asked whether he believed in God; but Virginia Woolf, like Heidegger, offers an explicitly secular description of feelings of patternedness, rift-experiences. If Heidegger had seen this passage, written about two years after his first lectures on the origin of the work of art, he might have thought Virginia Woolf a remarkably earthless woman, so literary, so caught up in verbal constructions, so exclusively residing in *world* that when *earth* rose up before her it seemed monstrous, the enemy, Leviathan with a blunt instrument. It is true that Virginia Woolf, like Nabokov in the Kuropatkin parable, speaks both as an author and as a character in a novel; these blows, these accessions into reality, provide for her a feeling of authoredness in the absence of an author. It is strange that the combination of cotton wool—the commonplace daily life we all spin out of ourselves like a spider's web—*world*—and the hammer shocks of *earth* would give a sense of profound order, like a Beethoven quartet; but that is the mystery of the rift-design, the lovely tracing that is itself an abyss. Previously in this passage she has described her passivity in the face of these hidden intense realities, and she, unlike Nabokov, seems to tremble at the edge of self-abnegation, vertigo; but she does herself exert creative force, tames and anesthetizes these effusions of reality on her spine by verbalizing them, making novels that demonstrate at once the brutal shock and the concealed harmony, the vital pulse, within the shock. The Heideggerian artist, whose central mission is not self-expression but the disclosure of a world that rises out of and falls back into a great concealedness, a carpenter of windows looking out into a world much hidden by the very frames of the panes of glass, may be described either as a creator or as an instrument almost passively receptive to the huge tensions of earth and world, the slipping and sliding of the continental plates on which our life is founded. Indeed, Virginia Woolf attributes her becoming an artist to her seismographic sensitivities. To have what Joyce's Stephen Hero calls an epiphany, one must be sensitive to a circumambient and pervasive meaningfulness; it is only a matter of spiritual focus, of choosing which object to attend to in the great ubiquity of meaning. But a rift-experience is the discovery of patterns of collapse, the tape measure across the Grand Canyon, the cartography of undersea mountain ranges after the floor of the earth has sunk; and such authors are always intimate with catastrophe, earthquake, unmeaning. In Nabokov's *Ada* the heroine once describes herself as "a pale wild girl with gipsy hair in a deathless ballad, in a nulliverse . . . where the only principle is random variation" (p. 416). The ballad of Ada, that is, the text of the novel, is deathless precisely because the world on which it operates is a nulliverse; intrinsic lack of meaningfulness is a necessary precondition of this kind of art. The first principle of semiotics is the arbitrariness of the sign; and the alogical patterns of which Nabokov is so fond—Kuropatkin and the matches have no logical affiliation—range themselves over the velvet backdrop of despair, the blessed failure of omens to be ominous. Because signs have no inherent, mechanical meaning-identifications—and this is nearly the whole of Nabokov's quarrel with Freud—because the symbol is a thing, freestanding and independent, random, before it is a symbol, the imagination is liberated, able to devise its own patterns of meanings without prior constraint from the racial unconsciousness, from the book of all dream interpretation, from any old, weary manual of emblems. The world's randomness is the artist's strength. If one imagines the Ada of the "deathless ballad" as someone like the girl in Wallace Stevens's "The Idea of Order at Key West," I think he will not be far wrong. Ada, caught in a world of stray symmetries and scrambled myths—Cinderella is one of her father's servants—sees herself as a persistent motif absurdly rearranged. But the principle of random variation can itself be elevated into art, song, ballad; indeed, aleatory music, in which the position of raisins in a fruitcake or birds on telephone wires is translated into musical notation, is a fine example of rift-design, the art of the uncomprehended lifted up into utterance, into purely arbitrary pattern, the art of the nulliverse. The persistence of identity, the persistence of song, makes livable our thick and annulled dwelling place, our comprehensive Nowhere. In this sense all of us live on Antiterra, unearth; but we hear a deep clanging-together, presentiments of concord underneath us, the disturbing and darkly comforting It Is.

The felicity of *Ada* comes from the satisfaction of the imagination's verging ever more closely upon the earth that it refers to and tries to represent, the encroachment of Antiterra on Terra. In Nabokov's previous novels—except for *The Gift,* in which the imagination is solidly grounded, terrestrial upon the hero's childhood and youth—the imagination is usually disjunct and perfervid, the mother of sylphs and chimeras, growing ever more estranged from the earth it has abandoned. *Pale Fire* is a kind of textbook of the failures and successes of imaginary worlds: the poet John Shade constructs in his autobiography a myth of his life that is at once wholly fantastic—a dream shoe worn during a dream revelry is found on the lawn next morning—and wholly real, justified at every turning by rich and lucid human experience. For Charles Kinbote, Shade's doomed editor, the constructed world of his paranoid fantasy, the kingdom he calls Zembla, has no such solidity. Earth, Terra, instead of supporting, converging on the fable of Zembla, continually bristles, threatens, offers competing, commonplace explanations for the phenomena Kinbote would attribute to black conspiracies, international terror. The objects on which Shade meditates—his little daughter's swing, the clockwork toy wheelbarrow, his shaving platform—serve the Heideggerian function of Van Gogh's shoes, opening up the wealth of a felt world for public delectation; but the objects on which Kinbote meditates elaborate floridly in a vacuum, then close themselves, disappear. Here is Kinbote describing a painting from the palace of the king of Zembla:

> While unable to catch a likeness, and therefore wisely limiting himself to a conventional style of complimentary portraiture, Eystein showed himself to be a prodigious master of the trompe l'oeil in the depiction of various objects surrounding his dignified dead models and making them look even deader by contrast to the fallen petal or the polished panel that he rendered with such love and skill. But in some of those portraits Eystein had also resorted to a weird form of trickery: among his decorations of wood or wool, gold or velvet, he would insert one which was really made of the material elsewhere imitated by paint. This device which was apparently meant to enhance the effect of his tactile and tonal values had, however, something ignoble about and disclosed not only

> an essential flaw in Eystein's talent, but the basic fact that "reality" is neither the subject nor the object of true art which creates its own special reality having nothing to do with the average "reality" perceived by the communal eye. But to return to our technicians whose tapping is approaching along the gallery toward the bend where the King and Odon stand ready to part. At this spot hung a portrait representing a former Keeper of the Treasure, decrepit Count Kernel, who was painted with fingers resting lightly on an embossed and emblazoned box whose side facing the spectator consisted of an inset oblong made of real bronze, while upon the shaded top of the box, drawn in perspective, the artist had pictured a plate with the beautifully executed, twin-lobed, brainlike, halved kernel of a walnut. [*Pale Fire*, p. 94]

The Soviets ransacking the palace in their search for the crown jewels pry open the box lid decorated with the painted walnut; the box "contained nothing, however, except the broken bits of a nutshell." We are promised an opening-up, a revelation, but we are led nowhere, offered only a bit of garbage; the painting, instead of penetrating into a graduated and profound world, has turned out to be the thinnest iridescence, a rainbow visible only from one side. The whole description is a parody of the process of representation, an illustration of the unbridgeable gap—I have returned to the vocabulary of Auden's *The Sea and the Mirror*—between the "special reality" of art and the earth that is neither its subject nor its object. Eystein—the name suggests that his eye has petrified, confused itself with what it is regarding—glues bits of "wood or wool, gold or velvet" next to his representations of them; thereby the painting, instead of representing a world outside itself, embraces that world and ingests it, incorporates it. The relation of the painting to its subject is therefore awkward, twisted, false; the painting is not content to be an image of what it represents, but instead competes with it as a kind of second version of the thing itself, defective in one dimension. Eystein paints a walnut, but "behind" the image is not a real walnut outside the painting that served as a model for it but a little box burrowing into the canvas, containing fragments of a walnut shell—as if the honest walnut, usurped and swallowed, had left behind only a few indigestible scraps. It is a parable of the ravenousness of a bad imagination, falsifying the earth, embellishing the void; it is an emblem of the sealed, nonreferential quality of the whole Zembla fantasy, which balloons out and covers the sad detritus of a wretched life—a fantasy that is not a representation of that life but an evasion of it. The novel hints frequently about the failure of Zembla to refer to anything. In the one passage of Shade's poem that actually treats the myth of Zembla—it is a continuing joke that Kinbote has done every-thing he could think of to encourage Shade to write the Zemblan epic instead of an autobiographical poem—Shade informs the reader of the attitude a sane mind would take toward Zembla:

> There are events, strange happenings, that strike
> The mind as emblematic. They are like
> Lost similes adrift without a string,
> Attached to nothing. Thus that northern king,
> Whose desperate escape from prison was
> Brought off successfully only because
> Some forty of his followers that night
> Impersonated him and aped his flight—
> [*Pale Fire,* p. 72]

This is why Zembla is lunatic: not because it is bizarre or uncanny but because it is a *world* that has no relation to *earth:* a helium-filled simile floating off into the sky, a trope without reference. It is no wonder Kinbote dreams of committing suicide by falling from an airplane with-out a parachute.

The imagination becomes insatiable when it feeds on airy nothings, and this is why Kinbote seems so much more imaginative, more attrac-tive even, than the true hero of the novel, John Shade. For Shade there is truth to be told, and when it is told he is finished, can die content; but Kinbote, whose imagination lacks its proper object, must exuberate into ever more vertiginous and nonsensical constructions. Shade is the master of restricted form, the heroic couplet, while the phantasmagoria of Kinbote requires the amplitude of prose. Indeed, it is hard for Nabokov not to make his first-person narrators into models of the novelist; and Kinbote, though he is only a demented professor and editor, is nevertheless an ideal novelist, useful for defining problems of the relations of fiction to reality. Our first hint that there is something wrong with the verbal surface of the text comes on the first page:

> A methodical man, John Shade usually copied out his daily quota of completed lines at midnight but even if he recopied them again later, as I suspect he sometimes did, he marked his card or cards not with the date of his final adjustments, but with that of his Corrected Draft or first Fair Copy. I mean, he preserved the date of actual crea-tion rather than that of second or third thoughts. There is a very loud amusement park right in front of my present lodgings. [*Pale Fire,* p. 7]

Neither editors nor novelists are supposed to break into their texts with news about the actual present, a complaint about distraction; and yet editors edit, and novelists write, and readers read, by the grace of an act of will to shut out the continual clamor of the present moment, which everywhere thwarts, defies, the concentration necessary to maintain one's immersion in a verbal and constructed, illusory world. Shade, according to Nabokov's premise, is the kind of artist who can use the vitality of the present moment to perfect his art—his fourth canto ends with an exact description of his immediate surroundings, the sharp second before Jack Grey's bullet will kill him—while Kinbote is the kind of artist who is balked, impeded, perturbed by the earth that his fantasy neglects, conceals. And yet Kinbote's struggling against interruption—the whole poem and all the commentary on the poem constitute a vast interruption in the story of Zembla, making the novel a long tissue of interruption—is a faithful depiction of every novelist's struggle to keep attention focused on the text. Kinbote's novel, then, is a metaphor for the very process of reading and writing. Every reader reads in a constant tension of distractedness, holding erect the pseudo-reality evoked by the words while it is being penetrated by sewing machines, BB guns, random humming, amusement parks. The very light that illuminates the page is a glare and an annoyance; some other responsibility—the flowers need watering, a poem needs editing—preys on our mind as our eyes try to stay keen on the printed page. What I am reading becomes a thin veil, a scrim continuously violated by the more urgent but perhaps less interesting place in which I am sitting; and it is this sense, of the glittering unreality of the verbal and of its constant penetratedness, its transparency to the banal, that the Zembla fable embodies almost perfectly. These interruptions, these sudden breakthroughs of an earth with which the fiction has nothing to do, work rather like the incompetent singers in Auden's imaginary grand opera; they remind us of the dangerous inadequacies of art, or of a certain kind of art, to our present condition.

Nabokov employs, then, two different kinds of fantasy: heroic fantasy, which is a continual convergence upon the earth of experience, the leap of a flying fish gliding ever closer to the surface of the sea, a metamorphosis in a prolonged state of disenchanting itself back to its original form, Proteus about to achieve the shape of an old man after his dazzling experiments in identity—the kind of fantasy found in Antiterra or in the autobiographical poem of John Shade or in the Central Asian exploration of Fyodor in *The Gift*—and evasive fantasy, which is a continual exclusion of the earth of experience, the leap of a flying fish drowning in the upper air from the effort of holding itself out of the water, Proteus the dragon claiming that he never was and never will be an old man. This latter kind of fantasy is also common in Nabokov's novels and is highly elaborated in *Pale Fire* and in the unfinished novel on which *Pale Fire* was to some extent based, two chapters of which became the short stories "Ultima Thule" and "Solux Rex." In these stories a destitute painter, Sineusov, receives a mysterious commission to illustrate a poem, *Ultima Thule,* written in a Scandinavian language he does not know, a poem he dimly gathers to be about the king of a distant northern land and the political machinations against him. Sineusov, despondent over the death of his wife, grows so engrossed in the visual world he imagines around the unreadable text that his days and his nights lose touch with sensuous reality, become absorbed in the contemplation of the northern king, K, who becomes a fantastic surrogate. It is as if the reader were shown what is only hinted at in *Pale Fire,* the process by which Kinbote constructs his fantasy of being Charles the Beloved, king of Zembla; and these two stories also show how ingeniously dismal a fantastic world can grow without the counterbalance of the stable earth provided by John Shade in *Pale Fire.* One can see why Nabokov had to abandon the tale, for as the distant northern land proliferates it grows sterile, untenable, impossible for the novelist to support. "Solus Rex" and *Pale Fire,* taken together, will enable us to set forth a list of rules for distinguishing good imaginary worlds from bad ones, heroic from evasive fantasy.

1. *Symmetry.* If every element corresponds relentlessly to another, the reader will feel that the fable develops only by the slow rotation of mirrors mounted around a cylinder, static, stifling, enclosed, having only an ocular, speculative, and impalpable reality. Just as every member of Charles the Beloved's court has his exact counterpart among the regicidal Shadows—faithful Odon has an evil and epileptic half-brother named Nodo—so Charles Kinbote has his own antiself in the person of the assassin Gradus, who is a gray cannibal to the colorful vegetarian Kinbote, heterosexual and castrated while Kinbote is homosexual and insatiable. The excess of symmetry suggests the high magnification, the overblownness of the image, at the tangible center of which is only a broken bit of nutshell, or nothing at all:

> He awoke to find her standing with a comb in her hand before his—or rather, his grandfather's—cheval glass, a triptych of bottomless light, a really fantastic mirror, signed with a diamond by its maker, Sudarg of Bokay. She turned about before it: a secret device of reflection gathered an infinite number of nudes in its depths, garlands of girls in graceful and sorrowful groups, diminishing in the limpid distance, or breaking into individual nymphs, some of whom, she murmured, must resemble her ancestors when they were young—little peasant *garlien* combing their hair in shallow water as far as the eye

could reach, and then the wistful mermaid from an old tale, and then nothing. [*Pale Fire,* p. 81]

Sudarg of Bokay is, of course, Jakob Gradus spelled backward. At the center of the image of the imaginary seductress Fleur is an ordinary peasant girl; but as we try to focus our eyes on the referent of the image of Fleur, to get to the bottom of it, it veers into a mermaid, into unreality, and vanishes.

2. *Emptiness.* The "nothing" in the center of the mirror is a common image pattern in evasive fantasy; what is nonreferential will crumble, blow away, if one searches too assiduously for a referent. The fantastic aspects of the Zembla fable perhaps reach their culmination in a passage in which the deposed Kinbote, escaped from Communist Zembla and on his way to America, visits Disa, his former queen, in southern France and remembers a dream he once had of her, a dream provoked by his guilt over her sexual humiliation at his hands, over his confession that he did not love her. The Zembla fable has here extended itself to the most intimate reaches, and we have arrived at the innermost fantasy, a dream at the heart of a dream:

> And he absolutely had to find her at once to tell her that he adored her, but the large audience before him separated him from the door, and the notes reaching him through a succession of hands said that she was not available; that she was inaugurating a fire; that she had married an American businessman; that she had become a character in a novel; that she was dead. [*Pale Fire,* p. 151]

The unreal has almost admitted its unreality, as the note announces that Disa had become a character in a novel; and the last message, of Disa's death, is a dispelling and evacuation of the queen. The death of Sineusov's wife, we remember, induced his Kinbote-like insanity in "Solus Rex," and it is possible that there is an actual dead wife behind Kinbote's Queen Disa; but she seems so implausible and literary, so contingent—her features are stolen from Shade's description of *his* wife Sibyl—that it is hard to believe her more than a ghost, a hollow image.

3. *Predictability.* The circle-of-mirrors effect leads at times to a bizarre monotony, a rigidity of form. For instance, the invariant rain of "Solux Rex" falls "for precisely three hundred six days out of three hundred sixty-five or six, so that the weather's peripeties had long ceased to trouble anyone."

4. *Obsessive repetition.* This is another aspect of the hermetic rigidity of evasive fantasy. The razor of *Pale Fire* is a good example: the actual

lunatic who mistakenly murdered Shade, Jack Grey, the model for Gradus, slit his own throat with a razor; and throughout the novel whenever Kinbote imagines Gradus it is in the act of shaving, or of playing with a razor, or of directing the carving of the king's body in an infernal feast. This persistence of theme is not, as in the case of Kuropatkin's matches, a luminous discovery of design, but, like the others, a symptom of disease of an imagination helpless and spastic before its own images.

5. *Instability*. A general statement, inclusive of rules 3, 4, and 5, is that things that should keep changing become frozen, stuck, while things which should remain stable become subject to fits of change; it is again the contrariness, the unnaturalness, the backward quality of mirror images. The best example of perverse instability is the celebrated passage in *Pale Fire* in which Kinbote adorns a fauve youth, Gordon, with the steamy apparatus of a homosexual wet dream. His brief swimming-pool apparel, which is never far from Kinbote's eyes, is described, in the course of a single page, as a leopard-spotted loincloth, a wreath of ivy about his loins, black bathing trunks, white tennis shorts (pp. 143–44). The sheer pressure of Kinbote's gaze mottles, plaits, blanches, sunburns those slim hips; the liquefaction of the garment under the stress of attention shows the play of a lascivious imagination seeking every variety of enhancement, of slow undressing of the desired object. This unworldly plasticity is as compulsive, as uncontrolled as the previous rigor; because nothing is truly *there*, the sham objects are at once too skittery and too immobile, the kaleidoscopic recombinations of the same inescapable forms.

6. *Confusion of dimension*. This is a special case of instability, in which there is an unsteady wavering between the two-dimensional and the three-dimensional, a dissembling of images. "Solus Rex" is a tissue of such confusion, as its last paragraph shows:

> As K advanced toward the exit, he had the nightmare sensation that, maybe, the door was a still-life painting, that its handle was *en trompe-l'oeil,* and could not be turned. But all at once the door became real, and, escorted by a youth, who had softly come out of some other room in his bedslippers with a bundle of keys, K proceeded to go down a long and dark staircase. [*A Russian Beauty and Other Stories,* p. 218]

As in the parable of Eystein in *Pale Fire,* the world of Sineusov's evasive fantasy is a "special reality," a disoriented and disspiriting world without subject and object, in which the representation and what is represented are so scrambled that the imagination is lost in a wilderness of images within images; the descent down the staircase is a recession into the mirror. The limit of befuddlement of layers of reality is perhaps reached in *Pale Fire,* when King Charles, disguised in a red cap and sweater as he tries to flee Zembla, bends his head down to a mountain pool:

> In its limpid tintarron he saw his scarlet reflection but, oddly enough, owing to what seemed to be at first blush an optical illusion, this reflection was not at his feet but much further; moreover, it was accompanied by the ripple-warped reflection of a ledge that jutted high above his present position. And finally, the strain on the magic of the image caused it to snap as his red-sweatered, red-capped doubleganger turned and vanished, whereas he, the observer, remained immobile. He now advanced to the very lip of the water and was met there by a genuine reflection, much larger and clearer than the one that had deceived him. He skirted the pool. High up in the deep-blue sky jutted the empty ledge whereon a counterfeit king had just stood. A shiver of *alfear* (uncontrollable fear caused by elves) ran between his shoulderblades. He murmured a familiar prayer, crossed himself, and res-olutely proceeded toward the pass. At a high point upon an adjacent ridge a *steinmann* (a heap of stones erected as a memento of an ascent) had donned a cap of red wool in his honor. [*Pale Fire,* p. 103]

The king's loyal supporters have all donned red caps and sweaters to help him escape by multiplying his image in a thousand mirrors. In this passage we see that, even to King Charles himself, his image has grown helplessly indistinct, confused, suffering a declension from the king to his water reflection to the water reflection of one of his doubles—an image of an image of an image—to the red-capped stone dummy; as always, in the core of the mirror there is something dead, mocking, annulled. A charming and lightly fanciful variant of the confusion-of-dimension theme occurs inside the mirage of Fyodor's expedition to Central Asia in *The Gift,* when he beholds an elderly Chinaman throwing buckets of water over the *reflection* of flames on the wall of his house, though he is a safe distance from the fire (*The Gift,* p. 234); but for the heroic Fyodor these fantasies are explicitly, deftly unreal. Unlike Kinbote, Fyodor is always in control, never the wizard of Novalis who grows lost in his own labyrinth.

7. *Dissolution into irrelevance.* Evasive fantasy is a kind of water-color or pentimento underneath which another reality can be glimpsed. As it grows more detailed, more extensive, more incoherent in its

teeming false symmetries, disquieting apparitions become visible
through its holes, its inconsistencies, like the ruinous light that pen-
etrates the once-sealed, decrepit palace tunnel through which King
Charles crawls to freedom. The very elaborateness of its invention
destroys it; as the tension between it and terra firma becomes too great,
the fantasy collapses of its own proliferation, an iridescent butterfly's
wing stretched to cover the whole sky. Nabokov's madmen, like R. D.
Laing's, are generally moving toward illumination.

There remains only one more aspect of Nabokov's fantasy worlds to
be discussed: the manner in which solid objects take the shape of
words. The infiltration of verbal relationships into the fictive worlds of
Nabokov is often remarkable. Sineusov in "Ultima Thule" apos-
trophizes to his dead wife, "Oh my angel, perhaps our whole earthly
existence is now but a pun to you, or a grotesque rhyme, something
like 'dental' and 'transcendental'" (p. 153); and it is often the case in
Nabokov that purely verbal transformations can effect strange
metamorphoses. The sensitive man, looking at his environment, sees
an alphabet trying to form messages before his eyes, as if the world
itself were possessed a verbal will, an eagerness to resolve created
things into verbal significance. The hero of Nabokov's early short story
"A Guide to Berlin" writes,

> Today someone wrote "Otto" with his finger on the strip
> of virgin snow and I thought how beautifully that name,
> with its two soft o's flanking the pair of gentle con-
> sonants, suited the silent layer of snow upon that pipe
> with its two orifices and its tacit tunnel. [*Details of a
> Sunset,* p. 92]

The pipe utters its name by the resemblance of its shape to the printed
characters "Otto"; the name writes itself in the snow and is in turn
expanded into the phrase "two Orifices and its Tacit Tunnel" which is
at once a description of the pipe and an acrostic or cryptogram of
Otto. Kinbote in *Pale Fire,* considering the miraculousness of the art of
writing as he holds the index cards containing Shade's poem in his
hands, remarks,

> Solemnly I weighed in my hand what I was carrying
> under my left armpit, and for a moment, I found myself
> enriched with an indescribable amazement as if informed
> that fireflies were making decodable signals on behalf of
> stranded spirits, or that a bat was writing a legible tale of
> torture in the bruised and branded sky. [*Pale Fire,* p. 204]

Early in the novel Kinbote offers an account of Hazel Shade's attempts
to decode a will-o'-the-wisp flitting about a haunted barn, although in
that case the sprite produced nothing more intelligible than "pada ata

lane pad not ogo" (p. 135); but here it seems as if there is a genuine pressure in the cosmos toward verbal expression. This excess of verbality seems to be related to the dimensional confusions, to the jumbling of images and things, to Kinbote's attempt to pour water onto Fleur's shoulder in order to quench a moonbeam, as if light were tangible dust (p. 81); it seems, in short, to be another example of Kinbote's lunacy, of the distortions of evasive fantasy. But it is not.

John Shade, who is unequivocally sane—in an interview Nabokov points to him and to Fyodor in *The Gift* as preeminent examples of healthy and attractive geniuses (*Strong Opinions,* p. 119)—speaks of his world as replete, wealthy with verbal signs; his heroic fantasy is every bit as word-dominated as Kinbote's evasive one. In the first few lines of Shade's poem a pheasant's tracks in the snow become a kind of code (p. 23); and this motif, the uncanny settling of natural phenomena into rebus, semaphore, or alphabet, continues throughout the poem, as a bicycle leaves a lemniscate track on wet pavement (p. 26), as a rubberband drops into an accidental ampersand (p. 37). Indeed, the great revelation of Shade's life is his discovery that verbal manipulations take precedence over physical laws, that the real taxonomy of the universe is that of rhyme. He has a heart attack and is, in a sense, dead for a few moments; during this syncope he sees a tall white fountain playing on a dark background. He reads a magazine article about a woman who has undergone a similar experience, seen a similar fountain. In his desire to find further confirmation of his unexpectedly public, verified vision of the truth of the afterlife, he visits the author of the article:

"It's accurate. I have not changed her style.
There's one misprint—not that it matters much:
Mountain, not *fountain.* The majestic touch."

Life Everlasting—based on a misprint!
I mused as I drove homeward: take the hint,
And stop investigating my abyss?
But all at once it dawned on me that *this*
Was the real point, the contrapuntal theme;
Just this: not text, but texture; not the dream
But topsy-turvical coincidence,
Not flimsy nonsense, but a web of sense.
Yes! It sufficed that I in life could find
Some kind of link-and-bobolink, some kind
Of correlated pattern in the game,
Plexed artistry, and something of the same
Pleasure in it as they who played it found.

[*Pale Fire,* p. 44]

I take it that "not text, but texture" means "not the meaning of the words, but the alogical relations of them"—such relations as rhyme, such accidents as typographical botches, misprints. I have said that, for Nabokov and his more respectable characters, the earth has no intrinsic meaning, is a nulliverse or black backdrop upon which unexpected illuminations, miracles of insight, take place. Shade's shift upward from prosaic, logical meanings to accidents and ornaments of trope, sound pattern, and typesetting is an example of this tendency in Nabokov's thought: if the universe is verbal, its meaning is obscure, but verbal sensitivity can reveal important cross-references, rhyme-coincidences, homonym-identities. The story of Kuropatkin is an investigation of the recurrent imagery of fate, not of fate's meaning. Thus Shade can write *"Man's life as commentary to abstruse/Unfinished poem"* (p. 48), as if our lives were lived in annotations to an illegible text, that is, the universe itself—just as Kinbote lives his life in the annotation to the text of Shade's poem, abstruse and illegible only to him. Fyodor in *The Gift* is still more explicit:

> Funny that I have thought of death all my life, and if I have lived, have lived only in the margin of a book I have never been able to read. Now, who was it? Oh, years ago in Kiev...Goodness, what was his name? Would take out a library book in a language he didn't know, make notes in it and leave it lying about so visitors would think: He knows Portuguese, Aramaic. *Ich habe dasselbe getan.* Happiness, sorrow—exclamation marks *en marge,* while the context is absolutely unknown. A fine affair. [*The Gift,* p. 323]

The lunatic Kinbote claims actually to read the book of the universe, though it is he who has planted the meaning in it, the "tale of torture"; the wise Shade, the wise Fyodor claim only that the universe is verbal and illegible, closed. We do not know what it signifies, but we know its meter:

> And if my private universe scans right,
> So does the verse of galaxies divine
> Which I suspect is an iambic line.
> [*Pale Fire,* p. 49, lines 974–76]

Aesthetic appreciation of nature is in this way calligraphic, aural, the harmony of assonance and the brilliant fullness, acuity of gesture, of a typeface in an unknown alphabet, seraphs and serifs, a foretaste of the Elision Fields.

The end of heroic fantasy is the convergence of *earth* and *world,* of reality and the dream of reality that is our only knowledge of it; and, at such moments of superposition as the end of Shade's poem, it seems as if earth rises into an approximation of verbal form in order to greet the fantasy that is collapsing, merging into it. The concealedness of Heidegger's earth—the obscure ground of our experience, supersensibly concrete—assumes, as it ascends to the light, the aspect of the written word, for perhaps only the verbal is capable of disclosure to the human mind. Heidegger himself makes poetry preeminent among the arts. The very disclosure, the rising into utterance, is in a sense a falsification; *earth* is unutterable, while *world* is glib. And yet through the metaphor of the unreadable word Nabokov holds in a tense unity both the openness and the concealment; it is one of his best devices for describing the absolute point of convergence of the fantastic and the terrestrial. It also allows us to hope that the language of the earth, though now illegible, may someday be solved, that the hiddenness at the bottom of experience will turn out to be not the dim volumes, the receding and emaciated surfaces of the unknowable, but something overt, declared, decisive.

> The answer to all questions of life and death, "the absolute solution" was written all over the world he had known: it was like a traveller realising that the wild country he surveys is not an accidental assembly of natural phenomena, but the page in a book where these mountains and forests, and fields, and rivers are disposed in such a way as to form a coherent sentence; the vowel of a lake fusing with the consonant of a sibilant slope; the windings of a road writing its message in a round hand, as clear as that of one's father; trees conversing in dumbshow, making sense to one who has learnt the gestures of their language. [*The Real Life of Sebastian Knight,* pp. 178–79]

But this accommodation, this obliging legibility of nature, is venturesome, and in its extreme form it is nearly madness. A lunatic in Nabokov's short story "Signs and Symbols" suffers from "referential mania," in which "the patient imagines that everything happening around him is a veiled reference to his personality" (*Nabokov's Dozen,* p. 49). In the throes of this delusion the protagonist imagines that "His inmost thoughts are discussed at nightfall, in manual alphabet, by darkly gesticulating trees" (p. 50). This is clearly no good state of mind. Nabokov suggests that he does not believe in the fundamental verbality either of nature or of the human mind. In a quarry of notes assembled for, but not included in, *Pale Fire,* he remarks, "We think not in words but in shadows of words. James Joyce's mistake in those otherwise marvelous mental soliloquies of his consists in that he gives too much verbal body to thoughts'' (*Strong Opinions,* p. 30). The unstated corollary to this is that the universe is not verbal but a congeries of presences that shadow themselves forth in words, a world caught in the act of worlding by means of language. The act of novel-writing, then, is a mediation of shadows, an arranging of congruent silhouettes. There is a parable in *Bend Sinister* about the nature of translation, as Adam Krug meditates on his friend Ember's translation of *Hamlet:*

> It was as if someone, having seen a certain oak tree (further called Individual T) growing in a certain land and casting its own unique shadow on the green and brown ground, had proceeded to erect in his garden a prodigiously intricate piece of machinery which in itself was as unlike that or any other tree as the translator's inspiration and language were unlike those of the original author, but which, by means of ingenious combinations of parts, light effects, breeze-engendering engines, would, when completed, cast a shadow exactly similar to that of Individual T—the same outline, changing in the same manner, with the same double and single spots of suns rippling in the same position, at the same hour of the day.
> [*Bend Sinister,* pp. 119–20]

If we revise this passage to be a parable, not of translation from one language to another, but of translation from an already half-verbal reality to the secondary reality of a novel, it seems to me an important refinement in the history of representation: the artist does not produce an imitation of his subject, a mimetic counterfeit, but he erects a verbal device to cast a shadow identical to the shadow cast by the thing itself, a matching of umbras and impressions of mass, comet tails, rather than of entities. In this way Nabokov becomes, for all his prodigality of fancy, the most tightfisted of realists.

Plates

PLATE 1 Schoenberg was fond of painting self-portraits, and I believe all three of the pictures on the wall were painted by Schoenberg himself. The lowest is of special interest: although the mouth is only half-open, almost crooning, the face seems related to the famous face in Munch's *The Shriek*, the primal scream of expressionism. Schoenberg began painting in 1907, and, though he never considered himself more than an amateur, he found that painting and musical composition served the same goal: "In fact it [painting] was to me the same as making music, it was to me a way of expressing myself " (from an interview with Halsey Stevens, recorded on Columbia M2S 709). For artists like Kandinsky and Schoenberg, to whom matter was less important than spirit, a certain disinterest toward the particular medium is often noticed; music and paint count for little, the expression sinks into submission before the thing expressed. The photograph appears on page 7 of the booklet accompanying Deutsche Grammophon record 2711 014, Schoenberg-Berg-Webern—Karajan, and is used by permission of Universal Edition, Vienna.

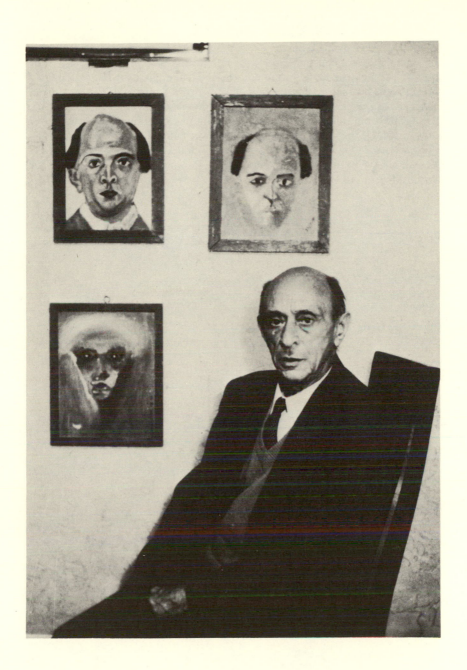

PLATE 2 This is Edvard Munch's *The Shriek*, 1893, from the Nasjonalgalleriet, Oslo. Munch described the experience behind the painting as follows: "The sun was setting—the clouds were colored red—like blood—I felt as though a scream went through nature—I thought I heard a scream" (*Edvard Munch: Symbols and Images* [Washington, D.C.: National Gallery of Art, 1978], p. 39). It is not far from this to the magical end point of expressionism, "I thought I *was* a scream," the complete collapse of viewer and field of vision, hearer and heard. Munch wrote in the bloody stream of cloud at the top of the painting, "Can only have been painted by a madman." Reproduced by permission of the Munch Museum of Oslo.

PLATE 3 Wassily Kandinsky, *Improvisation "Klamm,"* 1914, from the Städtische Galerie, Munich. *Klamm* means "ravine" in German, and one can make out in the lower center of the painting a waterfall, a platform, and a couple in Bavarian costume. The cataract, the stress between the formed and the formless, reminded Frank Whitford, in his book *Kandinsky* (London: Paul Hamlyn, 1967, p. 34), of a passage from Kandinsky's *Autobiography:* "Painting is a thundering conflict of different worlds, which in and out of the battle with one another are intended to create the new world, which is called the work of art. Each work arises technically in a way similar to that in which the cosmos arose—through catastrophes, which from the chaotic roaring of the instruments finally create a symphony, the music of the spheres. The creation of the work is the creation of worlds." Reproduced by permission of the Städtische Galerie im Lenbachhaus, Munich.

PLATE 4 Jefferson David Chalfant, *Which Is Which?* ca. 1890, Fort Lauderdale, Collection Ernest Jarvis. When the painting was new the stamp and the image were nearly indistinguishable, but now the stamp has faded. M. L. d'Otrange Mastai, in her book *Illusion and Art: Trompe l'Oeil: A History of Pictorial Illusionism* (New York: Abaris Books, 1975), quotes a comment on this painting by Alfred Frankenstein: "There exists no more perfect demonstration of the relative permanence of reality and illusion." Reproduced from Mastai, *Illusion and Art,* by permission of Abaris Books.

uine, Mr. Chalfant proposes to paste a
real stamp on the canvas beside his
painting, and the puzzling question will
be "Which is which?"

PLATE 5 Of several paintings by van Gogh entitled *A Pair of Shoes*, this one, painted in late 1886 and now in the Rijksmuseum Vincent van Gogh, Amsterdam, seems most likely to have inspired Heidegger's famous meditation in which the whole world of human toil and suffering emanates from an image of sad leather. Reproduced by permission of the Rijksmuseum Vincent van Gogh, Amsterdam.

PLATE 6 This untitled oil painting by Bram van Velde is from Beckett's personal collection and is a good illustration of Beckett's earlier theories about van Velde's art. In Beckett's article of 1945, "La peinture des van Velde; ou, Le monde et le pantalon," he develops a fairly orthodox expressionistic theory of art; responding to a hypothetical philistine, Beckett says, "There is no such thing as painting. There are only pictures. Pictures, not being sausages, aren't good or bad. All that one can say is that they express, with more or less loss, absurd and mysterious urges toward the image, that they are more or less adequate with respect to obscure internal tensions." Bram van Velde is an artist peculiarly gifted in freezing these interior images; his art is a presentation of "dead things," of "ignorance, silence and the immobile sky," of images "congealed in a lunar vacuum." The compliments that Beckett used for Proust in 1931 are adapted to van Velde: he is the hero who has turned his eyes from the exterior chaos of time, from spatial representation, in order to seize the "ideal real." The specimen here illustrated, painted between 1936 and 1941, shows this congealing, this airlessness: flat, slightly menacing images—one can see something like a row of knives in the upper center—are fixed against a dark blue background. Reproduced by permission of Jacques Putman.

PLATE 7 This untitled gouache—it can be dated only approximately, between 1945 and 1958—illustrates the postwar work of van Velde, as described in Beckett's "Three Dialogues" of 1949. Van Velde is praised not, as he was in 1945, as the master of coagulated interior images, but as the first painter in history who has freed himself from the chimerical goal of image-making, whose works embody the impossibility of expression or representation. We see here, unlike the previous plate, no definite foreground or background; the colors are predominantly light, light blues, pinks, beiges, with a few dark grays and browns, but the effect is not of brightness but of something washed out, etiolated; the tones are receding, fading away before our eyes. Most of the separate, insected areas contain only one pigment, and many of them are divided by black boundary lines; but the pigment has been applied sloppily, the boundary lines are continually transgressed, as if a hasty child were coloring in a coloring book. Beckett must have seen in such pictures as this a visible demonstration of forms laboring to achieve formlessness, it is the undoing of that triumphant cosmos described by Kandinsky in plate 3, for here creation seems to disarticulate itself into conflict, catastrophe. Reproduced by permission of Jacques Putman.

PLATE 8 Here are three illustrations by van Velde to Beckett's "The Calma-tive" (1941). The task of illustrating Beckett seems to have encouraged van Velde to unusual extremes of spareness or blackness. A passage written by Beckett in 1949 seems to suggest that, in his own mind, Beckett illustrated *The Unnamable* with images derived from van Velde: "In the immovable masses of a being shut away and shut off and turned inward forever, pathless, airless, cyclopean, lit with flares and torches, coloured with the colours of the spectrum of blackness. An endless unveiling, veil behind veil, plane after plane of imperfect transparencies, light and space themselves veils, an unveiling towards the unveilable, the nothing, the thing again. And burial in the unique, in a place of impenetrable nearness, cell painted on the stone of cell art of confinement" (*Bram van Velde,* ed. Jacques Putman [New York: Harry N. Abrams, 1962]). If, to Plato, painting is ontologically deficient because it is only the copy of a copy, van Velde seems capable of restoring the prestige of painting by an opposing process, by dispersing layer after layer of images, apparitions; art has access to a superior reality. Reproduced by permission of Jacques Putman.

PAR
SAMUEL
BECKETT

LE CALMANT
PAR SAMUEL BECKETT

3|Kafka

Most fiction creates an intelligible world and then disperses it in order to endow the reader with the hope that, in real life, the converse process may occur—that our obscure earth may be construed into intelligibility; every disenchantment offers the promise of enchantment, enlightenment, if only we can learn to say that magic spell backward. But the conjuring trick in Kafka's novels is different. To Kafka all that has form and mass—walls, furniture, the whole oppressive earth—is a distorted, debased expression of the spiritual, the real; and the language the artist employs is equally low, contaminated, heavy:

> For all things outside the physical world language can be employed only as a sort of adumbration, but never with even approximate exactitude, since in accordance with the physical world it treats only of possession and its connotations. [*The Great Wall of China*, p. 173]

The structure of language, its strings of predicates like pearl necklaces trying forever to declare the subject's attributes, possessions, a flagrant form of miserliness or conspicuous consumption, is itself analogous to the physical world, as greedy and complacent. How, then, can one speak in this fallen, covetous tongue of our authentic state of dispossession, humility? By using language against itself; by becoming a realist as fierce and precise as any and then exploding one's fable, hoping that the physical world, so complicit with illusion and evil, will perish along with its verbal representation. Kafka's books, like the bureaucracies shown in them, keep proliferating and breaking down, ramifying toward their own extinction. Disillusionment can never be complete—"what crumbles, crumbles, but cannot be destroyed" (*Great Wall of China*, p. 180)—but to some extent illusion can be mitigated, lightened, as false expressions, accurate expressions of terrestrial falsehood, continually abolish themselves, verge on silence, verge on the world at the center of Kafka's imagination, the world without gravity.

> What is ridiculous in the physical world is possible in the spiritual world. *There* there is no law of gravity (the angels do not fly, they have overcome any force of gravity, it is only we observers in the terrestrial world who cannot imagine it in any better way than that), which is, of course, beyond our power of conception, or at any rate conceivable only on a very high level. [*Dearest Father*, p. 65]

Mahler intended one of the movements in his original plan of the Fourth Symphony to be a scherzo called "The World without Gravity," and in a sense much of Kafka's career is a long laboring to produce a scherzo of that name, an ironical effect of levity rather more frightening than anything Mahler ever wrote. Gravity is the enemy of enlightenment, but the life of an unenlightened man, though it is heavy, sodden, pedestrian, is nonetheless perfectly acceptable. But enlightenment is a condition of terror. Alexander the Great, in Kafka's version, is so balked by the mere weight of his body that he stands at the bank of the Hellespont too corpulent to budge, unable to move let alone conquer the world (*Great Wall of China*, p. 169). Yet on the other hand the ecstasy of the disembodied—the phrase is from Plotinus—seems to be a kind of despair or even damnation; the Bucket Rider of Kafka's parable, so famished and shrunken that he can glide in an empty coal bucket at rooftop level through his town, goes begging for coal, but the coal dealer's wife shoos him off, and a single wave of her apron wafts him off into the ice mountains, making him lost forever.

Like many of Kafka's more extreme fantasies, this is a parable on the operations of the imagination. Flight, the vertigo of the mind's free building and unbuilding of images, is easy to achieve, but only by cutting one's ties to the physical, by marasmus, by loss of relation to other people, by loss of one's own ego, an oblivion at one with delirium. Kafka's fables are quests for various commonplace goals—coal, social recognition, business success—that hide the actual goal, which is to be dispossessed, to get lost. In his last novel, *The Castle,* K., who wishes to be appointed the court land surveyor, has an inkling of his true direction:

> K. was haunted by the feeling that he was losing himself or wandering into a strange country, farther than ever man had wandered before, a country so strange that not even the air had anything in common with his native air, where one might die of strangeness, and yet whose enchantment was such that one could only go on and lose oneself further. [*The Castle,* p. 54]

Kafka's heroes wander around in a depressing periphery, a representation of urban life that keeps growing more complicated, crumbling into fantastic absurdity as their wandering continues; and in the midst of this dissolving and disarticulating labyrinth come glimpses of a world of greater lightness, greater intensity, the place where one is at last lost and weightless, the blessed perdition.

This gnostic tendency in Kafka's thought complicates the problem of representation. Too careful scrutiny of an object will lead not to its apprehension but to its dissolution:

> There is only a spiritual world; what we call the physical world is the evil in the spiritual one, and what we call evil is only a necessary moment in our endless development.
>
> In a light that is fierce and strong one can see the world dissolve. [*The Great Wall of China,* p. 172]

If Kafka were to wish to describe the pencil in his hand, it would not offer an impression of accurate hue, texture, mass, history; it would fade, shrink from the acuity of his gaze. But Kafka does not generally describe such things as pencils; he prefers to represent a different class of objects, objects that are exceptionally light. If heaviness is a measure of distance from the spirit, of evil, of illusion, the enlightened mind will concentrate on objects of peculiarly diminished gravity. Sometimes these objects are wholly imaginary: for instance, in the story "Blumfeld, an Elderly Bachelor," the protagonist finds in his apartment "two small white celluloid balls with blue stripes jumping up and down side by side on the parquet; when one of them touches the floor the other is in the air, a game they continue ceaselessly to play'' (*Complete Stories*, p. 185). Their jumping is not due to electricity or clockwork or any other explicable cause; they are simply inspired, celestial. It is noteworthy that Blumfeld finds this uncanny spectacle quite unpleasant; and indeed most of Kafka's heroes find the sudden immanence of the spiritual to be source of disturbing giddiness, the nausea of free fall. The narrator of this story informs us that if Blumfeld had been not an elderly bachelor but a child he might have been delighted by these marvelous toys; and these intrusions from the world without gravity are often marked in Kafka's writings by a sudden childishness, an angelic or demonic playfulness, like the sound of the telephone exchange of *The Castle,* a hum of children's voices singing at an infinite distance.

Kafka's representations of reality, then, are either depictions of a heavy world lapsing, lapsing, caught in the process of dispelling itself, or else of unnaturally light things. One of Kafka's central parables about the difficulties of capturing the phenomenon is ''The Top'':

> A certain philosopher used to hang about wherever children were at play. And whenever he saw a boy with a top, he would lie in wait. As soon as the top began to spin the philosopher went in pursuit and tried to catch it. He was not perturbed when the children noisily protested and tried to keep him away from their toy; so long as he could catch the top while it was still spinning, he was happy, but only for a moment; then he threw it to the ground and walked away. For he believed that the understanding of any detail, that of a spinning top, for instance, was sufficient for the understanding of all things. For this reason he did not busy himself with great problems, it seemed to him uneconomical. Once the smallest detail was understood, then everything was understood, which was why he busied himself only with the spinning top. And whenever preparations were being made for the spinning of the top, he hoped that this time it would succeed: as soon as the top began to spin and he was running breathlessly after it, the hope would turn to certainty, but when he held the silly piece of wood in his hand, he felt nauseated. The screaming of the children, which hitherto he had not heard and which now suddenly pierced his ears, chased him away, and he tottered like a top under a clumsy whip. [*The Complete Stories,* p. 444]

The top, like Blumfeld's balls, is a child's toy, though a more ordinary one. At rest it is only a ''silly piece of wood,'' banal and uninteresting;

but when it is spinning it becomes mysteriously weightless, immaterial, the key to the understanding of the universe. The philosopher is un-comprehending, even nauseated, when he tries to seize the truth before him; it is the truth of the ascent from matter to spirit, the truth of the genuine masslessness hidden in commonplace things. The nausea he feels is the sensation well known to children who spin round and round to provoke a disturbance in the equilibrium of the inner ear: a loss of vertical orientation, an insecurity of wall and floor, floor and ceiling, a sense that the solid earth is whirling uncontrollably. To observe a top too closely makes the observer toplike. The philosopher tottering away "like a top under a clumsy whip" has achieved the vertigo of the enlightened, though presumably he was searching for an enlightenment of a more erudite and complacent nature; he is only one stage away from becoming one of Kafka's helpless and compulsive levitators, like the flying lapdogs of "Investigations of a Dog" or the sad acrobat of "First Sorrow" who needs a second trapeze so he need never come down to earth at all, may become a denizen of the middle air.

As is usual in these cases, the close student of a thing becomes deformed by the thing he studies; to be engrossed by something is to be enchanted, compelled to imitate, for one sacrifices one's sense of self in order to attend with care. In Auden's sonnet sequence "The Quest" the poet remarks of the magician-Platonist, lost in abstract speculation at the summit of his tower, "Those who see all become invisible"; and Kafka's seer develops a similar attenuation:

> He sees in two ways: the first is a calm contemplation, consideration, investigation, an overflow of life in-evitably involving a certain sensation of comfort. The possible manifestations of this process are infinite, for though even a woodlouse needs a relatively large crevice in which to accommodate itself, no space whatever is required for such labors; even where not the smallest crack can be found they may exist in tens of thousands, mutually interpenetrating one another. That is the first stage. The second is the moment when he is called upon to render an account of all this, finds himself incapable of uttering a sound, is flung back again on contemplation, etc., but now, knowing the hopelessness of it, can no longer dabble about in it, and so makes his body heavy and sinks with a curse. [*The Great Wall of China*, p. 155]

The wood louse, the angel who dances on the head of a pin, is not so small as the contemplator. Just as the philosopher of the tops grew dizzy and elevated by the act of contemplation, so the seer of this passage from "He" dwindles, grows remote and spectral, spiritual, simply from the act of looking, from the application of the intellect's world-dissolving light. But this high bliss is broken by the necessity of expression: since even the most primitive thing, a child's toy, is incomprehensible, inexpressible, the spirit's ease in itself is balked by a descent into speech, formulation. Just as the philosopher and his top grew light together, so the seer and the thing seen now grow heavy together, return to slow, blunt earth. The greatest felicity is to be a wood louse, invisible in the beholding of an invisible world; but Kafka is an artist, must call himself to account, must show, must represent, must sink into language; and the artist's agony is that he must try to discover combinations of thick, palpable words to embody the state of invisibility, must show a balloon floating upward by juggling cannonballs. Few writers have ever had such a sense of the squalor, the heaviness of language:

> It is as if I were made of stone, as if I were my own tombstone, there is no loophole for doubt or for faith, for love or repugnance, for courage or anxiety, in particular or in general, only a vague hope lives on, but no better than the inscriptions on tombstones. Almost every word I write jars against the next, I hear the consonants rub leadenly against each other and the vowels sing an accompaniment like Negroes in a minstrel show. My doubts stand in a circle around every word, I see them before I see the word, but what then! I do not see the word at all, I invent it. Of course, that wouldn't be the greatest misfortune, only I ought to be able to invent words capable of blowing the odor of corpses in a direction other than straight into mine and the reader's face. When I sit down at the desk I feel no better than someone who falls and breaks both legs in the middle of the traffic of the Place de l'Opéra. [*Diaries I*, p. 33]

One may rest happy in the abstract contemplation of the inexpressible; but to describe it, to bring it down to earth, involves the writer in a clumping boot dance of obese vowels and consonants, fragrant with human rot, a vulgar minstrel show that, outlandishly, is asked to enact the high comedy of the spirit, as if the various clowns of the commedia dell' arte were required to perform Dante's *Paradiso*. Auden's sonnet "Words" makes a similar point:

> Were not our fate by verbal chance expressed,
> As rustics in a ring-dance pantomime
> The Knight at some lone cross-roads of his quest?
> [*Collected Shorter Poems*, p. 321]

The verbal formulation is a comically debased analogue to the noble drama of the soul caught at the decisive moment of choice. Again, Kafka in this early diary entry imagines himself growing extraordinarily heavy, corpse-inert, as he tries to grasp the ungraspable: he is first petrified into his own tombstone, finally so ridden by his own body weight that his legs snap in the middle of traffic. The writer must in all cases deal with dim and ponderous analogies of the world without gravity and must suffer the consequences of contamination by his own medium. One offers representation at one's peril.

We have seen how Kafka has seized two denatured objects, a top and a magical celluloid ball; a third example should suffice to show the disturbing, deranging properties of very light things. This is a kind of household god called Odradek, from the story "The Cares of a Family Man":

> At first glance it looks like a flat star-shaped spool for thread, and indeed it does seem to have thread wound upon it; to be sure, they are only old, broken-off bits of thread, knotted and tangled together, of the most varied sorts and colors. But it is not only a spool, for a small wooden crossbar sticks out of the middle of the star, and another small rod is joined to that at a right angle. By means of this latter rod on one side and one of the points of the star on the other, the whole thing can stand upright as if on two legs.
>
> One is tempted to believe that the creature once had some sort of intelligible shape and is now only a broken-down remnant. Yet this does not seem to be the case; at least there is no sign of it; nowhere is there an unfinished or unbroken surface to suggest anything of the kind; the whole thing looks senseless enough, but in its own way perfectly finished. In any case, closer scrutiny is impossible, since Odradek is extraordinarily nimble and can never be laid hold of. [*The Penal Colony,* p. 160]

Odradek is perhaps the lightest, the most deft and elusive, of all Kafka's light objects; it—he—eludes all categories, for he is at once animate and inanimate, unintelligible, senseless, and perfect, so indefinable that the mere act of looking at him makes him go away, a retinal floater always at the edge of vision. It is a remarkable attempt to represent an unrepresentable object, to make a hovering vagueness precise in its every lineament. The reader could make a little Odradek of his own out of spool and thread, and yet Odradek recedes, dances away from the reach of the captious intellect. Like the two previous light objects, Odradek is a kind of toy, but he is at the same time a child: "you treat him—he is so diminutive that you cannot help it— rather like a child" (*The Penal Colony,* p. 161). In the heavy world of experience there is a separation between seer and seen; but Odradek suggests that in the world without gravity a further breakdown of category obtains, for subject and object are one, the philosopher has grown so intimate with the top that they are consubstantial. "Gravity" in this story has a special sense, as the title "The Cares of a Family Man" suggests; the Family Man is oppressed, weighted down with children, responsibility, while Odradek is so carelessly light—his laughter is lungless, like the rustling of fallen leaves—that he is immortal, will entertain the narrator's children's children, those countless dying generations. The narrator's household is commonplace; but in Kafka the most commonplace household has an elusive, impalpable, endlessly shifting spiritual center, though it may look like a silly child, too thoughtless to be malevolent.

Even in the earliest part of Kafka's career his imagination is always engaged at a task with few precedents in fiction, the task of representing ordinary life, the swollen, tender middle class so dear to all novelists, and of representing at the same time its higher nonexistence, a sort of desolating absurdity or vacuum with which the quotidian cannot cope and into which it collapses. In one of his most memorable statements of the plight of the artist, Kafka compared himself to a carpenter—Kafka liked carpentry and, according to Gustav Janouch (*Conversations with Kafka,* p. 15), near the end of his life even took lessons in it—laboriously, painfully constructing a table and simultaneously not doing anything at all, in such a way that it could be said of him, "'Hammering a table together is really hammering a table together to him, but at the same time it is nothing'" (*Great Wall of China,* p. 155). Something of the wood louse's happy nonentity, his unimpeded spiritual ease of contemplation, can be retained, apparently, even when the artist descends to the nuts and bolts of his craft. This, Kafka explains, is the kind of art appropriate for a vision of life that "while still retaining its natural full-bodied rise and fall, would simultaneously be recognized no less clearly as a nothing, a dream, a dim hovering." When one opens one's eyes one sees the lower world and its state of nonexistence at once; therefore the artist's task is to represent a condition of replete and tangible illusion mysteriously verging on unbeing. In all earthly deeds, from hammering tables to writing novels, there is a turbid and vigorous circle of action enclosing a central *nihil.* The rift-experience, if I may adapt Heidegger's language, of Kafka's fiction is just this manifestation of a commonplace world confronting the intuition of its own vanishing, the horn of plenty tapering to an empty point at the end of a curlicue, the water that defines in its disappearance down the drain the bright shape of a funnel of air. Odradek is a simple, benign example of this lively vacuum at the center of the ordinary, a rift-design that properly takes the shape of a spool, a cylindrical wooden hole.

Kafka's later protagonists have often grown so wearily accustomed to the incomprehensible, the clamorous nothing at the center of their lives, that they construct an elaborate but dubious mythological history to account for its presence, like the accounts of the origin of the Great Wall of China; but in the early fiction the discovery of the absurd center is shocking, devastating. In Kafka's earliest long work extant, the "Description of a Struggle" of 1904–5, the narrator leaves what seems to be an ordinary, rather boring party for a late-night walk with a new acquaintance and enters an unprecedented and deranged world; Kafka's career as a writer begins with the wildest fantasy he ever wrote. The acquaintance, who seemed at first merely a slightly obnoxious guest, talking of sexual adventures to a lonely narrator drinking his schnapps, begins to speak in an increasingly improbable, disturbing, and intimate manner; the narrator feels like kissing him, thinks his acquaintance is going to murder him, accepts unquestioningly the fact that a stranger arouses such odd feelings of complicity and terror in him. At one point, thinking of the housemaid who kissed the acquaintance on the staircase, the narrator says to himself,

> when they kiss him they also kiss me a little—with the corners of their mouths, so to speak. But if they carry him off, then they steal him from me. And he must always remain with me, always. Who is to protect him, if not I? And he's so stupid. Someone says to him in February: Come up the Laurenziberg—and off he goes. And supposing he falls down now, or catches cold? Suppose some jealous man appears from the Postgasse and attacks him? What will happen to me? Am I to be just kicked out of the world? [*The Complete Stories*, pp. 13–14]

It is clear that something is wrong; the acquaintance is not a separate human being but an aspect of the narrator, as if the narrator were the soul and the acquaintance the body, a body susceptible to amorous yearnings, to stupid provocations of disease, to the attacks of thieves, while the soul remains in solitary meditation, aloof, yet lightly affected by the mechanical rhythms of the body, those housemaid's kisses. The realistic novel has been subverted into phantasmagoria, a dance of projected aspects of the self. As Kafka would say much later, "There exist in the same human being varying perceptions of one and the same object which differ so completely from each other that one can only deduce the existence of different subjects in the same human being" (*Great Wall of China*, p. 175). What is interesting is that the "different

103

subjects'' comprised by a single self are so tense, discordant; the narrator of ''Description of a Struggle'' regards his ''acquaintance'' with a kind of intimate revulsion. For Kafka's mature writing as well, it will generally hold that characters who seem to be independent entities will prove to be participants in the protagonist's psychomachia. In ''Description of a Struggle'' the acquaintance is credible *only* as such a participant, but in the later fiction such ancillary characters will have a twi-formed nature, will be at once figments in an interior struggle and the precisely delineated personages of traditional fiction. By Kafka's later standards the penumbra of verisimilitude in ''Description of a Struggle'' is too faint; everything after the second page is a depiction of the null world, the spiritual center.

It is literally a world without gravity. The narrator of ''Description of a Struggle'' on his midnight excursion through Prague discovers that he can fly, can swim in circles above the statues of saints—a more drunken, less desperate flight than that of the Bucket Rider many years later. A pain in his knee brings him to earth. The second part of the story begins with the narrator's leaping onto the acquaintance's shoulder and urging him to trot up a steep slope, though the ride ceases when the acquaintance, badly wounded in the knee, collapses and is abandoned. We see here the old figure of the soul's relation to the body as that of rider to horse, grotesquely literalized; the astonishing fluidity of these incoherent personages is shown by the transference of the narrator's knee pain to his acquaintance, who is only separable, independent, to the extent that the narrator wills him to be. But all this is prelude to the narrator's solitary walk up the mountain, one of Kafka's most remarkable passages:

> I walked on, unperturbed. But since, as a pedestrian, I dreaded the effort of climbing the mountainous road, I let it become gradually flatter, let it slope down into a valley in the distance. The stones vanished at my will and the wind disappeared.
>
> I walked at a brisk pace and since I was on my way down I raised my head, stiffened my body, and crossed my arms behind my head. Because I love pinewoods I went through woods of this kind, and since I like gazing silently up at the stars, the stars appeared slowly in the sky, as is their wont. I saw only a few fleecy clouds which a wind, blowing just at their height, pulled through the air, to the astonishment of the pedestrian.
>
> Opposite and at some distance from my road, probably separated from it by a river as well, I caused to rise an enormously high mountain whose plateau, overgrown with brushwood, bordered on the sky. I could see quite

clearly the little ramifications of the highest branches and their movements. This sight, ordinary as it may be, made me so happy that I, as a small bird on a twig of those distant scrubby bushes, forgot to let the moon come up. It lay already behind the mountain, no doubt angry at the delay.

But now the cool light that precedes the rising of the moon spread over the mountain and suddenly the moon itself appeared from beyond one of the restless bushes. I on the other hand had meanwhile been gazing in another direction, and when I now looked ahead of me and suddenly saw it glowing in its almost full roundness, I stood still with troubled eyes, for my precipitous road seemed to lead straight into this terrifying moon. [*The Complete Stories,* p. 22]

With the body and the thick, clotted "real" world left behind, we enter a condition of the complete freedom of the imagination. Clouds, mountains, forests, all gather, pullulate, and disperse at the most casual wish, a landscape so drenched with the soul that the narrator peeks out from the edges of everything he beholds, a small bird negligent of its responsibility to create the moon. Yet even in this state of utter plasticity and obedience there is a sudden access of terror, the imagination frightened by the wilderness of its images. The soul has grown so huge, so incoherent, that it cannot behave with a single will, a single purpose; aspects of it keep suddenly appearing, dangerous and enigmatic, just as the characters in the story—the acquaintance, the fat man, the supplicant—keep rising out of nowhere, demanding an eerie confrontation. The landscape of pure psyche is a congenial, obliging, wholly lapsed world and also a kind of hell, queasy from involution, from compulsive self-referentiality. It is the hellishness of such a place that Auden emphasizes in *The Sea and the Mirror,* in a passage where Caliban speaks of the chimerical world created by Ariel when the imagination is absolute, transcendent:

All the phenomena of an empirically ordinary world are given. Extended objects appear to which events happen—old men catch dreadful coughs, little girls get their arms twisted, flames run whooping through woods, round a river bend, as harmless looking as a dirty old bearskin rug, comes the gliding fury of a town-effacing wave, but these are merely elements in an allegorical landscape to which mathematical measurement and phenomenological analysis have no relevance. . . .

Again, other selves undoubtedly exist, but though everyone's pocket is bulging with birth certificates, in-

surance policies, passports and letters of credit, there is
no way of proving whether they are genuine or planted or
forged, so that no one knows whether another is his
friend disguised as an enemy or his enemy disguised as a
friend (there is probably no one whose real name is
Brown), or whether the police who here as elsewhere are
grimly busy, are crushing a criminal revolt or upholding a
vicious tyranny, any more than he knows whether he
himself is a victim of the theft, or the thief, or a rival thief,
a professionally interested detective or a professionally
impartial journalist. . . .

. . .Everything, in short, suggests Mind but, sur-
rounded by an infinite extension of the adolescent difficulty, a rising of the subjective and subjunctive to ever
steeper, stormier heights, the panting frozen expressive
gift has collapsed under the strain of its communicative
anxiety, and contributes nothing by way of meaning but a
series of staccato barks or a delirious gush of glossolalia.
[*Collected Longer Poems*, pp. 245–46]

This collapse of a sheerly imaginary world is related to the figure of the
failed opera, which is the climax of Caliban's speech; art that removes
itself too far from crude nature, Caliban, cannot sustain itself, can only
burble off into subjective delusion, a disoriented impressive in-
consequence. The difficulties of "Description of a Struggle"—and the
story has repelled many of Kafka's finest critics—are due to its deliberate adoption of this technique; it aspires to be glossolalia, idiolalia,
for it admits the existence of no tongue but the narrator's. The demonic
aspects of such an improvised, elevated, chimerical world are as clear
to Kafka as to Auden; but Kafka, to whom the low world of Caliban
was much less genuine, much more despicable than to Auden, found a
kind of refuge in this hallucinatory void created by the imagination. At
the center of "Description of a Struggle" we see a deliberate destruction of language, a cultivated unmeaning:

I guessed from the very beginning the state you are in.
Isn't it something like a fever, a seasickness on land, a
kind of leprosy? Don't you feel it's this very feverishness
that is preventing you from being properly satisfied with
the real names of things, and that now, in your frantic
haste, you're just pelting them with any old names? You
can't do it fast enough. But hardly have you run away
from them when you've forgotten the names you gave
them. The poplar in the fields, which you've called the
"Tower of Babel" because you didn't want to know it
was a poplar, sways again without a name, so you have to
call it "Noah in his cups." [*The Complete Stories*, p. 33]

The Babylonians, we remember, had their language confounded by God because of their impious zeal for spiritual ascent; Kafka plays with a kind of backward magic, the notion that a trance of babbling may be rewarded with the levitation of the spirit. *Nomina sunt consequentiae rerum,* as Kafka suggests in "The Cares of a Family Man," and the fleeing entities of the psychic landscape require names as evanescent and unstable, as shimmery, as themselves. If vowels and consonants are leaden or smelly, these giddy chains of transient epithets may be as close as it is possible to come to the speech proper to the interior truth, the unspeakable.

According to the wisdom of Kafka's maturity, this victory over the strictures of matter and language is achieved too easily:

> All is deception: one can try to live with the minimum of illusion, take things as they are, or try to live with the maximum of illusion. In the first case one betrays good by wanting to make its achievement too easy, and evil by imposing overwhelmingly unfavorable fighting conditions upon it. In the second case one betrays good by refusing to strive towards it even on the earthly plane. In the third case one betrays good by sundering oneself as far as possible from it, and evil by hoping that through its ubiquity it may be rendered innocuous. From this it seems that the second course is the one to be preferred, for in every case one betrays good, but in this case one does not betray evil, at least in appearance. [*The Great Wall of China,* p. 172]

I know of no work of Kafka's that espouses the third course, that of the complacent man avid of illusion, the happy materialist; but the dilemma of choosing between the first two is never resolved. The psychic landscape of "Description of a Struggle" is, despite its chaos of images, an example of extreme disillusion; the rigor, the weight, of the lower world is effortlessly abolished, and the narrator strides through an unusually ductile, unusually real world. It is a story disrespectful of the tenacity of material illusion, and in all of Kafka's later work the perspective is not of the Canaanites reveling in milk and honey but of sad blasted Moses, tantalized by the Pisgah glimpse of the country he may never enter. Indeed much of Kafka's writing recommends, as does this reflection, the second course, the making of some compromise or accommodation with material illusion: the chamberlain in "The Warden of the Tomb" calmly announces that he is prepared to bear the unbearable situation (*Complete Stories,* p. 216); in "The Refusal" the citizens know that the government will refuse all petitions, yet they submit their petitions anyway and return "if not exactly strengthened or happy, nevertheless not disappointed or tired" (*Complete Stories,* p. 267); Frieda in *The Castle* advises K. never to refuse the gifts of the authorities, whether they in their divine arbitrariness offer incompetent assistants or a dubious wife (p. 458); and the speaker of "He," accused of making a virtue of necessity, says "I do not drain the swamp, but live in its feverish exhalations" (*Great Wall of China,* p. 158). Kafka felt a good deal of sympathy with those who abandon striving, who simply try to cope; but those who have the fortitude of endurance usually seem to slip into disenchantment, find themselves cut free of the sensuous world, struggle as best they can to survive in a region where customary behavior is useless, where physical laws no longer hold. In an oddly charming conversation with Gustav Janouch (*Conversations,* p. 16), Kafka compared himself to a *kavka,* a jackdaw, hopping bewildered in the cage of existence; it was not necessary to clip his wings, for his wings had atrophied. This will provide an image for the desperation that Kafka's heroes feel at the crisis, at the moment of illumination: they are flightless birds let out of their cages, struggling in midair to soar on their featherless arms.

The narrator-protagonist of "Description of a Struggle," compared with the later heroes, has the wingspread of an albatross, is almost like the footless bird of paradise that never needs to land; his successors in Kafka's fiction feel much less overt estrangement from the natural world, from their bodies, yet they feel a dim longing for the other place, the landscape of the spirit. Karl Rossmann in Kafka's first characteristic novel, *Amerika,* is a high-spirited, in many ways competent youth, whose parents pack him off to America after he is seduced by a maidservant. He becomes involved in a dispute among the ship's mechanics and unexpectedly is rescued by his rich uncle, Senator Edward Jacob; despite his poor preparation for his journey, his doubtful prospects, he is told that he has a brilliant career ahead of him (p. 24). This seems like the opening of a conventional novel of Great Expectations, but the traditional or Dickensian qualities—Kafka called the novel an imitation of Dickens (*Diaries II,* p. 188)—are quickly subverted: Germany is the abandoned world of the senses, of commonplace order; America is the locus of the imagination, a realm of diminished gravity. America has often been asked to play a similar role in European literature—one thinks of Chateaubriand's Niagara, or of the vast desert near New Orleans in which Manon Lescaut perishes—but it is hard to find an image of America as fantastic as Kafka's, where mountains loom behind New York City, the Statue of Liberty carries an upraised sword, and the state of Oklahoma is converted into a gigantic theater, a pageant of costumed angels and devils, Spenser's House of Alma or the *Psychomachia* of Prudentius.

The conventional plot of the immigrant youth's struggle to make good in the land of opportunity is rendered interior, involuted, by the use of two simple devices, often in combination: the reversal of fate and the hero's substitution of role with other characters. In the first chapter, "The Stoker," the stoker, who feels unjustly persecuted by his co-worker, Schubal, tells Karl he is leaving the ship and points out that Karl could take over his job. There is nothing particularly strange about this, but Karl and the stoker, like the narrator and the acquaintance of "Description of a Struggle," quickly develop an uncanny intimacy; soon the stoker turns his eyes on Karl "as if Karl were his heart, to whom he was silently bewailing his grief" (*Amerika,* p. 13). And it is not surprising that Karl becomes the stoker's passionate champion, offers to testify before the captain in the stoker's quarrel with Schubal. In the latter part of the chapter the stoker, who had seemed a sullen mechanic, a traditional sort of minor character, becomes oddly insubstantial; the whole hearing with Schubal, the orderly development of justice and discipline, is abrogated, canceled out by the appearance of Senator Jacob. Not only is Karl snatched away by a deus ex machina, but the proceeding itself seems to fade away. Karl feels guilty about abandoning the abject stoker, but everyone, even the stoker himself, seems to agree that if the petty dispute was the cause of Karl's discovery of his uncle, then it was all for the good:

> There would be no stoker pestering the head office any more with his ravings, yet his last effort would be held in almost friendly memory, since, as the Senator expressly declared, it had been the direct cause of his recognizing his nephew. The nephew himself had several times tried to help him already and so had more than repaid him beforehand for his services in the recognition scene; it did not even occur to the stoker to ask anything else from him now. [*Amerika,* pp. 32–33]

Karl at the beginning seemed not very important, a worthless and ill-educated youth, but it turns out that he is the favorite child, that he is the mysterious center of all that he beholds. The quarrel between the stoker and Schubal was only a pretext for Karl's advancement, as if all participants were enacting a script in which Karl Rossmann was the only actor of significance—the phrase "recognition scene" is the technical term of a scenario. The stoker, who began by suggesting that Karl trade places with him, ends by resigning himself utterly in favor of Karl; and the chapter ends with Karl and his uncle in a rowboat leaving the ship and heading toward New York—"it was now as if there were really no stoker at all." The stoker not only disappears from Karl's future, he disappears from the past as well, is superseded, annulled. It is wrong to claim that he never was anything but a casual component of Karl's being—one cannot simply identify him, as in the case of the acquaintance in "Description of a Struggle," with an aspect of Karl's psyche—but he does seem partial, ominous, like some minor, inarticulate, persecuted, laborious version of Karl, bound to the ship just as some fraction of Karl is bound to his German past. Kafka once told Gustav Janouch, in the course of a denunciation of abstract characters, that the stoker was a concretely real human being put in Karl's path: "Like every concrete human being, he was a messenger from the outer world. Abstractions are only caricatures of one's own passions, ghosts from the dungeons of the world within" (*Conversations with Kafka*, p. 94). The stoker is real, but from Karl's point of view he is a messenger, requires interpretation into the significant and private myth of Karl's career. The stoker is content to play a small role and vanish into a comprehensive egocentric drama, in which he does not very forcefully exist.

It is instructive to compare *Amerika* with Mann's short story "Felix Krull." It is one of the remarkable coincidences of literary history that these two works were written in the same year, 1911–12, for they share as protagonists a labile youth who in chameleon fashion keeps switching roles with everyone he meets, compelling human society to become a satisfying drama in which he is the sole actor. Mann boasted in later life that Kafka admired "Tonio Kröger," and it is far from impossible that Mann's thematic preoccupations influenced Kafka; it is even possible that *Amerika* influenced the 1954 expansion of *Felix Krull*, in which the hero, as in Kafka's book, works as an elevator boy; but they must be considered primarily as independent converging works. Both are comedies, both heroes learn the extremes of wealth and poverty; and yet there is a great difference. Felix Krull, the confidence man, himself exerts the shaping force, alters his body deliberately into the configurations of those he mimics; Karl Rossman is Felix turned inside out, passive, even obtuse, always finding himself impressed into the roles that befall him. He is in danger of becoming all whom he meets, no matter how little he wishes to usurp them. The stoker, so to speak, wishes to put his cap on Karl's head and hand him a shovel. When Karl comes to the hotel he takes the place of the liftboy Giacomo (p. 135), while the manageress's secretary Therese fears that Karl will be made secretary in her place (p. 141). Much later in the novel the wicked Robinson arranges that Karl will be made a slave so that he can go free (p. 242). These substitutions continue until Karl attains the Nature Theatre, the heaven of identity, where he and Giacomo sit side by side, without jostling for position, where there is room for everyone and everyone at last has a stable, assigned place. In this manner the convention of the picaresque novel is subverted, for those who seem to be minor characters are only the shadowy premonitions, the temporary placeholders, of the roles that Karl himself will be assigned to enact. By playing master and slave alternately, by frantically changing from one position to another, he manages to occupy all positions, to become the only genuine character. The contours of the later plot episodes are mostly simple repetitions of earlier episodes, but skewed 90 or 180 degrees; for instance, in the hotel Karl accepts humiliating punishment from his master the head waiter (p. 173), just as his alter ego the stoker suffered persecution in the first chapter. And, just as Karl failed in his attempt to help the stoker, he must behold in turn the failure of an intercessor, the manageress, who tries to intervene on his behalf (p. 189). What Karl saw the stoker endure foreshadowed his own fate. The plot of the novel is a tissue of peripeties, for the minor "characters" are systematically reversed in value. Uncle Edward begins as a benefactor but becomes an enemy, disinheriting Karl for a trivial act of negligence; the longer Karl knows the people around him, the more in-comprehensible, undefined, they become. The minor characters are all "American," that is, imaginary, fluid; they evolve from the quirky individualities of the nineteenth-century novel into figments of interior struggle, dancers in an elusive morality play. The last chapter, with its costumed angels set on pedestals and blowing trumpets, replaced at regular intervals by men dressed as devils, is only the final simplifica-tion into the imaginary, the spiritual, all event stylized into a shifting, abnormally light and airy spectacle. Karl is to be the humblest techni-cal laborer—not the engineer he aspired to become—in the Nature Theatre of Oklahoma; but despite his smallness the reader feels that the whole tableau is conducted for his delectation. Indeed, the hero's puniness is a sign of grace; as Bürgel will explain to K. in the heart of *The Castle,* smallness and insignificance are the requisites of revelation, for only the tiniest grain can pass through "the incomparable sieve" (*The Castle,* p. 347). To impinge on the central void, the world without gravity, one must be smaller than a wood louse. *Amerika* is ingenious in its solution of the difficulties of writing a novel in which all furniture, all peripheral characters, move toward illusion and allegory, in which the protagonist is engaged without knowing it in a continual re-linquishing of identity, a contraction to the manageable zero.

"There is a goal, but no way," as Kafka says in a famous aphorism, repeating Kundry's curse in act 2 of *Parsifal,* and Karl, though he is recruited by the Nature Theatre, never arrives in Oklahoma; the novel breaks off during Karl's train ride through the infinite expanses of America. Max Brod suggests in an afterword what Kafka intended for Karl to find:

> In enigmatic language Kafka used to hint smilingly, that
> within this "almost limitless" theatre his young hero was
> going to find again a profession, a stand-by, his freedom,
> even his old home and his parents, as if by some celestial
> witchery. [*Amerika,* p. 299]

It is easy to believe that Brod was right; during the recruitment scene,
the antetheater to Oklahoma, Karl is startled to discover that the head
of the bureau closely resembles "a teacher who was presumably still
teaching in the school at home" (*Amerika,* p. 285). Despite a transat-
lantic crossing and a train ride over plains and cataracts, Karl has
somehow never left the bosom of his family; the whole journey is only
a metaphor for a new way of perceiving the reality of his home, an
imaginative disenchantment of the commonplace, a penetration into
higher truth. Karl's career is a series of evictions, from Germany, from
his uncle's mansion, from the hotel, presumably from Brunelda's
apartment; but one is expelled from home only that its recovery may be
keener, more thorough. A paragraph from "He" states this condition
in more general terms:

> He was once part of a monumental group. Around
> some elevated figure or other in the center were ranged in
> carefully thought-out order symbolical images of the mil-
> itary caste, the arts, the sciences, the handicrafts. He was
> one of those many figures. Now the group is long since
> dispersed, or at least he has left it and makes his way
> through life alone. He no longer has even his old voca-
> tion, indeed he has actually forgotten what he once repre-
> sented. Probably it is this very forgetting that gives rise to
> a certain melancholy, uncertainty, unrest, a certain
> longing for vanished ages, darkening the present. And yet
> this longing is an essential element in human effort,
> perhaps indeed human effort itself. [*The Great Wall of
> China,* p. 156]

Amerika, in effect, grants this wish for a return, for a recovery of the
lost symbolic value formerly visible in medieval guild portraits or in
group photographs of one's family. Indeed, the angels and devils of the
Nature Theatre suggest that Paradise Regained is stripped of all that is
not direct meaning; family and society—and all professions, all art and
technology, are represented in the Theatre—have become incorporeal,
attenuated into pure symbol, a ballet of immaterial referents. Auden, a
fine critic of Kafka, diagnosed the Kafka hero as the "I without a Self"
(*Dyer's Hand,* p. 159)—an identity struggling toward some historical,
accredited role, as K. strives to be recognized as a land surveyor; but
what Auden calls selfhood is for Kafka a supernatural condition, avail-

able only to those who have passed beyond, the residents of Oklahoma. In Kafka's later work he usually makes this world of ether and rapture, of high suffering, seem much less fantastic, much more closely affiliated with the ordinary sensuous world that is a low expression, a parody, of it. The spirit may be remote, but it is not necessary to travel across continents to approach it.

Amerika is one of the first fables in which Kafka is concerned with the mechanism of transmission between the higher and the lower. If there is a goal but no way, only a wavering, how can we understand that there exists a goal at all? By the antimasque of angels and devils that entices us to join, or discourages us from joining, the Theatre; by directives from above, such as the senator's notes to Karl, which by their alternate rewarding and smiting prove themselves to be signs of the genuine arbitrariness of the divine; and, most of all, by the telephone switchboard and the information bureau of the hotel. No passage in *Amerika* offers the authentic shiver of Kafka more than the description of the information bureau, where two harried underporters are crowded by at least ten inquiring faces, "a perfect babel of tongues":

> Mere talking would not have sufficed for their work; they gabbled, and one in particular, a gloomy man with a dark beard almost hiding his whole face, poured out information without even taking breath. He neither looked at the counter, where he was perpetually handing things out, nor at the face of this or that questioner, but straight in front of him, obviously to economise and conserve his strength. His beard too must have somewhat interfered with the clearness of his enunciation, and in the short time that he was standing there Karl could make out very little of what was said, though possibly, in spite of the English intonation, it was in some foreign language which was required at the moment. Additionally confusing was the fact that one answer came so quickly on the heels of another as to be indistinguishable from it, so that often an enquirer went on listening intently, in the belief that his question was still being answered, without noticing for some time that his turn was past. You had also to get used to the under-porter's habit of never asking a question to be repeated; even if it was vague only in wording and quite sensible on the whole, he merely gave an almost imperceptible shake of the head to indicate that he did not intend to answer that question and it was the questioner's business to recognise his own error and formulate the question more correctly. This in particular kept many people for a long time in front of the counter. To help the

> under-porters, each of them was allotted a messenger
> boy, who had to rush to and fro bringing from a bookcase
> and various cupboards whatever the under-porter might
> need. [*Amerika*, pp. 196–97]

The confusion of language, the gibbering, the muffledness, is always a
sure sign of sudden elevation, of an accession to the spirit. But what is
chiefly of interest is the complexity of rules—if the auditor does not strain
to hear he will lose his chance—the ritualization, the hierarchy of errand
boys whose fetched objects will be casually knocked to the floor by the
impassive underporters if a mistake has occurred. The mediation from
authority to the lower earth has begun the astonishing proliferation, the
teeming of middlemen, that will eventually become the whole bureaucracy of *The Castle*. The hotel's telephone system is similar:

> out of each couple one did nothing but note down con-
> versations, passing on these notes to his neighbour, who
> despatched the messages by another telephone. The in-
> struments were of the new-fashioned kind which do not
> need a telephone box, for the ringing of the bell was no
> louder than a twitter, and a mere whisper into the mouth-
> piece was electrically amplified until it reached its destin-
> ation in a voice of thunder. For this reason the three men
> who were speaking into the telephones were scarcely au-
> dible, and one might have thought they were muttering to
> themselves about something happening in the mouth-
> piece, while the other three, as if deafened by the thunder
> coming from their ear-pieces, although no one else could
> hear a sound, drooped their heads over the sheets of
> paper on which they had to make their notes. Here too a
> boy assistant stood beside each of the three whisperers;
> these three boys did nothing but alternately lean their
> heads towards their masters in a listening posture and
> then hastily, as if stung, search for telephone numbers in
> huge, yellow books: the rustling of so many massed pages
> easily drowned any noise from the telephones. [*Amerika*,
> pp. 199–200]

Karl hears only faint, unintelligible twitters, like the thin whistling
noise that disturbs the protagonist of "The Burrow," but he knows that
messages of devastating import are being recorded, passed on. Someone will at last hear the word of thunder, will be struck with the lightning bolt from above, but only if it can make its way through the thick
clog of intermediaries. These passages are only brief interpolations in
Karl's journey, but such myths will sophisticate themselves into the
major structures of Kafka's later fiction: networks of passageways,

conduits of messages sent by no one and decisively received by no one, but from which vague murmurs leak out.

> The choice was put to them whether they would like to be kings or king's couriers. Like children they all wanted to be couriers. So now there are a great many couriers, they post through the world, and, as there are no kings left, shout to each other their meaningless and obsolete messages. They would gladly put an end to their wretched lives, but they dare not because of their oath of service. [*The Great Wall of China*, p. 171]

The most enlightened understanding one can have of the sordid world of experience is that it is everywhere manipulated from above, that we are all childlike couriers of messages we should not read, that may indeed have lost all pertinence. The rift-design of Kafka's later fiction may be compared to the flow chart of a government office or the circuit board of a radio, through which information is transmitted, a diagram that is perfectly intelligible even though the information conveyed through it is in itself garbled. The dog in "Investigations of a Dog" looks back to a dim era when "the true Word could still have intervened":

> the Word was there, was very near at least, on the tip of everybody's tongue, anyone might have hit upon it. And what has become of it today? Today one may pluck out one's very heart and not find it. [*The Great Wall of China*, p. 25]

We all live in a condition of estrangement from the Word, no matter how we belabor our organs to hear it. A writer who cannot speak the Word is in an unenviable position; he must use words to denote their own inadequacy, their failure to denote. The poplar of "Description of a Struggle," whose name keeps being forgotten and reinvented, shows one device for emblematizing this state of wordlessness; but the strategy of Kafka's mature writing is to construct a ramifying pattern of message delivery and message interpretation, a labyrinth of garblers and deniers, a design that stands as a kind of hieroglyph of our condition of estrangement from the Word. The Word is blocked—the messenger with the emperor's personal instructions to us has not been able to get out of the palace, let alone to the city limits of Peking, let alone across the immensities of China—but the mechanisms of transmission elaborate endlessly, twine the subtlest tendrils to evade this blockage, to circumvent the loss of the Word; but it is only the elaboration of capillaries to feed the blockage itself, like some great tumor.

For Kafka it may be said the connections between things are

more vivid than things in themselves. It is generally true of the psychomachia that its subordinate entities have little external existence but are chiefly signs of some aspect or relation in the protagonist's mind. This is one reason Kafka makes so much of the fiction a crisscross of messengers; he cares only about one character—whose name usually bears some resemblance to "Kafka"—and about that character's relations with the spiritual and the terrestrial, a network of chains connecting him to heaven and to earth, throttling him both on his descent and on his ascent (*Great Wall*, p. 174). The protagonist is Everyman faced with a series of helpers and obstacles, except that the usual case in Kafka is that the helpers *are* the obstacles. In Kafka's story *The Judgment* (1912), written just after the major part of *Amerika*, Kafka tries to solve the difficult problem of portraying a character who is not a character at all but explicitly an emblem of relation. Georg Bendemann, a young merchant whose business has grown very successful as he has taken the reins from his aging father, maintains a correspondence with a friend in Saint Petersburg whose career is going downhill, who is lonely, diseased, and estranged from local society. Georg feels he must treat his friend with extreme tact, withhold all important local news—such as Georg's recent engagement to be married—for fear of upsetting him, of altering his tranquil, static image of society at home. But at last he does write to his friend about the engagement and tells his father about the letter. His father, inexplicably, says that he does not believe that Georg has a friend in Saint Petersburg; then, no longer a semiinvalid, he rises from his bed like a colossus, denounces Georg, and claims that Georg's friend has been like a true son to him and that Georg has plotted against them both. He accuses Georg of profaning his dead mother by his engagement and finally orders Georg's suicide. Georg, through all of this, has behaved in a mild, unassertive, appeasing fashion, the most thoughtful friend and child; yet he rushes to his death at his father's command. *The Judgment* is the only work of his for which Kafka offered an extended explication:

> The friend is the link between father and son, he is their strongest common bond. Sitting alone at his window, Georg rummages voluptuously in this consciousness of what they have in common, believes he has his father within him, and would be at peace with everything if it were not for a fleeting, sad thoughtfulness. In the course of the story the father, with the strengthened position that the other, lesser things they share in common give him—love, devotion to the mother, loyalty to her memory, the clientele that he (the father) had been the first to

acquire for the business—uses the common bond of the friend to set himself up as Georg's antagonist. Georg is left with nothing; the bride, who lives in the story only in relation to the friend, that is, to what father and son have in common, is easily driven away by the father since no marriage has yet taken place, and so she cannot penetrate the circle of blood relationship that is drawn around father and son. What they have in common is built up entirely around the father, Georg can feel it only as something foreign, something that has become independent, that he has never given enough protection, that is exposed to Russian revolutions, and only because he himself has lost everything except his awareness of the father does the judgment, which closes off his father from him completely, have so strong an effect on him. [*Diaries I*, pp. 278–79]

Kafka's readers should recall, when they find puzzling characters in his works, that a mere common bond between members of a family can acquire a personality, a business, a case of jaundice; in a notebook sketch a swoon, dressed in a long dress and a feathered hat, visits the narrator's apartment (*Dearest Father*, p. 54); and Kafka once wrote to Milena Jesenská that their conversations about an unreal future in which they lived together resembled a search for a missing dear friend, whom they kept calling, calling by lovely names, but who never came, who could not answer because he was not there (*Letters to Milena*, pp. 207–8)—another failed relationship embodied in a remote third party. This turning inward from exterior characters to the relations between characters is another example of the attempt to represent what is abstract, spiritual. The friend is a kind of pretext for an endless proliferation of unheeded messages: for Georg and his father do not talk to each other, but only make stilted and impersonal allusions to what they cannot really share or confront—the death of the mother, Georg's engagement—as if each only wrote carefully censored letters to a third party. The friend's skin disease and business failure are signs of the attrition, the wasting away, of the relation of father and son; and, as Kafka explains, each uses the "friend"—what they have in common—for his own purposes, the son to keep the father piously quiet, smothered, ineffectual, the father to destroy his son in the sudden shock, the immediate recognition of the strong subliminal current of feeling between them. What Kafka does not explain is the incredibility of the father. I believe that the father, as well as the friend, cannot be taken as a literal character according to the canons of realistic fiction; he must himself be a kind of aspect or relation, what Freud would call an imago, the vigorous caricature of the paternal that Georg carries suppressed within him. The father has attenuated into the face on a picture postcard possessed by a friend in Saint Petersburg. *The Judgment,* then, is a story about deliberate alienation from the real, about the multiple thicknesses of insulation in which we swaddle ourselves from the truth, and about the impossibility of maintaining this ingenious contraption for estrangement—the necessary collapse of illusion into an enlightenment meaning, in this case, death.

When Georg's father first reveals himself in his strength, Georg retorts, "'You comedian!'" to which his father responds, "'Yes, of course I've been playing a comedy! A comedy! That's a good expression! What other comfort was left to a poor old widower?'" (*Penal Colony,* p. 60). He means that he has acquiesced in a false, submissive role urged on him by Georg. But in a larger sense the whole of *The Judgment,* despite the horror of its outcome, is a comedy. As Kafka remarked to his much younger friend Gustav Janouch, who was almost like a son to him:

> "The revolt of the son against the father is one of the primeval themes of literature, and an even older problem in the world. Dramas and tragedies are written about it, yet in reality it is material for comedy. The Irishman Synge was right in realizing this. In his play *The Playboy of the Western World* the son is an adolescent exhibitionist who boasts of having murdered his father. Then along comes the old man and turns the young conqueror of paternal authority into a figure of fun."
>
> "I see that you are very sceptical about the struggle of the young against the old," I said.
>
> Kafka smiled.
>
> "My scepticism does not alter the fact that this struggle is usually only shadow boxing."
>
> "What do you mean—shadow boxing?"
>
> "Age is the future of youth, which sooner or later it must reach. So why struggle? To become old sooner? For a quicker departure?" [*Conversations with Kafka,* pp. 68–69]

It is not easy to compare *The Judgment* with *The Playboy of the Western World,* but *The Judgment* too is a kind of shadowboxing of father and son, a story of imaginary murder, a theater of figments; the central combat is not son versus father, but the comfortable and the deluded versus the real. Kafka suggests that all struggles between son and father are actually between the son and an image of something latent within him, an image that he palliates, refuses to acknowledge, consigns to the sickbed. Just as at the heart of America Karl Rossmann

finds a theater expanded nearly to the size of a continent, so Georg
Bendemann discovers that his well-upholstered family life, at the
crisis, stiffens into a theater of enlightenment, of disillusion.

Much of Kafka's subsequent fiction shapes itself around theatrical
spectacles, such as the circus of "First Sorrow," the ape vaudeville of
"Report to an Academy," even the public execution of *In the Penal
Colony;* but even when the locale of the fiction is simply the family
apartment, an apparatus of theatrical metaphor will usually be erected.
Kafka's most celebrated story, *The Metamorphosis,* written in 1912,
two months after *The Judgment,* is in simplest form an ordinary commercial traveler's discovery that he is playing the lead role in a drama,
a dark comedy. The central event of the tale—Gregor Samsa's awak-
ening one morning as a giant dung beetle (I employ Nabokov's, and the
charwoman's, entomological classification of him, for the narrator calls
him only an insect)—exaggerates, stylizes a certain preexistent drama
latent in Gregor's homelife. Gregor has been more or less happily
playing the role of his family's sole provider, a role they are only too
happy to assign to him. He takes pride in being the provider, the
dispenser of bounty, and enjoys the magnanimity of being about to give
his sister violin lessons at the conservatory for a Christmas present
(*Penal Colony,* p. 95). Yet he feels that his family has "no special
uprush of warm feeling" in return for his benevolence; further, he
suspects that he is not esteemed at his office and tries to tell the chief
clerk that he understands the prejudice against commercial travelers,
who are considered an overrewarded and funloving lot (p. 83). His
metamorphosis into a beetle is a kind of fantastic aggrandizement of
these feelings of contemptibleness. Gregor, instead of being taken for
granted as an untroublesome provider, makes himself the sole object of
everyone's attention, the cynosure, the star in the drama of his family
life. One of the most interesting aspects of the fable is the way Kafka
has combined a little story of The Worm Turns with the high comedy of
spiritual enlightenment. The commercial traveler who plots how he
could spectacularly resign, tell the chief "exactly what I think of him"
(p. 69), if only he were not responsible for his family's welfare, discovers that his metamorphosis makes him so frightening that the chief
clerk leaps down the staircase yelling "Ugh!" in an agony of disgust (p.
85). The worm turns by making himself more vermiform, monstrous,
and exacts his petty revenge in the most unexpected way. Indeed, it is
easier for a worm to turn than it is for a man; Kafka's *Letter to His
Father* records how his career as a writer helped him escape from
his father, "even if it was slightly reminiscent of the worm that, when a
foot treads on its tail end, breaks loose with its front part and drags
itself aside" (p. 85). One diminishes into worm or beetle because the

smaller being is more adaptable, plastic, accommodating—a vehicle in which it is easy to escape from or to dramatize one's problem. By the latter parts of the story Gregor has learned to try to take advantage of his theatricality, to accept and deploy his monstrousness. He deliberately plays the bogeyman to frighten the insulting charwoman, who, alas, is immune from revulsion and fear and threatens to squash him (*Penal Colony,* p. 116); and when he enters the living room to show his human sensitivity to his sister's violin-playing, he becomes an entertainment for the lodgers and makes his apartment into a kind of freak show (p. 122). It is perhaps remarkable that his family's shame on his account prevents them from thinking of selling tickets to look at him, as happens to the humanized ape Red Peter in "Report to an Academy."

Yet Kafka's heroes learn to see themselves in a dramatic light only at the price of being victimized, degraded. Karl Rossmann in *Amerika* must sink to slavery before he can go to Oklahoma; and Georg Bendemann in *The Judgment* knows no comedy except the one in which he is first fool, then sacrifice. The play in which Gregor Samsa finds himself is the drama of his self-abnegation, self-contraction, vanishing; his every action ends in his further estrangement, mutilation. As he undergoes metamorphosis, becomes abased and grotesque to his family, more central and more excluded than ever before, the signs of lightening, revelation, disenchantment become prominent; an expansion in wisdom, a greater detachment and indifference, accompanies his contraction in stature. His voice, during the act of metamorphosis, acquires the fraying edge of silence that suggests proximity to the spirit:

> Gregor had a shock as he heard his own voice answering hers, unmistakably his own voice, it was true, but with a persistent horrible twittering squeak behind it like an undertone, which left the words in their clear shape only for the first moment and then rose up reverberating around them to destroy their sense, so that one could not be sure one had heard them rightly. [*The Penal Colony,* p. 70]

His abstraction into complete unintelligibility shows that he has left one form of corrupt expression behind him. As he withdraws from participation in family life, his comprehension of his family's situation becomes keener, clearer. He learns that they were by no means as dependent on him as he had thought, that his father had concealed financial resources, and that mother, father, and sister alike were capable of gainful employment. Even in these simple ways retreat and alienation are the conditions of insight. The whole family had been conspirators in maintaining certain complacent illusions, and Gregor's insecthood is a metamorphosis into disillusion.

The Metamorphosis is a parable about disembodiment, about the distorted forms enlightenment takes when seen from the vantage point of the terrestrial. As the narrator and the acquaintance of "Description of a Struggle" together constitute a soul and body, so Gregor's discarnate soul takes the appearance of a beetle in *The Metamorphosis*. This is explicit in a famous passage from Kafka's very early fragment "Wedding Preparations in the Country" (1907–8), in which the hero, faced with a trying and unpleasant journey, remembers how as a child he merely dispatched his "clothed body" on painful errands, while he himself remained cozy in bed, having assumed the shape of "a stag beetle or a cockchafer":

> "The form of a large beetle, yes. Then I would pretend it was a matter of hibernating, and I would press my little legs to my bulging belly. And I would whisper a few words, instructions to my sad body, which stands close beside me, bent. Soon I shall have done—it bows, it goes swiftly, and it will manage everything efficiently while I rest." [*The Complete Stories*, p. 56]

The passage has an idle, langorous, dreamy tone, far removed from the horribly specific, point-blank realization of *The Metamorphosis;* but the insectile nature of the soul is the same, I believe. As one ascends, one becomes disembodied, inconsequent, insignificant, a wood louse demure to the point of vanishing. Gregor as a beetle is anorectic, wastes away from lack of food, wonders at the insensitivity of his chiton (*Penal Colony,* p. 91); and this supersession of the body is accompanied by increasing lack of interest in the matters that engaged him in previous life. In the middle of the story Gregor becomes alarmed by his apathy, his loss of human considerateness—Beckett refers to this condition as "loss of species"—and tries to prevent his mother and sister from removing from his room two souvenirs of his former humanness, his writing desk and the picture he has framed. But this is a rearguard action, a last stand of his humanity; for the most part he is happily assimilated into beetlehood, has abandoned his family for the joys of involution, bare uncluttered walls, the kingdom of the spirit. Gregor metamorphoses, and his world metamorphoses at the same time:

> For in reality day by day things that were even a little way off were growing dimmer to his sight; the hospital across the street, which he used to execrate for being all too often before his eyes, was now quite beyond his range of vision, and if he had not known that he lived in Charlotte Street, a quiet street but still a city street, he might have believed that his window gave on a desert waste

where gray sky and gray land blended indistinguishably into each other. [*The Penal Colony,* p. 97]

It is an appalling vacancy, but it has been successfully evacuated of all that is merely corporeal; it is a city landscape seen without illusion. And Gregor abandons himself to the felicity of his utter freedom, that place so persistent in Kafka's writings, the world without gravity:

> During the daytime he did not want to show himself at the window, out of consideration for his parents, but he could not crawl very far around the few square yards of floor space he had, nor could he bear lying quietly at rest all during the night, while he was fast losing any interest he had ever taken in food, so that for mere recreation he had formed the habit of crawling criss-cross over the walls and ceiling. He especially enjoyed hanging suspended from the ceiling; it was much better than lying on the floor; one could breathe more freely; one's body swung and rocked lightly; and in the almost blissful absorption induced by this suspension it could happen to his own surprise that he let go and fell plump on the floor. [*The Penal Colony,* p. 100]

Thus, in an inverted manner, the insect alone can manifest the sublimity of the imagination.

In the end Gregor and his family all agree that it is time for him to vanish; he dies and is mysteriously eliminated by the charwoman, his body so "completely flat and dry" that one supposes that the slightest wind could blow it away. This metamorphosis into extreme lightness—the suction pads on his rapid little legs have at last lifted him out of the world entirely—is not, in the Ovidian manner, an escape from the parlousness of the human into the beauty of rapt and careless nature, Daphne the laurel and Philomel the nightingale, but is a heightening of despicableness. However, it is like Ovid in that it is anesthetic, a release from suffering, a vehicle into the imagination's unearthly joy. One of the most Kafkaesque stories written after Kafka's death is Mann's *The Holy Sinner* (1951), in which Grigorss— the resemblance of the name to Gregor is a remarkable coincidence— expiates his unwitting crime by being chained on a rock in the middle of a lake, becomes horny-skinned and granular, shrunken, at last a kind of hedgehog, nearly legless, armless, mouthless; but at the end of the appointed time he is loosed, restored to humanity, and, beyond humanity, is assumed into the papacy as Gregory the Great. He too sees his life as a play and says, "We have thought to offer God an entertainment" (*Holy Sinner,* p. 225). It is a drama of ascension into glory by means of a corporeal transformation, and, though Kafka's entertainment is the stuff of nightmares, it is still a related kind of comedy. *The Metamorphosis* could with equal justice have been titled *The Transfiguration*.

What makes Kafka's fiction hard to understand is the method of persistent inversion, the invention of deliberately fake worlds that can manifest the truth only by collapsing, by turning themselves inside out, by growing unintelligible. "What is called suffering in this world is, without any alteration, except that it is freed from its opposite, bliss in another" (*Great Wall of China*, p. 181). By means of such reflections Kafka tells the reader to read "white" whenever "black" appears on the page; as things above, so, in exactly opposite fashion, are things below. Gregor as a beetle is a representation of an anti-man, a person grown so unlike a human being that he is a fit emblem of the spiritual self; the cramped prison of Gregor's room is a similarly inverted emblem of the limitless heaven. It is especially proper that the keenest of Gregor's sufferings are derived from being forced through a narrow door, for all of Kafka's doors are emblems of the passage between states of being, like the door in "A Report to an Academy," forced from behind with an immense pressure of wind, through which Red Peter leaves his apehood and enters the human race (*Penal Colony*, p. 173). Kafka's stories are representations of the falseness of false things, the manner in which each thing we observe is simultaneously itself and nothing at all:

> "Everything sails under a false flag, no word corresponds to the truth. I, for instance—I am now going home. But it only looks as if I were. In reality, I mount into a prison specially constructed for myself, which is all the harsher because it looks like a perfectly ordinary bourgeois home and—except for myself—no one would recognize it as a prison. For that reason, every attempt at escape is useless. One cannot break one's chains when there are no chains to be seen. One's imprisonment is therefore organized as a perfectly ordinary, not over-comfortable form of daily life. Everything looks as if it were made of solid, lasting stuff. But on the contrary it is a life in which one is falling towards an abyss. It isn't visible. But if one closes one's eyes, one can hear its rush and roar." [*Conversations with Kafka*, pp. 53–54]

The Metamorphosis is just such a home-prison, at once tenacious and fragile, in which Gregor, by concentrating on the roar of the abyss under it, eventually drowns out the consciousness of the prison itself. Every display of the false is an adumbration of the true.

Perhaps Kafka's most daring experiment in demonstrating that suffering is bliss is *In the Penal Colony* (1914). This is one of Kafka's most abstract stories, set not in the usual too-familiar city but in a remote and fabulous kingdom; and, like Oklahoma and all the other remote places, it is a schematic representation, spiritual, at once a model of our dwelling place and a proof of its unreality. The world of experience has dwindled to a diabolical machine, a device for executing condemned criminals by engraving, in a florid and embellished script, the broken commandment on their skins with vibrating needles. It is a simple two-part fable: in the first part the presiding officer describes to an explorer—who is a bourgeois liberal, horrified by inhumane punishment—how the machine operates, how it has operated in the past; the criminal's death is reached at a moment of terminal enlightenment:

> "Enlightenment comes to the most dull-witted. It begins around the eyes. From there it radiates. A moment that might tempt one to get under the Harrow oneself. Nothing more happens than that the man begins to understand the inscription, he purses his mouth as if he were listening. You have seen how difficult it is to decipher the script with one's eyes; but our man deciphers it with his wounds." [*The Penal Colony*, p. 204]

In former times executions were great public festivals in which men, women, and children alike rejoiced at the spectacle of the "look of transfiguration on the face of the sufferer" (p. 209). But now the institution has fallen into public disfavor and the new Commandant—the old Commandant was the builder of the machine, at once "soldier, judge, mechanic, chemist and draughtsman" (p. 196), in short, God—is clearly abolishing the custom, letting the machine fall into disrepair. In the second part the officer, the last true believer in the machine, has failed to persuade the explorer to plead on the machine's behalf; he then decides to undergo the enlightening torture himself, to execute himself on his own machine. He sets the controls to write "Be Just!" on his body, but the machine goes haywire, spews out its cogwheels in all directions, jabs him to death without writing anything—"no exquisite torture," but just "plain murder" (p. 224). The first part is a kind of stylization of the system of justice as we might wish it to be, a smooth, easy transition from divine commandment to our comprehension of it in our wounds. It is the ideal justice of the Old Testament, in which the least sin is punishable by a measured death, in which the condemned man grows wise in a bloody clarification of his guilt. The radiance of the condemned man seems to prove that suffering is bliss; but it is in reality not so simple as the officer wishes it to be. The second part is the collapse, the abolition of the first part. Justice does not operate as theory suggests it should; the commandment, already embellished into near-illegibility in the first part, grows so complicated and random that it ceases to be any sort of sentence at all; as the Designer, the box that contains the encoded commandments, and the Harrow, the apparatus of needles, fall apart, the links between spirit and nature are severed, and the manifestations of justice reduce to freakish whorls and arbitrary punctures, neither signs nor symbols. The pretty letters of the alphabet are elaborated into unmeaning; this is the real enlightenment, not the sham radiance of the officer's indulgent memory, but the confrontation with "plain murder," stark, unmitigated by the Word. The pattern of jabs that ought to have read "Be Just!" is instead a symbol denoting a lack of symbols, a visible unintelligibility, a rift-design traced by its failure of meaning. The hope of justice is to convert the sinner into a text, a kind of illuminated manuscript in which he is a signal denunciation of his own sin; and even at the end of the story the sinner is a text—what the Harrow does to the officer is still a kind of writing—but it is a lapsed text, a verbal absurdity. The twentieth century has been intrigued by machines like Jean Tinguely's, which are built solely for the purpose of shaking themselves to pieces; Kafka's story is a self-destroying fable, a concatenation of words designed to impinge upon, to frame, a condition of wordlessness. It is a theater in which the stage machinery is erected to annihilate the sole actor in the process of its own collapse, a drama ended by the exit of the sole spectator, as if nothing had ever happened at all.

> "But then he returned to his work as if nothing had happened." That is a saying which sounds familiar to us from an indefinite number of old tales, though in fact it perhaps occurs in none. [*The Great Wall of China,* p. 184]

It would be the proper last line of *In the Penal Colony,* perhaps of all of Kafka's tales. Not only must we learn to read "bliss" for "suffering," "white" for "black," we must learn to unread the whole fictive world erected for our contemplation.

In the Penal Colony is a verbal approximation to reality achieved by an act of self-contradiction, by a dismantling of the artifice of itself. It is one of Kafka's favorite techniques; at the end of *Letter to His Father,* written five years later, Kafka imagines a long rebuttal his father might make against the whole of the *Letter:*

> Naturally things cannot in reality fit together the way the

> evidence does in my letter; life is more than a Chinese
> puzzle. But with the correction made by this rejoinder—a
> correction I neither can nor will elaborate in detail—in
> my opinion something has been achieved which so
> closely approximates the truth that it might reassure us
> both a little and make our living and our dying easier.
> [*Letter to His Father*, p. 125]

Words can approach reality only by including denials of themselves. It is a lawyerly aspect of Kafka's mind, this notion that the sifting of competing claims and denials is the best method for attaining truth; but what is not good legal practice is Kafka's habit of being both prosecutor and defendant at once. In the *Letter* Kafka does not invite his father to present his case; and this was sometimes in fact Kafka's practice as a lawyer, for Janouch tells us that Kafka occasionally hired and briefed in secret a defense attorney for old pitiable laborers whose accident claims Kafka was required to dispute, thereby transforming a court of law into a theater of competing Kafkas (*Conversations*, p. 66). Similarly, the officer of *In the Penal Colony* is a hangman who of his own will becomes the victim, who expels the ignorant condemned man from the bed of execution as if he could not bear another actor to intrude in the solitary drama in which all roles are played by one man.

In this way, and in many others, *In the Penal Colony* is an exercise preliminary to the composition of *The Trial* (1914–15), a blueprint for the operations of a justice to be realized in the detailed hideous city of that novel. Its protagonist, Joseph K., is at once the condemned man and the officer: like the condemned man he understands little or nothing of the workings of justice; like the officer he has a certain drive to play all the roles. When he tries to show Fräulein Bürstner how he was arrested, he literally assumes the role of his accuser:

> "You must picture to yourself exactly where the various
> people are, it's very interesting. I am the Inspector, over
> there on the chest two warders are sitting, beside the
> photographs three young men are standing. At the latch
> of the window—just to mention it in passing—a white
> blouse is dangling. And now we can begin. Oh, I've for-
> gotten about myself, the most important person; well,
> I'm standing here in front of the table." [*The Trial*, p. 27]

As in *Amerika*, Kafka describes the mysterious oneness of insignificance and centrality: K. is the most minor and trivial case before the court—no one seems to pay more than perfunctory attention to him—and yet the court seems in other ways so preoccupied with him that the whole world seems one vast apparatus for his prosecution. One of the meanings of the famous parable "Before the Law" is that there is a door into the law, and a doorkeeper for that door, assigned uniquely to Joseph K.; and at many points K. has intuitions that he is the sole center, agent, and audience of all the spectacles he beholds. He is the congregation to whom the priest speaks (p. 208); at work in his office "all this activity rotated around K. as if he were the center of it" (p. 202); and in an unfinished chapter he has a dream in which "he thought of himself as the only defendant and all of the others as officials and lawyers thronging the corridors of a law court" (*Trial*, p. 247). The novel contains one scene in which it seems apparent that K. is the central power behind the whole fable: he sees his warders, Willem and Franz—it is significant that Kafka's first name turns up as one of K.'s harassers, as if Franz and K. were aspects of the same entity—being flogged (p. 84). They explain that the flogging is due to his complaint; K. protests that he never complained. It is as if a secret whim of K.'s were so potent that it could cause a whip to fall on his persecutors' backs, as if every event in the book, every obstacle in K.'s path to vindication, even his own execution, were an expression of some aspect of his hidden will. In a letter to Milena Jesenská, Kafka calls himself the pawn of a pawn who dreams of becoming first queen, then king, then the whole board (*Letters to Milena*, p. 73); and *The Trial* is a fantastic realization of this omnipotent triviality.

Just as *In the Penal Colony* is concerned with the amazing distortions that occur between the spirit's commandments and their expression on the backs of the condemned, so one of the important themes of *The Trial* is the distortion of expression between high and low, inner and outer. *The Trial*, like all the rest, is a comedy; indeed, K. announces in the opening pages that "if this was a comedy he would insist on playing it to the end" (p. 5); and it could be described as a comedy of the lack of reticence. The Inspector gives K. in the first chapter the best piece of advice he will receive in the whole book:

> "However, if I can't answer your questions, I can at least give you a piece of advice; think less about us and of what is going to happen to you, think more about yourself instead. And don't make such an outcry about your feeling innocent, it spoils the not unfavorable impression you make in other respects. Also you should be far more reticent, nearly everything you have just said could have been implied in your behavior with the help of a word here and there, and in any case does not redound particularly to your credit." [*The Trial*, p. 12]

All that mysteriously befalls K. is due to his lack of silence: by uttering protests, by struggling and expostulating, he erects around himself the whole machinery of prosecution and defense, creates a pair of warders to seize him and a magistrate to examine him, creates a battery of doubtful helpers to intercede for him, creates his death. If K. were at ease with himself, were tacit about guilt and innocence, he would be solitary and worldless, for everything in the world is a frightening literalization of self-accusal, self-justification, an infernal psychomachia. Kafka described in his *Letter to His Father*—an autobiography in which he explicitly compares himself (p. 73) to K. in *The Trial*—how his father's belittling him, annihilating him, drove the boy into such utter silence that he "lost the capacity to talk" (p. 33). And in *The Trial* also there is a sense in which every expression of thought and feeling, every descent from self-absorption into speech, will be quickly punished, will itself constitute a punishment.

Where utterance is the crime, declarations of guilt and innocence alike condemn. Several times in the novel K. is tempted; and these temptations are usually temptations to speak. In the "Leni" chapter, K. meets one of a series of female helpers whose aid he will enlist until, near the end, the priest tells him to stop casting about "for outside help . . . especially from women" (*Trial*, p. 211). Leni warns him that he cannot fight the court, that he must confess to guilt, as she presses her breasts against his body (p. 108). It is as if she were really urging him to grow explicit about his sexual interest while she ostensibly urges confession to the court; in either case it is a declaration, an utterance, a self-expression that she wants; she tempts him to a violation of his integrity, his self-containedness. K. does not succumb to the temptation to confess, but in a later chapter, "Painter," he succumbs to the matching temptation of declaring himself innocent, savors his elation by repeating it (p. 149). This leads Titorelli, in one of the most awesome passages in all of Kafka, to explain to K. the kinds of acquittal that can be obtained, the court's rules of evidence, the remote, naive judges—K.'s declaration implicates him in the labyrinth of justice from which he never escapes. Self-expression is a binding of oneself to a corrupt exterior world; silence frees one from this complicity with illusion. This is why the affiliation of the law with sex is so prevalent in the novel: the law books K. discovers contain obscene drawings (p. 52), and K.'s lawyer hints to him that Leni sleeps with all accused men, who grow attractive to her, beautiful, because of their accusal (p. 183). *The Trial* is the comedy of the spirit's seduction, its taking the interplay of its figments as a solid external world; and sex is a useful metaphor for this temptation into unreality. It is a recapitulation of the fall of man. Indeed, it is possible that the unspecified crime that leads to K.'s arrest is mere physical existence, having a body. At the end of "The Offices" chapter, K. becomes dizzy, seasick, as if the room were rolling and pitching (p. 72)—a sign of the interiority, the projectedness of the psychic cityscape—and K. wonders, "Could his body possibly be meditating a revolution and preparing a new trial for him?" (*Trial*, p. 73), as if the trial were never anything but a coming to terms with the body, an inquiry into the hardness, the false expressions of the corporeal.

K. is bedeviled by the mock substantiality of his own utterances; and throughout the novel there is a remarkable prevalence of false images, images that give no true likeness. Few novels are quite so dense with descriptions of pictures; indeed, *The Trial* is an offshoot of the aesthetic novel and could justly have been titled *A Rebours, Against Nature*. The world of *The Trial* is almost completely unnatural, with its Piranesi architecture, low galleries in which no one can stand upright (p. 37), halls and ceilings riddled with impossible holes (p. 116), masonry oozing yellow fluid (p. 141), unlit and oversteep staircases, identical lobbies and passageways whose forms are exactly prescribed by regulation (p. 164)—in short, the torture machine of *In the Penal Colony* elaborated into a city. Nature has been reduced to a few heathscapes painted by Titorelli, now unfashionably somber and depressing to his clientele (p. 163). Kafka, thinking of the rich who feed on the misery of the poor, told Gustav Janouch that the Marquis de Sade was the real patron of our era (*Conversations*, p. 131); but another aspect of de Sade's thought, the delight in the unnatural, the perverse, the ingenuity in the construction of torture machines—there is a device described at the end of *120 Days of Sodom* that shoots darts in a regular sequence at the victim until her skin is invisible under the mass of tufts—perhaps shows itself in *The Trial*. The aesthetic novel of the nineteenth century, in which the protagonist grows involute in velvet and mirrors, wraps himself in the shivering of his delighted senses, only to discover that his life is ashes, his appetite famished by shadow fruit, is oddly mutated in the career of Joseph K., whose confrontations with the law are mostly a matter of staring at painted images. Titorelli gives this secret away: "'If I were to paint all the Judges in a row on one canvas and you were to plead your case before it, you would have more hope of success than before the actual Court'" (*Trial,* p. 150). It is no accident that K.'s closest accession to the mysteries of the court is gained not from his lawyers, not from the well-connected women whose support he enlists, but from the court painter, Titorelli; indeed, I am not sure that the "Painter" chapter is not the most impressive in the novel. The affairs of the spirit—sin, pain, hope, and the true way—are, without being in any manner less ethically demanding, intuited or understood only by aesthetic means, by the imagination, which distorts in the very act of apprehension. We have seen that purely mental contemplation, the wood louse lost in the bliss of invisibility, is easy, rapid, felicitous, but that he who attempts to manifest, to utter his vision, grows heavy and bloated, incompetent. The paintings of Titorelli are representations of the judges, the officers of the spirit, but they are poor images, ludicrous and misleading, deliberately falsified. The first such likeness that K. beholds is in the "Leni" chapter:

> It represented a man in a Judge's robe; he was sitting on a high thronelike seat, and the gilding of the seat stood out strongly in the picture. The strange thing was that the Judge did not seem to be sitting in dignified composure, for his left arm was braced along the back and the side-arm of his throne, while his right arm rested on nothing, except for the hand, which clutched the other arm of the chair; it was as if in a moment he must spring up with a violent and probably wrathful gesture to make some decisive observation or even to pronounce sentence. The accused might be imagined as standing on the lowest step leading up to the chair of justice; the top steps, which were covered with a yellowish carpet, were shown in the picture. "Perhaps that is my Judge," said K., pointing with his finger at the picture. "I know him," said Leni, and she looked at the picture too. "He often comes here. That picture was painted when he was young, but it could never have been in the least like him, for he's a small man, almost a dwarf. Yet in spite of that he had himself drawn out to that length in the portrait, for he's madly vain like everybody else here. But I'm a vain person, too, and very much upset that you don't like me in the least."
> [*The Trial*, p. 107–8]

Leni further explains that the thronelike chair was also an invention, for he was sitting "on a kitchen chair, with an old horse-rug doubled under him" (p. 108). The examining magistrate portrayed here seems awesome and ferocious, an eagle about to pounce, but it is all artistic license, exaggeration, invention; the subject is a dwarf, and the awesomeness and the ferocity are theatrical, conventional, even sentimental. But can we be sure that Leni's image is the proper one, that the subject was really a dwarf? Block says in a later chapter that this same painting represents not a lowly examining magistrate but a high judge (p. 168). It seems likely that all representations are dubious— Titorelli's, Leni's, Block's; the image of the magistrate is presented, then its accuracy is denied, then the denial is denied. Any attempt to capture Justice, to bring it down to earth, is deception, flattery, evasion; Justice is incapable of representation, and Leni's puncturing of the painted image is Kafka's means of representing the un-representability of the spirit.

In Titorelli's studio K. sees an unfinished portrait of another judge, also menacing, bracing himself to rise, but in this painting there stands a dim figure in the background, Justice, complete with the usual scales and bandaged eyes, but shown flying, with wings on her heels; Titorelli says he has been instructed to paint "Justice and the goddess of Victory in one" (*Trial*, p. 146). K. remarks, smiling, that the scales will waver if Justice is airborne, making a just verdict impossible. Titorelli continues to paint, adding a halo to the judge's head, and the background figure alters until "it no longer suggested the goddess of Justice, or even the goddess of Victory, but looked exactly like a goddess of the Hunt in full cry" (p. 147). Justice as Artemis, persecution for persecution's sake, is a closer approximation of Justice than the usual icon, just as the torture machine of *In the Penal Colony* is a closer approximation of justice in its breakdown than it was in its designed function. This is the most accurate likeness Titorelli has to offer; but it is not a genuine realization of the spirit, only a statement of its floating, its hovering, its refusal to descend. The gap between the conception of Justice, flying above in an abstract sky, and such concrete manifestations of justice as the warders Franz and Willem is in no way bridged. Justice threatens, impends, but cannot declare itself. Titorelli, K. soon learns, is an expert in the discrepancy between legal theory and the practice of the law; and Titorelli's paintings are chiefly concerned with the impossibility of matching the spirit with its material representation. Images are deceitful, duplicitous, precisely because in the absence of a real referent one can claim any interpretation one wishes; the subject of a painting may be a dwarf, it may be a high judge, but the image is of no help in deciding. It is similar in the "Cathedral" chapter with the priest's summary of commentary about the parable "Before the Law": the doorkeeper may be incomparably great, an avatar of the law, or he may be the deluded servant of the man who beseeches him. The parable, like the painting, is only a tease, an inducement to intellectual wavering, a representation of unknowability. We are told that K. has "some knowledge of art" (*Trial*, p. 199), is in fact "a member of the Society for the Preservation of Ancient Monuments"; and the fable in which he is the hero, perhaps the sole agent, engages him in a series of acts of art criticism, for his mission is the interpretation of omens, peculiarly corrupt images. In a sense K. summons up Titorelli in order to give substantial weight, specificity, to his continuous phantasmagoria of the operations of his soul; but by miring himself in such vividly precise images he becomes lost in a twilight of double vision in which every image seems equally conducive to salvation or damnation, in which the concrete embodiment itself is an estrangement from meaning. The only enlightenment possible for K. is a kind of toleration of ambiguity, a resting content with confusion. It is uncertain whether Kafka wished the final chapter to follow "Cathedral," but the printed sequence does make some sense. K. might well go to his death at the hands of the two "tenth-rate old actors" (p. 224)—the last apparitions in K.'s monodrama—after hearing the priest, for he is left so bewildered by conflicting interpretations, so stranded between images of self-aggrandizement and self-nullity, that he could indeed abandon there the quest for specious clarity, for forcing an impossible congruence of the *is* and the *ought,* the world of experience and Justice. The lack of justice in this world is, at best, a proof of justice in another, where suffering is bliss.

The continual undermining of the truth of paintings and the meaning of parables suggests that the whole urban landscape of *The Trial* is, in a way, the perfection of Kafka's artistic method, for never before or afterward did Kafka realize the world of illusion in such full horror of oppressiveness, and at the same time show the hollowness, the abyss at the center of it; it is at once hideous and nonexistent, hideous because nonexistent, the Medusa who petrifies us precisely because she is only a poetical invention, a fable.

> The means this world employs to seduce us, and the seal of the warrant that this world is only a passing stage, are one and the same. Rightly so, for only thus could this world seduce us, and besides it squares with the truth. The worst of it, however, is that after being successfully seduced we forget the warrant and so find ourselves tempted by good into evil, tempted by woman's eyes into her bed. [*The Great Wall of China,* p. 183]

The world announces plainly that it is transitory, an illusion, and seduces us nevertheless into crediting its reality, its hard diuturnity, by means of its very transitoriness, its beguiling agitation of brief images. The city of *The Trial* proclaims its contingency, its debasedness, its inadequacy at every turn; and when Titorelli tells K. that in the attic of almost every building there are Law Court offices (p. 164), it is abundantly clear that there is a higher referent hovering above the ceiling of every earthly structure—indeed, that the earth itself is only an obscure and unintelligible outer office or antechamber of the spirit. The city's architecture consists of dead ends, circular passages, blind galleries, everything that baffles and frustrates; but when one has grown used to the foul light one sees concealed doors, sudden holes in walls, for the final secret of the architecture is that it is transparent. The city is a labyrinth from which one can escape at any point; and disorientation, getting lost, is the necessary prelude to revelation.

The Trial is a turning point in Kafka's career, for the detailed, minute descriptions of interesting squalor become less important from here on; there is a lightening of tone, and the true subject of Kafka's fiction becomes, overtly, the presentation of ecstasy. In many of the stories collected in *A Country Doctor,* written in 1916–17, the plot may concern itself with rape, disease, murder, or starvation, but these matters are intertwined with a dreamlike exhilaration or vertigo. The narrator of "A Country Doctor" takes a mad sleigh ride that deafens and blinds him with a rush of snow, an instantaneous journey; the narrator of "The Bucket Rider"—intended for *A Country Doctor* but not included in it—ascends above the rooftops, out of this world. Indeed, the appalling crimes, the despair, seem to be only added stimuli to induce a kinesthetic frenzy, a derangement of balance. The reader's orientation in a secure fictive world is increasingly precarious. In *The Metamorphosis* and *The Trial* Kafka had set up such a terra firma in order to shake it to pieces, as if one had to establish equilibrium in order to disturb it; but in the *Country Doctor* stories the solidity of the setting is dispensed with from the start. An agreeable playfulness, clear in "Description of a Struggle" but generally absent from Kafka's work of 1911–15, begins to manifest itself in such stories as "The Cares of a Family Man," or "Eleven Sons," in which Kafka describes eleven of his stories as if they were flawed children—self-deprecation turned into a kind of sportiveness, deadpan humor. *The Metamorphosis* and *The Trial* labored to produce a few devastating surprises, but in the *Country Doctor* stories the surprises are so various and rapid that the reader follows in a state of expecting only more unexpectedness. The musical analogy for these stories is perhaps the unpredictable successions of chords in Debussy, related by no clear tonic center of gravity. Debussy in 1916, slowly dying of cancer, had recently abandoned plans for an opera based on Poe's "The Fall of the House of Usher," a tale of hyperesthesia, of collapsing structures, like so many of Kafka's, and one wonders whether the composer would have been interested in setting Kafka if he had known of him.

Surprises in fiction tend to look like holes in the text; when Alice falls down the rabbit hole in *Alice in Wonderland,* she falls through a gap in a realistic story into pure fantasy, just as K. in *The Trial* walks over Titorelli's bed and through a little door into the fetid and irrational world of the law. There are a good number of such holes in *The Trial,* but as Kafka enters the last phase of his development, these holes proliferate until they become more urgent, more "visible" than the buildings or landscapes they riddle. The whole premise of the story

"The Great Wall of China" (1917) is an apology for the piecemeal system of constructing the Great Wall, in which tiny bits of wall are built along its entire length and slowly connected, a system that elevates the principle of random discontinuity into the philosophy of the nation. As the narrator tells the history of China it becomes clear that time is discontinuous as well, that the people are compelled to obey the edicts of long-dead emperors, that they confuse the dead rulers with the living. The only intelligible order is a pattern of holes, a rift-design. The world of experience is a prison, to be sure, but of an unusual sort:

> it was a barred cage that he was in. Calmly and insolently, as if at home, the din of the world streamed out and in through the bars, the prisoner was really free, he could take part in everything, nothing that went on outside escaped him, he could simply have left the cage, the bars were yards apart, he was not even a prisoner. [*The Great Wall of China*, p. 154]

Our world, despite its closedness, its fetor, is not self-contained but full of gaping cracks; we cannot escape it though it is open on every side; it is oppressive but unreliable, dependent. The central task of Kafka's late fiction is to represent the flaws, the holes, in the low, heavy historical world; to show it as a lie that cannot sustain itself, by making representations of fictive worlds that cannot sustain themselves, that disintegrate before the reader's eyes. A wall consisting entirely of holes cannot support, cannot repel.

During the later years of World War I and for two years thereafter, Kafka was not especially productive; the war, the collapse of his second engagement, and the onset of his tuberculosis doubtless made writing difficult. As Susan Sontag has said, the myth of tuberculosis is that it is a watery and airy disease, a condition of lightening, and there is perhaps a tubercular lightness to the works written just before Kafka's death, from 1921 to 1924. *The Castle* (1922), by far Kafka's longest work, is a gigantic scherzo, a depiction of a world so puffed with absurdity that it is feather light, though it turns out that the *pneuma* of the soul contains no oxygen and does not support life. The K. of *The Castle* is a land surveyor, avid for precise demarcation and measured coordinates, a lover of neat rectilinear order; but he has ascended to a realm where no clear limits obtain, where lines grow smeared, where the eye loses focus as it attempts to distinguish walls that are walls from walls that are not walls at all:

> "And you mustn't imagine that these barriers are a definite dividing-line; Barnabas is always impressing that on me. There are barriers even at the entrance to the rooms

> where he's admitted, so you see there are barriers he can
> pass, and they're just the same as the ones he's never yet
> passed, which looks as if one ought not to suppose that
> behind the ultimate barriers the offices are any different
> from those Barnabas has already seen. Only that's what
> we do suppose in moments of depression. And the doubt
> doesn't stop there, we can't keep it within bounds." [*The
> Castle*, pp. 228–29]

K. wishes to be a surveyor, but here there is nothing capable of being
surveyed; so he surveys his prospects for becoming a surveyor, but
they are not capable of being surveyed either. This K. differs fundamentally from the K. of *The Trial*, I believe, in that he is childish,
Chaplinesque, almost happy. It is true that no one could be more
exquisitely frustrated than he, who is stripped of public rank, of self-
esteem, condemned to dwindle to a grain of sand; but there is a kind of
joy in this massive dispossession. I hesitate to disagree with two such
distinguished critics of Kafka as Auden and Erich Heller, but I believe,
as Thomas Mann did, that the bureaucracy of *The Castle* is a description of the kingdom of the spirit, indeed Kafka's most potent fantasy of
heaven. The K.s of *The Trial* and *The Castle* make a common error:
they struggle to find a one-to-one correspondence between the spirit
and the lower world—in *The Trial* by hoping to find the rules of the law
stated as intelligible commandments, images, in *The Castle* by applying
the tools of land surveying to a cloud. But these strategies are futile, for
the truth is imageless.

> The expulsion from Paradise is in its main significance
> eternal: Consequently the expulsion from Paradise is
> final, and life in this world irrevocable, but the eternal
> nature of the occurrence (or, temporally expressed, the
> eternal recapitulation of the occurrence) makes it
> nevertheless possible that not only could we live con-
> tinuously in Paradise, but that we are continuously there
> in actual fact, no matter whether we know it here or not.
> [*The Great Wall of China*, p. 174]

Paradise, being eternal, is not to be constrained by the rules of clock
time, yardstick space; and so in the failure of measurement, in the
destruction of categories, in the discontinuity in our comprehension,
we may be brought closer to the intuition of the Garden of Eden that we
have never left, are always leaving. If de Sade is one patron of our era,
it is possible, as Valéry, Borges, and Italo Calvino have alleged, that
Zeno of Elea is another. K. in *The Castle* is, as Borges says
(*Labyrinths*, p. 199), a kind of personification of Zeno's moving object,
plunging toward a destination that comes closer and closer without

ever arriving, caught in an infinitesimal crack in time, fascinated by the splitting fractions that crumble aroung him. Thus K., amorous of integers, gets lost amid surds; by the end his once-discriminating and exact mind "revolves as though in a kaleidoscope" (*Castle*, p. 423). This confusion, this state of moving motionlessness, is itself a kind of peace: "Zeno, pressed as to whether anything is at rest, replied: Yes, the flying arrow rests" (*Diaries I*, p. 34). Enlightenment, as K. has not entirely learned even as late as the nineteenth chapter, consists of imitating the moth:

> Does not even the nocturnal moth, the poor creature, when day comes, seek out a quiet cranny, flatten itself out there, only wishing it could vanish and being unhappy because it cannot? [*The Castle*, p. 368]

Kafka once compared himself to "A jackdaw [*kavka*] who longs to disappear between the stones" (*Conversations*, p. 17); and his fiction at the end of his life is a construction of crevices, clefts through which the protagonist keeps slipping away. As with Beckett, the protagonist finds himself in a continual state of vanishing without ever having at last vanished.

The imagination's task, then, is not to represent things but to represent the holes between things; and Kafka is not the only writer of the century who sets himself this remarkable work of evacuation. Kafka's parable of the imagination in its hole-digging function is "The Burrow" (1923), his penultimate story. The burrow is a little world, constructed by a badgerlike narrator, but a world consisting entirely of tunnels, chambers, holes; the negative inverse of a world. He designed and executed it, he tells us, to protect himself from predators, but we do not see any creature other than the narrator, who seems the only agent in his cosmos. He is immensely proud and possessive of his burrow, his lifework, fashioned by the most arduous labor of his intellect, in the case of the tunnels, and of his body, in the case of the great central chamber, the castle keep:

> But for such tasks the only tool I possess is my forehead. So I had to run with my forehead thousands and thousands of times, for whole days and nights, against the ground, and I was glad when the blood came, for that was a proof that the walls were beginning to harden; and in that way, as everybody must admit, I richly paid for my Castle Keep. [*The Great Wall of China*, p. 48]

This passage may be compared with an aphorism of 1919, from "He": "the bony structure of his own forehead blocks his way; he batters himself bloody against his own forehead" (*Great Wall of China*, p.

154). The whole design of the burrow is a kind of magnification of brain and body, an extension of the burrower's corporeal and intellectual being, its tunnels twisting like a tedious argument of insidious intent. His intimacy with his burrow is beyond the usual affection that a craftsman feels for his artifact: he feels that "I and the burrow belong...indissolubly together," that the burrow is "so essentially mine" that he could calmly accept in it an enemy's mortal stroke, knowing that his blood would ebb into its soil (*Great Wall of China*, p. 61). He counts his own life nothing in comparison to the survival of the burrow (p. 63); "any wound to it hurts me as if I myself were hit" (p. 77); and near the end of the story he imagines that the walls of the tunnel are looking at him, as if trying to read the answer to their salvation in his face (p. 80). The burrow has eyes, it bleeds. The burrower lives in a place shaped according to the image of his body, brown, yielding, warm, articulated, subtly responsive to his will, with air holes for nostrils, a castle keep for heart or pineal gland; but it is a body turned inside out, with its organs splayed, spread out into the circumferent depths, while its eyes stare inward at the "old architect," the little burrower it accommodates. The burrower often sighs over the burrow's inadequacies, such as the thin-walled, overingenious labyrinth of tunnels that disguises its entrance; but the burrow is nevertheless a great projection of his self-regard.

His life in the burrow is by no means settled or secure; it is a series of alternating frenzies. Sometimes his safety seems to require him to store all his food in the castle keep; at other times a competing train of thought will make him think that safety requires him to store his food in the outer, subsidiary chambers. Since the burrow has never been attacked, his jeopardy is entirely imaginary, his systems of defense untested. He tries to anticipate every contingency but gets lost in contradictory speculations. At one point he becomes momentarily lost in his own entrance maze; and he is indeed a wizard lost in a labyrinth of his own devising, like the schizophrenic whose mental defenses impoverish him more than any external threat could. In general the burrower has two major ways of enjoying his burrow. The first is to seal himself up, attend to its silence, roll around in its enormous stocks of food, the happiest miser of his own identity; the psychiatric analogy would be the autistic child who neither eats nor defecates, who imagines his body as a complicated machine for the ingestion and excretion of food, a machine over which he can gain control by sealing off its orifices—I am thinking of Bruno Bettelheim's case history in *The Empty Fortress* of Joey the Machine Child. Bounded in a nutshell, the burrower could count himself king of infinite space, but he has bad dreams. He is prey to fantasies of an enemy so strong, cunning, and rapacious that no defense could ever suffice to protect him. Indeed, he sometimes prowls around "as if I were the enemy" (p. 58), puts himself in his antagonist's place in order to anticipate attack, plays all the roles in the monodrama of his existence; it is his own forehead against which he batters himself bloody. He digs a complex hole to save himself, but the hole is too like a grave, the intricate locus of his perishing. At the beginning he speaks of a legendary creature, inconceivably fierce, who might invade his burrow: "it is of no avail to console yourself with the thought that you are in your own house; far rather are you in theirs" (p. 46). These meditations spoil the burrower's pleasure in the coziness of his burrow, make it seem alien, confining, choking. Kafka once showed Gustav Janouch the warehouses of his prosperous father but denied that he was rich: "Wealth is something completely relative and unsatisfying. Fundamentally, it is only a special situation. Wealth implies dependence on things which one possesses and which have to be safeguarded from dwindling away by new possessions and a further dependence. It is merely materialized insecurity" (*Conversations*, p. 24). The ramifications, the prodigious elaborations of the burrow demonstrate just this famishing, this attempt to cure by inflaming the disease. The burrower attempts to make himself secure, but he only succeeds in descending into a material image of his own insecurity.

When the burrower is too frightened by dwelling inside the palpable circuits of his anxiety, he must go to the surface; and on the surface he enters his second, and keener, mode of enjoying his burrow. He finds a hiding place near the entrance and spends most of his days and nights watching it from the outside: "At such times it is as if I were not so much looking at my house as at myself sleeping, and had the joy of being in a profound slumber and simultaneously of keeping vigilant guard over myself" (p. 54). This may be compared with another paragraph from "He":

> He is thirsty, and is cut off from a spring by a mere clump of bushes. But he is divided against himself: one part overlooks the whole, sees that he is standing here and that the spring is just beside him; but another part notices nothing, has at most a divination that the first part sees all. But as he notices nothing he cannot drink. [*The Great Wall of China*, p. 160]

This is the process of bifurcation, the soul's abstracting itself, becoming disinterested, infinitesimal, contemplative, a wood louse. The burrower can elevate himself into a kind of detached oversoul, peer at his expression, study it without being engrossed in it, a doorkeeper to his own being. The burrow now seems like the burrower asleep, a mere body in its supine, automatic, soulless state, remaining in a trance of nature while the restless burrower roams above. It is like the situation of one of Kafka's early diary entries, where, after a bad night, he writes, "I sleep alongside myself, so to speak, while I myself struggle with dreams" (*Diaries I*, p. 74). The burrower imagines that his greatest felicity would be to remain forever just outside the burrow, gloating perpetually about "how steadfast a protection my burrow would be if I were inside it" (*Great Wall of China*, p. 55). But he is not; by remaining outside his burrow he vitiates it, renders it vain. He is exposed to a thousand perils; "No, I do not watch over my own sleep, as I imagined; rather it is I who sleep, while the destroyer watches" (p. 55). He is right in both cases: he watches over his sleep; and he is himself the destroyer who threatens the burrow.

He descends again into the burrow; but, like the thirsty man of "He," no wisdom from his superior vantage point accompanies the descent; he remains again frenetic and anxious after the brief joy of homecoming, and he begins the cycle anew. But there comes a point in the story where the burrower ceases to describe the habitual patterns of his life and instead confronts an unprecedented event: he hears a whistling noise, constant in intensity from every section of his burrow; perhaps it is the sound of innumerable small burrowing animals or, more disturbingly, the noise of some enormous, as yet distant, antagonist making his way toward the burrow. He tries to stifle the latter explanation, but his "imagination will not rest," and conviction grows; he panics (*Great Wall of China*, pp. 75–76). Although his heartbeat sometimes drowns out the whistling noise (p. 72), he never considers the possibility that the whistling is only a disease of his ear, a confusion of internal and external. He instead grows obsessed with the grisly beast who could cause such a noise; he imparts a terrible flesh to every fantasy of calamity. The burrow becomes a huge cochlea straining for the whistling sound, for knowledge of its cause. Auden's Simeon, in *For the Time Being*, speaks of the imagination's vain fornication with its images; and here we see the extremes the imagination can reach when its power is operating on a nullity, or a thin sound that is almost a nullity. The imagination, which constructed the burrow to embody and protect a fantastic insecurity, reaches such a pitch of image-making that it starts to destroy the burrow. The burrower at first decides to sift the earthwork of his walls for small whistling animals by gouging trenches in them (p. 70); he finds nothing but succeeds in disfiguring his walls and clogging his tunnels with heaps of earth; his hasty attempt to restore them leaves "Hideous protuberances, disturbing cracks" (p. 72). Near the end, as he awaits catastrophe, he wishes he had erected a

system of "improvised landslides" that would have "not only concealed the burrow, but also entombed the attackers" (p. 78). The story,
like most of Kafka's major works, is unfinished; but it seems to be
moving, I believe, toward something difficult to illustrate within the
confines of the story, the collapse of the burrow, undermined by the
frantic burrower. The imagination is the instrument of disenchantment
as well as enchantment; it will efface what it has wrought as its images
grow intolerable. Indeed, it is possible that the anxiety the burrow
could not alleviate, only utter, could be alleviated by the burrow's
destruction. Kafka once wrote, in a memorable sentence, that "the
whole world is perhaps nothing more than the rationalization of a man
who wants to find peace for a moment" (*Great Wall of China*, p. 179).
The light, friable, delicate worlds of Kafka's later fiction are demon-
strations of this rationalized quality, this inventedness, this knowing
delusion; but these rationalizations are permeable, in fact are only
holes, vacancies. The shiver of derationalization, which is the effect
Kafka's fiction intends, is gained when the protagonist sees the inadequacy, the fragile monstrousness of his constructed world, sees that
he is living not only in a hole but in a lapsing hole. The means of safe
disappearance are themselves disappearing, the hole vanishes into a
still more profound zero of being.

The insubstantial, frangible worlds of Kafka's late fiction are, despite
their abstractness, models of the world in which Kafka dwelt. Prague is
itself a rationalization. Janouch's *Conversations with Kafka* recalls the
ideas of Kafka's last period, for Janouch did not meet him until 1920;
and there Kafka speaks of city streets in language similar to that of
"The Burrow," though he substitutes a submarine for the subterranean
metaphor of that story:

> As we passed by the Eiermarkt to the Schönborn palace,
> Kafka said: "This is not a city. It is a fissure in the ocean
> bed of time, covered with the stony rubble of burned-out
> dreams and passions, through which we—as if in a diving
> bell—take a walk. It's interesting, but after a time one
> loses one's breath. Like all divers, one has to come to
> the surface, otherwise the blood bursts one's lungs. I have
> lived here a long time. I had to go away. It was too
> much." [*Conversations with Kafka*, p. 117]

Prague is itself a fissure, a hole; the stroller slips through a crack into a
stony pit, littered with old shells, the corpses of illusions; but, as with
the burrower, the urge to return to the surface, to break out of involution, eventually becomes impossible to resist. Janouch's reply and
their subsequent discussion are also of interest:

"Yes," I said, "the roads to the Inner Town are not good. One has to cross ancient stone bridges and then through a maze of tortuous alleys. There's no direct route."

Kafka was silent for a few moments. Then he responded to my remark with a question, which he immediately answered himself.

He said: "Is there a direct route anywhere at all for us? A direct route is only a dream, and that only leads to error."

I looked at Kafka in bewilderment. What connection was there between dreams and the route from the Kleinseite to the Insurance Institution on the Pořič? [*Conversations with Kafka,* pp. 117–18]

Kafka had said some years earlier, in his "Reflections on Sin, Pain, Hope, and the True Way," that "There is a goal, but no way." He was talking about a spiritual quest, but it is clear from this conversation that the pedestrian difficulty of navigating the streets of Prague is itself an image of this spiritual truth; there is no road to the Insurance Institution, let alone a road to the castle. The "real" Prague, like the landscapes of Kafka's fiction, is a coarse embodiment, concrete and wooden, ugly, hollow, illusory, of something beyond itself, unspeakable and imageless; therefore Kafka is a realist, inventing abysses that imitate the primary abyss, his own family, Prague.

In the *Conversations* Kafka speaks in puzzling ways about the desirability of realism in art. The scenes from modern life depicted on magazine covers—zeppelins, Scottish bagpipers, policemen with revolvers, prizewinning dogs, ladies in feather boas—displeased Kafka: "They break the wings of the imagination. That's perfectly natural. The more the technique of painting improves, the weaker our eyes get. The instrument damages the organs" (p. 97). Photography seemed the perfection of this superficial, attenuated realism: Kafka rejected Janouch's statement, "'The camera cannot lie!'" with vehemence:

"Photography concentrates one's eye on the superficial. For that reason it obscures the hidden life which glimmers through the outlines of things like a play of light and shade. One can't catch that even with the sharpest lens. One has to grope for it by feeling. Or do you think that one can successfully apprehend the profound depths of this ever-returning reality, before which, through all former ages, whole legions of poets, artists, scientists and other miracle workers have stood in trembling longing and hope, by pressing the knob of a cheap machine?—I

> doubt it. This automatic camera doesn't multiply men's
> eyes but only gives a fantastically simplified fly's eye
> view." [*Conversations*, p. 144]

The material must be seen as an expression of something immaterial,
some flicker of shaded light from within; the photograph catches only
the corpse. And yet, with the proviso that realistic art must be, as it has
been with the "miracle workers" of the past, a penetration beneath the
surface, an attempt to grasp the hidden vivacity of things, Kafka is
explicitly against fantasy, in favor of realism:

> we talked about a new book of stories by a successful
> Austrian writer of fantastic novels and tales.
> "He has an immense talent for invention," I said in his
> praise. But Kafka only curled his lip slightly and said:
> "Invention is easier than discovery. To present reality in
> all its detailed, and if possible in its most comprehensive,
> diversity is certainly the hardest task there is. The faces
> one sees every day rush by one like a mysterious army of
> insects."
> For a moment he abstractedly contemplated the traffic
> at the road junction in the middle of the Wenzelsplatz,
> where we were standing at the corner of the Bruckels-
> and the Obstgasse.
> "What are all these meetings about? Every face is a
> fortress tower. Yet nothing vanishes so rapidly as a
> human face." [*Conversations*, pp. 111–12]

This is why nothing is so hard as realism: the author must be faithful
both to the solid, perdurable aspect of things—the face as a fortress
tower—and to the aspect of its evanescence. Hammering a table together is at once hammering a table together and nothing at all. The
camera, the slick modern artist, can presumably represent the bland
stasis, the fortress tower; but only the true artist, the wings of his
imagination unbroken, can represent the state of the boiling-away at the
center. Many of the passages of greatest imaginative intensity in
Kafka's writing, as we have seen, are just such seizures of vanishing.
Any tourist to New York can see the skyscrapers; what Kafka grasps,
in his early novel *Amerika*, is the image of traffic:

> From morning to evening and far into the dreaming night
> that street was the channel for a constant stream of traffic
> which, seen from above, looked like an inextricable
> confusion, for ever newly improvised, of foreshortened
> human figures and the roofs of all kinds of vehicles,
> sending into the upper air another confusion, more riot-
> ous and complicated, of noises, dust and smells, all of it

> enveloped and penetrated by a flood of light which the
> multitudinous objects in the street scattered, carried off
> and again busily brought back, with an effect as palpable
> to the dazzled eye as if a glass roof stretched over the
> street were being violently smashed into fragments at
> every moment. [*Amerika,* p. 39]

This is the city in its full ebullition, its full transparency: it is glass in a
continuous state of being smashed. Kafka's realism is dynamic, even in
a sense cinematic, though he detested the cinema (*Conversations,* p.
147): the heavy persistence of objective reality must be pictured as a
rapid fleeting succession of its states of perishing. All true apprehension is the apprehension of a passing away; Kafka told Gustav Janouch
that people should greet each other not with "How are you?" but with
"How are you withering? How goes your esteemed decomposition?"
(*Conversations,* p. 125). In 1913 Kafka recorded "the feeling that I was
the representative of my inner emptiness, an emptiness that replaces
everything else and is not even very great" (*Diaries I,* p. 323). By the
end of his career he was, so to speak, attempting to write the autobiography of that emptiness, the evaporation of the "representative," the
historical, physical Kafka.

The last preoccupation of Kafka's fiction was art itself. "A Hunger
Artist" (1922) suggests that the artist who represents vanishing things
is in fact only expressing the attrition of his own being. Art is not
something one does, but something one is. We remember that the
victim of *In the Penal Colony* himself became a kind of text; the whole
torture machine was only a kind of infernal tattooing device, by means
of which the officer managed to alter himself into a configuration of
justice. Again in "A Hunger Artist" the body is the vehicle of art; the
artist's material, the artist's production, the artist, and, ultimately, the
spectator of the artist are all one and the same. The hunger artist is a
kind of null dancer—when his fasts are ended the impresario shakes
him so that he totters and sways, the very picture of emaciation (*Penal
Colony,* p. 248)—a dancer indistinguishable from the dance. Art is a
kind of theater of marasmus, of self-effacement; it is a peculiar sophistication of expressionist theory, for the art is still a self-dramatization,
but a dramatization of the self's wasting. Kafka insisted many times on
the autobiographical nature of his fiction, on the pain of displaying his
botched self in such botched stories; for instance, he tried to tell his
father in *Letter to His Father* that "My writing was all about you; all I
did there, after all, was to bemoan what I could not bemoan upon your
breast" (*Letter,* p. 87). But even in such father-oriented stories as *The
Judgment* and *The Metamorphosis* the subject is not the self in the
depths of lamentation but the self in the act of superseding itself, of

dying, of metamorphosing into some airier, more evasive, more authentic shape. The hunger artist was once a celebrity, but his world contracts until he sits in a circus cage, invisible and ignored, with only the stench of the animals to interfere with his rapture of dwindling. Like Gregor Samsa in *The Metamorphosis,* his self-transformation is accompanied by an increasing destitution, emptying, derationalization of his world; and like Gregor he passes beyond the limits of the human, enters by the power of his imagination into an unheard-of dissolving of flesh:

> Why should he be cheated of the fame he would get for fasting longer, for being not only the record hunger artist of all time, which presumably he was already, but for beating his own record by a performance beyond human imagination, since he felt that there were no limits to his capacity for fasting? [*The Penal Colony,* p. 247]

The hunger artist differs from the earlier heroes in that he deliberately induces this famishing, asks to be admired for it; but this is a false pride, and his enlightenment, his death, cannot come until he grows oblivious of fame, stops counting the number of days of his terminal fast, admits modestly that he deserves no special credit, that he fasted only because he disliked the taste of food (p. 255). The artist must ask no special treatment from the world on account of his negative capability, his gift for offering images of attrition; he cannot help it, it is only his nature. Just as the use of cryptograms of the name Kafka—Kafka admitted that the name Georg Bendemann was arranged to resemble his own in a distant manner—and of the initial K. for his major characters makes the reader aware of the autobiographical component of his writings, so the use of an artist-hero, indeed a paradigm of all artists, makes the sequence of protagonists seem to converge on the historical Kafka. The reader of ''A Hunger Artist'' feels that it is a culmination of all that has gone before, that the populous world of Kafka's fiction is at last stripping itself down to the bare minimum, the single artist-hero whose undressing, self-dispossession, is his only theme. Art completes itself, gives moral satisfaction, by showing the destruction of the artist.

But ''A Hunger Artist'' is not the end of the evolution of this theme; Kafka's last story, ''Josephine the Singer, or the Mouse Folk'' (1924) is also a parable about art. Here the metaphor of art is not the dance of death but the songs of an ancient *Lieder* singer whose art has outlived her voice, a voice reduced to a mere whisper, a husky croak. Her art is little more than the gesture of trying to sing when no song will come; and indeed the silence she emits, evokes, is the most pleasing part of her performance: ''Is it her singing that enchants us or is it not rather the solemn stillness enclosing her frail little voice?'' (*Penal Colony*, p. 259). Kafka dealt once before, in ''Investigations of a Dog'' (1922), with the notion that art is a kind of silent music; in that story a troop of acrobatic dogs climb on each other's backs and make symmetrical patterns; although they are emphatically silent, ''from the empty air they conjured music'' (*Great Wall of China*, p. 5). Throughout the tale the doggy narrator finds all his questions greeted by silence, calls the race of dogs ''bulwarks of silence'' (p. 17), speaks of himself, the researcher, as one entombed in silence, ''never to be dragged out of it again''; the reason for this silence, he concludes, is that we have lost the true Word (p. 25). This is why art consists in making absence palpable, in drawing the contours of holes: without the Word nothing whatsoever can be said, realized, so that the task of art is to define significant vanishings, vanishings of significance. The dog ends his investigations of music with the observation that ''although what struck me most deeply at first about these dogs was their music, their silence seemed to me still more significant'' (p. 42). The dogs that were the subjects of these investigations were accomplished artists; but when Kafka returned to the theme of the music of silence two years later, he wished his artist, Josephine, to be someone decidedly less competent, clever, adept, than usual:

> To crack a nut is truly no feat, so no one would ever dare to collect an audience in order to entertain it with nut-cracking. But if all the same one does do that and succeeds in entertaining the public, then it cannot be a matter of simple nut-cracking. Or it is a matter of nut-cracking, but it turns out that we have overlooked the art of cracking nuts because we were too skilled in it and that this newcomer to it first shows us its real nature, even finding it useful in making his effects to be rather less expert in nut-cracking than most of us. [*The Penal Colony*, p. 258]

The charm of art is in its odd gracelessness, its faltering, its inadequacy; anyone can sing better than Josephine, but only Josephine is worth attending to. Like Moses in Schoenberg's opera *Moses und Aron* (1930–32), Josephine can offer special revelation precisely because she has a sort of speech impediment; what can be uttered has no great value, but the quaking, the stuttering that is the only earthly expression of the unutterable provides the audience with a kind of exaltation. It is nearly the strangest plea that an artist can make; Kafka through the fable is begging a kind of indulgence for his incorrect representations, his fragments, his wealth of broken images. Like the parable of the failed opera in Auden's *The Sea and the Mirror*, it is the gap between conception and execution—the singers know the melodies, but their voices are too feeble to hit the notes—that illustrates the existence of the truth and our condition of estrangement from it. Josephine sings with the greatest difficulty, strains into inaudibility; and like the tinny edge of silence that insinuates itself into Gregor Samsa's voice at the actual moment of his metamorphosis, it is a sign of passing beyond the personal. This is Kafka's theory of the impersonality of art: each stutters in his own peculiar way, but in silence we are all alike.

What benefit do the listeners gain from Josephine's singing? They hear an expression of the common condition of humankind, that is, mousedom:

> This piping, which rises up where everyone else is pledged to silence, comes almost like a message from the whole people to each individual; Josephine's thin piping amidst grave decisions is almost like our people's precarious existence amidst the tumult of a hostile world. Josephine exerts herself, a mere nothing in voice, a mere nothing in execution, she asserts herself and gets across to us; it does us good to think of that. A really trained singer, if ever such a one should be found among us, we could certainly not endure at such a time and we should unanimously turn away from the senselessness of any such performance. [*The Penal Colony*, pp. 265–66]

The quaver of her voice is an image of the precariousness, the incoherence, the wavering of our own state; she offers a representation of the general condition not by the content of her song, but by how she sings it—how badly she sings it. Furthermore, her voice is a kind of vox populi; the individual is superseded, the race hears its lament uttered. Kafka once remarked that he greatly deprecated individuality:

> "That is our original sin. We set ourselves above nature. We are not content to die and to survive merely as members of a species. Each of us wishes to preserve and possess his life for as long as possible as an individual organism. This is a rejection, by which we forfeit life." [*Conversations*, pp. 71–72]

Josephine's art removes what Schopenhauer called the delusion of individuation; her songs cause her listeners to grow transpersonal, to melt out into their species. It is an enlightenment, another kind of passing beyond oneself; but the irony is that Josephine herself is pettier, more obsessed with her ego than are any of her listeners. She demands that the mouse community exempt her from labor; she is so vain as to believe her hoarse voice incomparably beautiful. Near the end of the story she goes on strike and omits grace notes from her arias, though no one notices the omissions. When she hurts her foot she adopts an ostentatious limp to gain sympathy:

> Since she cannot very well go on limping forever, she thinks of something else, she pleads that she is tired, not in the mood for singing, feeling faint. And so we get a theatrical performance as well as a concert. We see Josephine's supporters in the background begging and imploring her to sing. She would be glad to oblige, but she cannot. They comfort and caress her with flatteries, they almost carry her to the selected spot where she is sup-posed to sing. At last, bursting inexplicably into tears, she gives way, but when she stands up to sing, obviously at the end of her resources, weary, her arms not wide-spread as usual but hanging lifelessly down, so that one gets the impression that they are perhaps a little too short—just as she is about to strike up, there, she cannot do it after all, an unwilling shake of the head tells us so and she breaks down before our eyes. To be sure, she pulls herself together again and sings, I fancy, much as usual; perhaps, if one has an ear for the finer shades of expression, one can hear that she is singing with unusual feeling, which is, however, all to the good. [*The Penal Colony*, pp. 275–76]

This is her last performance. It is a kind of writer's block elevated from petulance into art; her limp, her gestures of demurral, her breakdown into tears seem to be now the main substance of her performance. Antonin Artaud, whose "theater of cruelty" seems a gross literaliza-tion of the technique of Kafka's novels, once hired a stage upon which to go insane, and Roger Shattuck has described this last public monologue as the theater of the mind's self-combustion; the phrase is a good description of Josephine's behavior here. Her song derives from the pretty pathos of her inability to sing; and it is the best song of her career. Then she disappears, it seems forever—"of her own accord destroys the power she has gained over people's hearts" (p. 277). The tag *ars est celare artem* acquires a new meaning, for art not only hides art, it makes art vanish; it is the quality that Kafka once called the "self-canceling-out of art" (*Dearest Father*, p. 80). The people, despite her popularity, will not miss her for long:

> Not that it will be easy for us; how can our gatherings take place in utter silence? Still, were they not silent even when Josephine was present? Was her actual piping no-tably louder and more alive than the memory of it will be?

> Was it even in her lifetime more than a simple memory?
> Was it not rather because Josephine's singing was
> already past losing in this way that our people in their
> wisdom prized it so highly?
>
> So perhaps we shall not miss so very much after all,
> while Josephine, redeemed from the earthly sorrows
> which to her thinking lay in wait for all chosen spirits, will
> happily lose herself in the numberless throng of the
> heroes of our people, and soon, since we are no histo-
> rians, will rise to the heights of redemption and be for-
> gotten like all her brothers. [*The Penal Colony,* p. 277]

The art that is a form of audible silence is as potent in memory as it was
during the concert; it is an art past losing because silence is always
impinging on us—if one abstracts oneself from common cares the silence awaits. "A Hunger Artist" ended with the sense that art finally
demanded the destruction of the artist; "Josephine the Singer" ends
with the sense that art finally demands the destruction of art. The song
is imperishable because it is annulled, an unforgettable absence of
sound issuing from the stress of a cracked throat.

Art is at once imperishable and conducive to oblivion, imperishable
because conducive to oblivion. Josephine too must at last abandon
vanity, join the numberless throngs of the dead; it is, of course,
Kafka's own farewell to life and art. Kafka in his last months had to
write out some of his conversations on slips of paper, because tuberculosis had invaded his larynx; and his inability to speak, his consciousness of his pettiness, his sense of increasing remoteness—he
speaks of being on "another planet," of enjoying "on another plane the
freedom of movement completely lacking to me here" (*Diaries II,* pp.
210, 215)—and, most of all, a serene intuition that his fables had succeeded in compelling public attention to something beyond their poor
selves, all are embodied in the figure of Josephine, whose very inferiority has made her the wizard of mice. In his "Reflections" Kafka
had written: "Our art is a dazzled blindness before the truth: The light
on the grotesque recoiling phiz is true, but nothing else" (*Great Wall of
China,* p. 174). Art does not represent the truth; art represents the
light, the condition of illuminatedness of the truth, but the truth is
invisible in the dazzle of its shining. Semele knew for an instant that
Zeus existed but knew nothing of what he looked like. Art also represents our condition of recoil, revulsion, the aversion of our face from
the truth, all muscles pinched and tense from the shock of light. The
world of Kafka's fictions consists of the solid things we have erected to
shield ourselves from this light, a freely chosen state of dwelling in
tolerable untruth; and it is Kafka's intent to illustrate the hallucinatory

quality of this world, to show its lack of internal consistency, its flaws and discontinuities, the sunlight streaming through its gaps, its jagged margins, its frightening disintegration. He wrote his books to describe this untenability, to indicate light by the uncomfortable shiftings of opaque things that fail to sustain their opacity; and he may have instructed Max Brod to burn all his manuscripts after his death because he thought that such an immolation—"language clothes what is indestructible in us, a garment which survives us" (*Conversations*, p. 121)—would be a still more serious entry into oblivion, unmaking.

4 Beckett

Is there such a thing as a perfect act of the imagination? Modern literature is full of stories about the childhood of the artist, stories that usually culminate in a scene in which the young hero's imagination suddenly stands face to face with an image. This moment of power, at which the loosened imagination for the first time discovers, summons up, focuses on, or creates an image worthy of it, is always a difficult matter for the novelist to handle properly. It is hard to display a single Image that is ample yet precise, beautiful yet suggestive of the full richness of human life—in short, an Image that stands for the whole gamut of images upon which the imagination will dwell during a long career. The apparition of a lovely woman is most likely to meet these conditions: a woman who is actually present, neither vision nor waking dream—if she were too fantastic she would indicate that the artist's imagination was thin, worldless, caught up in the contemplation of the unreal—and yet a woman who is not personally involved with the artist—if she were too accessible, *complaisante,* she would suggest that the young artist's delirium of beholding was not an act of the imagination but simply a fever of sex. Joyce found just the right sort of Image for Stephen Dedalus in *Portrait of the Artist*:

> A girl stood before him in midstream, alone and still, gazing out to sea. She seemed like one whom magic had changed into the likeness of a strange and beautiful seabird. Her long slender bare legs were delicate as a crane's and pure save where an emerald trail of seaweed had fashioned itself as a sign upon the flesh. Her thighs, fuller and softhued as ivory, were bared almost to the hips where the white fringes of her drawers were like feathering of soft white down. Her slateblue skirts were kilted boldly about her waist and dovetailed behind her. Her bosom was as a bird's, soft and slight, slight and soft as the breast of some darkplumaged dove. But her long fair hair was girlish: and girlish, and touched with the wonder of mortal beauty, her face. [p. 171]

First Stephen sees a vision of the old Daedalus, who appears as "a quaint device opening a page of some medieval book of prophecies and symbols, a hawklike man flying sunward above the sea" (p. 169)—his own fledgeling imagination trying its wings—and then he seizes upon the girl on the beach; the elated artist drags an angel down. Her beauty is all the more wondrous for being "mortal beauty," but the design of seaweed on her leg suggests that the beholder and the beheld alike are resolving into hieroglyph, frontispiece, signature, that luminous apprehension is on the brink of resolving into verbal form, the text of the novel. The rhetoric of the paragraph, full of stately chains of chiasmus, dovetailings, suggests that the language is trying to embody a dove, feathery and aerial, the dove that the hawk grasps in its intensity of conception: "Her image had passed into his soul forever" (p. 171). Soon it is clear that the captured Image serves a mediating function; the girl on the beach, without knowing it, is a kind of intercessor, through whom Stephen is put into relation with the whole world of created things, the world from which he has been so often estranged:

> He felt above him the vast indifferent dome and the calm processes of the heavenly bodies; and the earth beneath him, the earth that had borne him, had taken him to her breast. [*Portrait,* p. 172]

Through the one Image the universe becomes viable for art; the imagination, having discovered its unique totem, is now capable of treating, manipulating, digesting anything at all; the world, formerly a heap of entangling and sometimes hostile appearances, is now a treasure house of images. The entities that have beguiled and will beguile Stephen's imagination—Dumas's Mercedes, the prostitute he seems to create from the sheer pressure of obsession, the temptress of the villanelle, who seems naked and literate on his very bed—are comprehended, epitomized, in the girl on the beach; from the earth that she has permitted him to touch he will endeavor "to express, to press out again" (p. 206) the images of beauty that are her premonitions and avatars. Stephen's human girl friend, Emma Clery, is a poor thing next to these celestial pinups, and his last act in Ireland will be to shut her out from his emotion and fantasy, to deny her any place among his images—yet she too is said to have "dove's eyes" (p. 220), as if she must, even against Stephen's will, take her part in the panoply of the Image, a continuum through the full range of the supernatural and the ordinary. One of the epithets of the temptress of the villanelle is "lure of the fallen seraphim" (p. 217), a languorous and decadent line reminiscent of a remark of Sara's in Villiers de l'Isle-Adam's *Axel,* "I think I remember having made the angels fall"; and indeed the Joycean Image has its precursors in the radical aestheticism of the late nineteenth century. The girl on the beach, like Pater's Mona Lisa, is older than the rocks among which she sits; the vampire, the pearl diver, Leda, Helen, and Saint Anne—Stephen in his piety has a tremulous vision of the Blessed Virgin's lucid loveliness (p. 116)—are all part of her permitted repertoire of invention, for she stands for Beauty independent of any finite beautiful form. Only such an Image, plastic, extensible, fecund, befits an imagination of genius.

It is easy to find scenes in other novels in which the imagination discovers the one Image that satisfies. For Mann's Tonio Kröger it is the likeness of Inge, a girl he never embraced, that illuminates his faculties long after the girl, and even his human affection for her, have passed away. For Woolf's Mrs. Ramsay it is a lighthouse; indeed, the rhythm of the scene is the same as that in Joyce's *Portrait,* for she attains her essential form—not quite the "quaint device" of a flying man, but a dark wedge capable of hovering over Rome or the Indian plains—as her imagination, receptive, heightened, prepares itself for the lighthouse beam. Mrs. Ramsay, like Stephen, is transfigured into union with her environment by the agency of the Image; and she will serve, after her death, just such a function for Lily Briscoe, a convenient ghost, as the imaginer becomes translated into an Image. Wilde's Dorian Gray is himself an Image, grown unruly, wild, desolating—even Pater's Mona Lisa had bloodsucking tendencies—by the loss of the discipline of the imagination, Basil Hallward's moral purity; it is as if the girl on the beach had murdered Stephen, as if the temptress of the villanelle, not content with luring seraphim, had gone on a rampage in the world of man and then, consumed by grief and self-hatred, had abdicated her status as Image, grown human and condemned.

The novelists who succeeded Joyce have for the most part been more interested in exploring, as Wilde had done, the possibilities for perversion, error, and failure in the bond between imagination and Image. Joyce himself seems to parody the beach scene of *Portrait* in the Nausicaa chapter of *Ulysses,* where Leopold Bloom masturbates as he watches lame Gerty McDowell on the beach; though it seems likely to me that in *Ulysses,* a book full of the delight of low, huddled, subsistent things, Joyce conceived the Image as no less sacred for being pathetic, ridiculous. A far more unsettling book in its treatment of the Image is Thomas Pynchon's *V.* (1963): the Lady V. herself is a direct descendent of Pater's Mona Lisa, Wilde's Salome, the rabid beauty who, in the guises of an English convent girl or Parisian dressmaker, a Maltese priest or a rat in the sewers of New York—vampire, Leda, Saint Anne—so manipulates historical events as to cause every major war from 1898 to 1945, purely out of an aesthetic delight in catastrophe. The central intrigue of the novel consists in the pursuit of this phantom of intelligible destruction by one Herbert Stencil, a keenly imaginative man—indeed the name Stencil indicates the image-making power in a most literal way—and I believe that the novel suggests that the imagination is the most corrupt of human faculties. To Pynchon every yearning for the ideal is depravity. One of the novel's villains is Dr. Schoenmacher, a plastic surgeon; and every attempt to improve, alter, or extenuate what is given us, the simple gross fact of existence, leads to the automaton. As Lady V. matures she replaces parts of her body with cunning prostheses: she has her feet amputated and replaced by ivory, with the veins in intaglio instead of bas-relief, has a star sapphire sewn into her navel. The Image, instead of reconciling us with the earth, draws us out of the human, into a false heaven of art in which Galatea bestows her magical, petrifying touch upon Pygmalion. The ethical basis of *V.* is that of the iconoclasts; indeed, there is a scene in which Botticelli's *Birth of Venus* is described, mocked for its thin gorgeousness, and torn from its frame, as if Pynchon would be a new Savonarola. The novel's hero is a coarse road worker, Benny Profane, a schlemihl, an obese, tasteless man; the man Pynchon values is the man who rests content in the provisional, the indiscriminate, the messy, who tolerates ambiguity without recourse to Stencil's dreams of malevolent order, the man without imagination.

Thus we see that the Image may be salvation or it may be damnation; but in the major novels of Samuel Beckett there is no such thing as an

Image. Paradoxically, this is both an impoverishment and a liberation.

In Beckett's earliest works there are a few vestiges of the Image, as if the author had to chase away the necessary angel of earth with a club before he could rejoice in its absence. In the brief story "Assumption," published in 1929, only fifteen years after Joyce's *Portrait*, we are offered an embryonic version of the Beckett hero, a solitary autochthon who sits in his room cultivating silence. The only public activity that gives him pleasure is his favorite parlor trick, a method of imposing silence on a voluble discussion with one carefully timed whisper; this contrivance seems to be a kind of art:

> The highest art reduces significance in order to obtain that inexplicable bombshell perfection. Before no supreme manifestation of Beauty do we proceed comfortably up a staircase of sensation, and sit down mildly on the topmost stair to digest our gratification: such is the pleasure of Prettiness. We are taken up bodily and pitched breathless on the peak of a sheer crag: which is the pain of Beauty. Just as the creative artist must be partly illusionist, our whispering prestidigitator was partly artist. [*Transition* (Paris) 16–17 (June 1929):269]

The mockery of the sublime is astringent, and the doctrine expressed here is nearly a burlesque of that of Kafka's "A Hunger Artist" and "Josephine the Singer, or the Mouse Folk": the highest kind of art is a kind of abolishing of meaning, a public rehearsal of the void. But in the silence of his room, the repressed sound takes its revenge: he feels "a splendid drunken scream" rising within him, an expression he is determined to stifle at all costs, lest it destroy him in one frantic instant of release. In the midst of this struggle, a woman comes to his room, an admirer of his genius, a petite-bourgeoise Salome:

> The eyes were so deeply set as to be almost cavernous; the light falling on the cheekbones threw them back into a misty shadow. In daylight they were strange, almost repulsive, deriving a pitiless penetration from the rim of white showing naturally above the green-flecked pupil. Now as she leaned forward beneath the light, they were pools of obscurity. She wore a close-fitting hat of faded green felt: he thought he had never seen such charming shabbiness. . . . When at last she went away he felt that something had gone out from him, something he could not spare, but still less could grudge, something of the desire to live, something of the unreasonable tenacity with which he shrank from dissolution. [p. 270]

To his horror she performs a function akin to that of the girl on the beach in Joyce's *Portrait:* she puts him into relation with the universe, she breaks down the barriers he has carefully constructed around himself, as her repeated visits loosen the stones of his "clumsy dam":

> he found himself alone in his room, spent with ecstasy, torn by the bitter loathing of that which he had condemned to the humanity of silence. Thus each night he died and was God, each night revived and was torn, torn and battered with increasing grievousness, so that he hungered to be irretrievably engulfed in the light of eternity, one with the birdless cloudless colourless skies, in infinite fulfillment.
>
> Then it happened. While the woman was contemplating the face that she had overlaid with death, she was swept aside by a great storm of sound, shaking the very house with its prolonged, triumphant vehemence, climbing in a dizzy, bubbling scale, until, dispersed, it fused into the breath of the forest and the throbbing cry of the sea.
>
> They found her caressing his wild dead hair. [p. 271]

Humanity is reticence, involution, keeping oneself discrete and uncontaminated; godhead is dissolution, a merging with the inanimate, as if the only god Beckett acknowledged were Nietzsche's Dionysus. I am not sure this is one of the great screams of modern art, worthy to rank with Munch's woodcut "The Shriek" or the memorable cries at the beginning of Kafka's "Unhappiness" and at the end of Schoenberg's *Erwartung,* but it is certainly an ambitious one. The Orpheus of Greek legend had such an efficacious lyre that beasts, stones, rivers, and the hellish heart of Pluto were moved; but he had no art to prevent the Furies from tearing his body asunder. The hero of "Assumption" is a kind of Orpheus who would prefer to remain in Hades, tacit and smiling, but Eurydice drags him to the surface of the earth, thrusts the lyre into his unwilling hands, herself grows claws and bloody teeth. Orpheus's unique song is the scream he makes at the instant of his *sparagma,* the shock of which seems to shake the fixed stars. Stephen Dedalus's lofty conception of the role of the artist is here reversed: instead of the indignant high priest of the imagination who tells his friend Cranly that his only goal is "to express myself in some mode of life or art as freely as I can and as wholly as I can" (p. 247), we have what is probably the first statement of Beckett's aesthetic: self-expression is death. It is an error to believe that Beckett presents art as a weak or impotent activity; the protagonists of his novels debilitate themselves from the effort of restraining from art, debilitate themselves further from the wounds inflicted on them by their artistic successes. If Amphion is a one-man demolition gang, if Orpheus is a suicide, then the power of art can be measured by the progress of the artist's disease.

Even in "Assumption," one of the first stories Beckett wrote, it seems he has reached an impasse: there is no middle ground between silence and the swan song; how can one write if the only possible expression is the death rattle in one's own throat? Beckett eventually mastered the trick of making his words look like sustained silences on one hand and sustained death rattles on the other, but he nevertheless had to find a way of adapting a medium not congenial to either extreme, the old verisimilar grab bag genre of the novel, to these unaccustomed urgencies. Beckett had to find a compromise to permit him to write anything at all, and the compromise he discovered about 1930 gave him such a rich vein of literary material that he was still mining it thirty years later. If art aspires to be a single brief, comprehensive cry of a man caught at the moment of his perishing, at once a summation and a farewell, if all expression that is not this piercing epitome is too trivial to bother with, there is a kind of prolonged discourse that can be derived from intricate apologies for the failure of expression, from witty pretenses of expression despite the fact of its absence, from groping attempts at expression embellished with self-deprecation, from expression performed so badly that no one would confuse it with the real thing.

"Assumption" states exactly why Beckett refuses to be an expressionist: expression is painful, important, irrepressible, murderous; it would be best to be silent, but that is too difficult. The only alternative—and this is what Beckett does in his early novels—is to make speech out of the evasion of the obligation to express. This evasion bears witness to the sacredness of what it evades.

Beckett would have liked to have been Mallarmé, the poet of the blank page and of unearthly intensities. Mallarmé's poem "Les Fenêtres" depicts an old man coughing, rotting, climbing out of his hospital bed to gaze outward at the blue sky, "l'azur," at golden boats, swanlike, that sleep on a river of purple and perfumes, cradling the wild and rich flash of their lines in a great apathy charged with remembrance. If the old man of this poem were taken to an anonymous asylum and placed next to a still more remarkable window, a window that changed its shape, sometimes even looked painted on the wall, "like Tiepolo's ceiling at Würzburg" (*Malone Dies*, p. 235), he would start to resemble Malone or Molloy or another member of Beckett's gallery of decaying rogues. "*Je suis hanté!* l'Azur! l'Azur! l'Azur! l'Azur!" Mallarmé says in a related poem, and Beckett too is haunted by a vision of supersensible repose, an aesthetic refuge from the bitterness of life. Worm in *The Unnamable* ''should have dragged himself away, no matter where, towards them, towards the azure, but how could he, he can't stir'' (p. 364); and in *Mercier and Camier* the pair of comedians are sitting on a bank by a canal, staring at the sky:

> I see our sister-convict Venus, said Camier, foundering in the skywrack. I hope it's not for that you dragged me here.
> Further, further, said Mercier.
> Camier screened his eyes with his hand. . . .
> I saw a few pale gleams, said Camier.
> You need to have the knack, said Mercier.
> I'd do better with my knuckle in my eye, said Camier.
> The ancients' Blessed Isles, said Mercier.
> They weren't hard to please, said Camier.
> You wait, said Mercier, you only barely saw, but you'll never forget, you'll be back.
> What is that grim pile? said Camier.
> A hospital, said Mercier. Diseases of the skin. [p. 121]

Most of Beckett's narrators resemble the lyrical speakers of *symboliste* poetry, possessed of a nearly inexpressible vision of things beyond their ken; but the inexpressible includes not only remote reflections of impossible purity but such homely objects as greatcoats, bicycles, sticks, beds, oneself. Amazing energies are lavished on describing a thing as familiar as a pencil, for it is all too likely that, in this general collapse of expression, it will elude the author, no matter how attentive he may be. A pencil may therefore be as tantalizing, as inconceivable, as the swan of Mallarmé's sonnet; and the author's stance toward his pencil will be that of the *symboliste* poet, unsteady, allusive, as if even the simplest nouns were losing denotative power, as if the most banal object were a film shifting in the air.

> The pencil on the contrary is an old acquaintance, I must have had it about me when I was brought here. It has five faces. It is very short. It is pointed at both ends. A Venus. I hope it will see me out. [*Malone*, p. 209]

> What a misfortune, the pencil must have slipped from my fingers, for I have only just succeeded in recovering it after forty-eight hours (see above) of intermittent efforts. What my stick lacks is a little prehensile proboscis like the nocturnal tapir's. I should really lose my pencil more often, it might do me good, I might be more cheerful, it might be more cheerful. I have spent two unforgettable days of which nothing will ever be known, it is too late now, or still

too soon, I forget which, except that they brought me the solution and conclusion of the whole sorry business, I mean the business of Malone (since that is what I am called now) and of the other, for the rest is no business of mine. And it was, though more unutterable, like the crumbling away of two little heaps of finest sand, or dust, or ashes, of unequal size, but diminishing together as it were in ratio, if that means anything, and leaving behind them, each in its own stead, the blessedness of absence. While this was going on I was struggling to retrieve my pencil, by fits and starts. My pencil. It is a little Venus, still green no doubt, with five or six facets, pointed at both ends and so short there is just room, between them, for my thumb and the two adjacent fingers, gathered together in a little vice. I use the two points turn and turn about, sucking them frequently, I love to suck. And when they go quite blunt I strip them with my nails which are long, yellow, sharp and brittle for want of chalk or is it phosphate. So little by little my little pencil dwindles, inevitably, and the day is fast approaching when nothing will remain but a fragment too tiny to hold. So I write as lightly as I can. But the lead is hard and would leave no trace if I wrote too lightly. But I say to myself, Between a hard lead with which one dare not write too lightly, if a trace is to be left, and a soft fat lead which blackens the page almost without touching it, what possible difference can there be, from the point of view of durability. Ah, yes, I have my little pastimes. The strange thing is I have another pencil, made in France, a long cylinder hardly broached, in the bed with me somewhere I think. So I have nothing to worry about, on this score. And yet I do worry. [pp. 222–23]

Quick quick my possessions. Quiet, quiet, twice, I have time, lots of time, as usual. My pencil, my two pencils, the one of which nothing remains between my huge fingers but the lead fallen from the wood and the other, long and round, in the bed somewhere, I was holding it in reserve, I won't look for it, I know it's there somewhere, if I have time when I've finished I'll look for it, if I don't find it I won't have it. I'll make the correction, with the other, if anything remains of it. Quiet, quiet. [p. 246]

Did I say I only say a small proportion of the things that come into my head? I must have. I choose those that seem somehow akin. It is not always easy. I hope they

are the most important. I wonder If I shall ever be able to
stop. Perhaps I should throw away my lead. I could never
retrieve it now. I might be sorry. My little lead. It is a risk
I do not feel inclined to take, just now. [p. 253]

18. You couldn't by any chance let me have the butt of a
pencil? 19. Number your answers. 20. Don't go, I
haven't finished.... 21. Could you lend me an India
rubber? [p. 272]

Lemuel is in charge, he raises his hatchet on which the
blood will never dry, but not to hit anyone, he will not hit
anyone, he will not hit anyone any more, he will not touch
anyone any more, either with it or with it or with it or
with or...
    or with his pencil or with his stick or
    or light light I mean
    never there he will never
    never anything
    there
    any more   [p. 288]

Malone's pencil lacks some of the solidity, the perspicuousness, of the
pencil in Nabokov's *Transparent Things*. It has five facets, then five or
six facets, is remembered to have been green and may still be green; its
representation is imperiled at every instant by the feebleness of Malone's senses of sight and touch, by his tendency to lose it beyond the
range of his faculties, by the continual wearing away of its substance.
Far from ever possessing any satisfying stability, any palpability, the
pencil is only an occasion for its own concealment, its own vanishing.
Yet, despite the pencil's elusiveness, it is a lethal instrument; for the
same thin tracing of lead upon the page that erects the little fictional characters in Malone's stories—Saposcat, Macmann, and the rest—is also
the agency of their murder, their undoing. Indeed, the pencil is the occasion for an elaborate coordination of synchronized vanishings, the
most important of which is Malone's death; it is a wooden conduit or
fistula connecting Malone, who is the most self-conscious artist in Beckett's novels, to the imaginary world of things that lapse, fall asunder,
a world designed to facilitate his own lapsing. In this mediating function, it resembles the Image of traditional fiction, like the girl on the
beach in Joyce's *Portrait*—Malone's stick, which also mediates between himself and the world, is at one point called "a little woman" (p.
247), and the pencil too is in a sense wifely, muselike, a real Venus—
but in an inverted manner: it is an anti-Image that disperses images and
imaginer alike. The heap of sand that Malone takes as an image of

himself, as he diminishes in ratio with his fiction, might just as well have been called a heap of pencil shavings: Malone is himself a human pencil sharpener, and the friction of pencil against author seems to erode them both in equal measure. In Beckett's novels the act of writing is seen as an act of destruction, and pencils are put to unusual uses: Molloy says that he "would do better, at least no worse, to obliterate texts than to blacken margins, to fill in the holes of words till all is blank and flat and the whole ghastly business looks like what it is, senseless, speechless, issueless misery" (p. 13); and the Unnamable wishes that he could live in the white gap between written words (p. 374). The rubble of graphite keeps smudging, smearing, widening, thinning, lightening until it attains the blessed candor of the white space at the bottom of the novel's last page. The plea for an India rubber is unnecessary, for the pencil is its own eraser.

It was not until 1949, just before Beckett began *The Unnamable,* that he stated explicitly the aesthetic governing his depiction of images, in the "Three Dialogues" by Samuel Beckett and Georges Duthuit. This treatise is the culmination of a long tradition of denunciations of the doctrine of self-expression, including Matthew Arnold's 1853 Preface and Eliot's "Tradition and the Individual Talent," and it is perhaps the most subtle and uncompromising. It alleges the impossibility of expression in a famous sentence in which Beckett announces his preference for "the expression that there is nothing to express, nothing with which to express, nothing from which to express, no power to express, no desire to express, together with the obligation to express" ("Three Dialogues," reprinted in Esslin, p. 17). Artists have always deluded themselves with the notion that they were expressing something in the natural world, or something of their own feelings; but, in fact, Cézanne's apple has nothing to do with an edible fruit, Zeuxis's grapes may have fooled the birds but were nevertheless bound exclusively to their worldless domain of paint. In 1912 Kandinsky and others were pleading for a nonrepresentational art; in 1949 Beckett declares that there never was any other kind of art and pleads for an art that admits its inescapable nonrepresentationality, its inexpressiveness. He thinks he has found such a painter, the Dutchman Bram van Velde, a plastic Samuel Beckett:

> It is obvious that for the artist obsessed with his expressive vocation, anything and everything is doomed to become occasion, including, as is apparently to some extent the case with Masson, the pursuit of occasion, and the every man his own wife experiments of the spiritual Kandinsky. No painting is more replete than Mondrian's. But if the occasion appears as an unstable term of relation,

the artist, who is the other term, is hardly less so, thanks to his warren of modes and attitudes. The objections to this dualist view of the creative process are unconvincing. Two things are established, however precariously: the aliment, from fruits on plates to low mathematics and self-commiseration, and its manner of dispatch. All that should concern us is the acute and increasing anxiety of the relation itself, as though shadowed more and more darkly by a sense of invalidity, of inadequacy, of existence at the expense of all that it excludes, all that it blinds to. The history of painting, here we go again, is the history of its attempts to escape from this sense of failure, by means of more authentic, more ample, less exclusive relations between representer and representee, in a kind of tropism towards a light as to the nature of which the best opinions continue to vary, and with a kind of Pythagorean terror, as though the irrationality of pi were an offence against the deity, not to mention his creature. My case, since I am in the dock, is that Van Velde is the first to desist from this estheticised automatism, the first to submit wholly to the incoercible absence of relation, in the absence of terms or, if you like, in the presence of unavailable terms, the first to admit that to be an artist is to fail, as no other dare fail, that failure is his world and the shrink from it desertion, art and craft, good house-keeping, living. No, no, allow me to expire. I know that all that is required now, in order to bring even this horrible matter to an acceptable conclusion, is to make of this submission, this admission, this fidelity to failure, a new occasion, a new term of relation, and of the act which, unable to act, obliged to act, he makes, an expressive act, even if only of itself, of its impossibility, of its obligation. I know that my inability to do so places myself, and perhaps an innocent, in what I think is still called an unenviable situation, familiar to psychiatrists. For what is this coloured plane, that was not there before. I don't know what it is, having never seen anything like it before. It seems to have nothing to do with art, in any case, if my memories of art are correct. (Prepares to go).

D.—Are you not forgetting something?

B.—Surely that is enough?

D.—I understood your number was to have two parts. The first was to consist in your saying what you—er—thought. This I am prepared to believe you have done. The second—

B.—(Remembering, warmly) Yes, yes, I am mistaken, I am mistaken.

["Three Dialogues," pp. 21–22]

Again, as in "Assumption," it seems that expressionism demands, continually labors toward, a condition of plenitude, an absolutely complete statement of the thing to be expressed. When he speaks of "more ample, less exclusive relations between representer and representee," we see that the perfect expressive act—that is, if expression were possible at all—would be either a conjuring of such divine intelligence that Cézanne could construct out of paint an actual apple that could nourish a man, generate a new tree; or alternatively the scream of "Assumption," whereby the artist attains the most ample and inclusive relation possible with the natural world, transcendental union, death. Since representation and expression cannot achieve these miracles, Beckett will not permit them to exist at all. On one hand is aliment—the artist's subject matter; on the other hand is dispatch—the work of art considered as excrement, a parody of the vocabulary in Freud's discussion of the creative process. Of the mysterious process of transmutation, digestion, Beckett will say only that it leaves dispatch and aliment in a state of dark unrelation, just as Beckett's Murphy knows that there is a mental experience and there is a physical experience but, feeling that his mind is "bodytight" (p. 109), cannot understand how any intercourse from one to other is possible. To Beckett, then, modern art is an uncomfortable attempt to supersede by increasingly desperate strategies this impassable division of subject from object: Kandinsky struggles to look inside himself, to depict his interior tensions and resolutions in a kind of spiritual autobiography, thereby obviating the need for an exterior subject to be represented; Masson tries to make of the search for a new subject matter for art a new subject matter for art, like Yeats in "The Circus Animals' Desertion"; but both fail, for they have not dispensed with aliment, only substituted a subtler, more rarefied aliment. To have intercourse with oneself, to eat oneself, is not to refrain from intercourse, from eating. Beckett also rejects the one argument that could make a peculiarly refined expressionist out of Beckett and van Velde, the argument that their art is "expressive of the impossibility to express" (Esslin, "Three Dialogues," p. 20); in a world where expression is impossible, the impossible and the possible are alike inexpressible. The "Three Dialogues" concludes with its best joke, Beckett's warm admission that he has made a mistake, that the theory of van Velde's art just described has nothing to do with van Velde's art, for van Velde's art is the aliment to the dispatch of the "Three Dialogues" and therefore unrelated to it. Beckett's aesthetic neatly vitiates criticism as well as other kinds of representation.

And yet when a writer writes the word "stick" it is hard for the reader not to visualize some piece of wood in the world of experience to which that word, despite Beckett, despite Wittgenstein, seems to refer. Beckett must therefore devise complicated strategies for betraying our habit of seeing through the mere verbality, the empty breath of air, to some tangible reality behind it. Words must be mollified, deadened, made to stop doing tricks, made to be noises, not words; the turd that looks like an apple must be shown to be only a turd. One such strategy is to say "pencil" when you mean a filament of bare lead, a vacant space where a pencil used to be; "pencil" is thereby gradually stripped of its referent, mapped into the null set. Another strategy is to describe tantalizing nonthings:

> It consisted of two crosses, joined, at their points of intersection, by a bar, and resembled a tiny sawing-horse, with this difference however, that the crosses of the true sawing-horse are not perfect crosses, but truncated at the top, whereas the crosses of the little object I am referring to were perfect, that is to say composed each of two identical V's, one upper with its opening above, like all V's for that matter, and the other lower with its opening below, or more precisely of four rigorously identical V's, the two I have just named and then two more, one on the right hand, the other on the left, having their openings on the right and left respectively. But perhaps it is out of place to speak here of right and left, of upper and lower. For this little object did not seem to have any base properly so-called, but stood with equal stability on any one of its four bases, and without any change of appearance, which is not true of the sawing-horse. This strange instrument I think I still have somewhere, for I could never bring myself to sell it, even in my worst need, for I could never understand what possible purpose it could serve, nor even contrive the faintest hypothesis on the subject. [*Molloy*, p. 63]

This imaginary object—I can call it only a miniature reversible branding-iron—seems, as Molloy says, to be neither useful nor decorative, to have no conceivable function, to lack any tissue of relations with other objects in the world we know. The description is clear, the thing described is clear, there is no implausibility anywhere, and yet the displacement, the feeling of dislocation from the reader's world of experience, is all the more intense because the shift is so slight. With its double Xs it seems like a reified cancellation mark. Another object, this time taken from Malone's inventory, demonstrates another way description avoids, shies away from, real representation:

> A needle stuck into two corks to prevent it from sticking

> into me, for if the point pricks less than the eye, no, that's
> wrong, for if the point pricks more than the eye, the eye
> pricks too, that's wrong too. Round the shank, between
> the two corks, a wisp of black thread clings. It is a pretty
> little object, like a—no, it is like nothing. [*Malone*,
> p. 247]

This is also an object without relations, unique, incapable of comparison or simile. It is very dangerous, despite the lavish insulation of the
two corks. Like the doubly sharpened pencil, it has two points, each of
which is likely to destroy the eyeball that stares at it; the organ of sense
and the object to which it attends, both sharpened—Dante speaks in a
famous passage of tailors who sharpen their eyebrows to thread a
needle—must never meet; the gaze turns aside, the object is never
spoken of again, and indeed all of Beckett's objects are seen only out of
the corner of the eye, never face to face:

> It took me a long time, my lifetime so to speak, to realize
> that the colour of an eye half seen, or the source of some
> distant sound, are closer to Giudecca in the hell of un-
> knowing than the existence of God, or the origins of pro-
> toplasm, or the existence of self, and even less worthy
> than these to occupy the wise. [*First Love,* pp. 32–33]

This suggests a method for showing our state of not knowing. Despite
the infernality, the excrementitiousness, of Beckett's fiction he displays only half-things, sidelong glances, objects in the process of dissolving themselves, a phantasmagoria of descriptions that fail to constitute themselves into recognizable images, that insist on giving no
satisfaction to the reader's appetite for representation. From Beckett's
viewpoint he is only being honest; a writer like Tolstoy can do no better
but panders to a taste for the illusion of a solidly established, persistent, complacent world.

This honest admission of art's incapacity to represent leads Beckett,
however, to a kind of realism. Beckett's descriptions of unreal objects
are self-debunking; all these calculated outrages of reference—not only
the pencils that vanish, the windows that change their shape from
square to round, but also the narrated impossibilities, such as Watt's
obtaining an absolutely unobtainable key—leave the reader with a
sense of fictions dispelling themselves, a collapsing of unrealities, as if
each Beckett hero were a puny, vermiform Samson shaking down around
his ears the temple of Dagon, still a house of idolatry even if it could be
bounded in a shoe box, leaving only the noise of those "fundamental
sounds," the authentic reality of the human, sounds that Beckett has
declared it his task to make as fully possible. The artist can never make

that single, wholly adequate scream that would constitute an expressive act; but he can give a certain impression of the pitch, the volume, the duration of that scream by careful depiction of the circumstances, the crumbling into dust of oneself and one's world, that would justify such a scream. It is an undertone beneath the scurry of words, spindly-legged, blighted, the inanities that constitute the text:

> No cries, above all no cries, be urbane, a credit to the art
> and code of dying, while the others cackle, I can hear
> them from here, like the crackling of thorns, no I forgot,
> it's impossible, it's myself I hear, howling behind my
> dissertation. [*The Unnamable*, p. 314]

Beckett, if he cannot express, can at least allude to expression; and the more empty of denotation he can render his stream of words, the more rapid and urgent their progress, then the more closely he can make his language approximate the ineffable, the forbidden scream, yet without violating the formal, syntactical nature of English or French. As Kafka said in a parable about the nature of art, hammering a table together is at once hammering a table together and nothing at all. Beckett is a verbal realist in that he scrupulously adheres in his usage to the real weakness, the real emptiness of language, a realist of wordlessness, antarctic night.

Beckett is also a realist in the sense Yeats meant when he called Blake a "too literal realist of imagination." His verisimilitude is not of the processes of sensation and apprehension, the exact grasping of the object beheld, but a verisimilitude of the processes of inventing and transcribing. Much of the traditional author's craft is the cultivation of a posture of continuity and organization, despite the fact that every author is to some extent ignorant of what he is saying until he has said it, despite the fact that he looks at his work with a certain startledness. A long written work must have the impossible appearance of being an ordained whole, as if it somehow preexisted before its writing. Beckett abolishes this simulacrum, which had been as characteristic of stream-of-consciousness fiction as of traditional fiction; instead, he seems to rejoice in the surprise he feels at what comes out of his pencil, like a small child trying to catch himself at the very instant of falling asleep. "Well, well," says Malone, says the Unnamable, seeing with a sardonic interest what has just popped out, making much of their novels a tissue of inferences from the data produced by invention: "I have the ocean to drink, so there is an ocean then" (p. 314); "Did I say I catch flies? I snap them up, clack! Does this mean I still have my teeth?" (p. 332)—although the Unnamable goes so far as to claim that he is a parrot (p. 335), that the inferences he makes, presumably even the statement that he is a parrot, are only part of a dictation in which he takes no personal part. This realism of language's self-referentiality, this accurate description of words locked into the process of analyzing themselves, reaches its climax in *How It Is* (1961), in which the fictive "world" has attenuated into a weary, farfetched, inconsistent, arithmetical fantasy of an infinite sequence of mud crawlers, but in which, correspondingly, the description of the operation of the imagination has proliferated beyond all bounds. The imagination is granted a pair of eyes different in color from the usual organs, set in a different part of the skull, capable of X-ray vision through the mud, trained upon a different, richer, brighter, more interesting, more acute world—gleams of childhood, snatches of young love—and the transcription of these inventions becomes the business of generations of scribes, equipped with tablets and lanterns, ceaselessly bent over the prone narrator to catch his every murmur. It is clear from Deirdre Bair's biography of Beckett (pp. 209, 557) that Beckett did regard inspiration as a seizure, a condition of automatism; and he is a realist of the creative process, a realist in his treatment of this blast, this burden of words that befalls him, not in his treatment of the world to which his images refer.

In addition to the realism of fundamental sounds and the realism of imagination, there is a third kind of realism pertinent to Beckett. Artistic representation is paradoxical: the more one tries to grasp the entirety of an object, to record everything knowable about it, the more elusive it becomes. It would not be surprising if this paradox had a further twist, that the more one tried to depict the elusiveness of an object, the more convincing its representation would appear. The doctrine of "Three Dialogues" requires Beckett to deny that a noun—say "pencil"—has any stable locus of reference, to frustrate our expectation that there subsists an invariant cylinder of wood beneath all this description. Yet many modern philosophers, such as Henri Bergson and T. S. Eliot, have stressed that the *real* object is discontinuous, obscure, volatile, just as the real subject who attends to it is essentially plural, a sequence of altering and faltering points of view. The river never feels the same foot in it twice. The description of Malone's pencil may be seen as an imitation of the way an actual pencil exists; in a sense the repudiated pencil flies back to the hand that casts it away, grows vivid and credible against the author's will. Many of Beckett's allegations about Proust's art in his early essay *Proust* (1931) seem valid for some of Beckett's own works. When he says, "the individual is a succession of individuals" (p. 6), or "the observer infects the observed with his own mobility" (p. 8), he seems to approach the concepts of subject and object that would allow Malone to be considered a kind of Bergsonian naturalist. Later in the essay Beckett discusses "the only paradise that is not the dream of a madman, the Paradise that has been lost"

(p. 55), discusses how it is evoked by the sudden striking superposition of a present and a remembered object:

> The identification of immediate with past experience, the recurrence of past action or reaction in the present, amounts to a participation between the ideal and the real, imagination and direct apprehension, symbol and substance. Such participation frees the essential reality that is denied to the contemplative as to the active life. What is common to present and past is more essential than either taken separately. Reality, whether approached imaginatively or empirically, remains a surface, hermetic. Imagination, applied—a priori—to what is absent, is exercised in vacuo and cannot tolerate the limits of the real. Nor is any direct and purely experimental contact possible between subject and object, because they are automatically separated by the subject's consciousness of perception, and the object loses its purity and becomes a mere intellectual pretext or motive. But, thanks to this reduplication, the experience is at once imaginative and empirical, at once an evocation and a direct perception, real without being merely actual, ideal without being merely abstract, the ideal real, the essential, the extratemporal. But if this mystical experience communicates an extratemporal essence, it follows that the communicant is for the moment an extratemporal being. [*Proust*, pp. 55–56]

It is as if Proust had discovered a solution to the impasse of the "Three Dialogues": although the imaginary and the real are mutually exclusive, although no amount of inquiry into the real world will succeed in discovering it, there do exist these shocks of revelation. I am not sure that Malone's pencil, like Proust's madeleine, does not attain to some extent this state of ideal realness, extratemporal because it is shown in all its degrees of contraction, vanishing, the whole span of its forthright extancy, its reticence, its wornness, its unbeing. The unused pencil reputed to be lost somewhere in the bedclothes may be taken as an emblem for this extramundane, almost Platonic object. The anti-image cannot help being an image. "I was not born Defoe," Beckett says in an early poem (*Collected Poems*, p. 22), but Defoe thrusts himself upon him.

The aesthetic of "Three Dialogues" is a secret glorification of the artist. The van Velde who is "the first to admit that to be an artist is to fail, as no other dare fail, that failure is his world" is a hero of self-abasement, a Saint Anthony whose Thebaid is an empty canvas, a Paul smiting himself as chief of sinners. It is an extension into giddiness of the doctrine of Browning's Andrea del Sarto, who knows that "the fault-less painter," the man capable of exact representation, is deficient in that sublimity of insight that makes great painters try to seize the inexpressible; the fact that Raphael draws an arm incorrectly manifests his loftiness of vision, his magnanimity. Van Velde is a Raphael with such a headache of genius that he cannot even draw stick figures on a blackboard.

In the field of literature, Beckett begins his career with the remark-able assertion that writing at its zenith is not a representation of some-thing; it *is* something. Here is the famous description of Joyce's *Work in Progress* (which ultimately progressed into *Finnegans Wake*), from the early essay "Dante . . . Bruno. Vico . . Joyce" (1929):

> Here form *is* content, content *is* form. You complain that this stuff is not written in English. It is not written at all. It is not to be read—or rather it is not only to be read. It is to be looked at and listened to. His writing is not *about* something; *it is that something itself.* . . . When the sense is sleep, the words go to sleep. (See the end of '*Anna Livia*') When the sense is dancing, the words dance. Take the passage at the end of Shaun's pastoral: "To stirr up love's young fizz I tilt with this bridle's cup cham-pagne, dimming douce from her peepair of hideseeks tight squeezed on my snowybreasted and while my pear-lies in their sparkling wisdom are nippling her bubblets I swear (and let you swear) by the bumper round of my poor old snaggletooth's solidbowel I ne'er will prove I'm untrue to (theare!) you liking so long as my hole looks. Down." The language is drunk. The very words are tilted and effervescent. How can we qualify this general esthe-tic vigilance without which we cannot hope to snare the sense which is for ever rising to the surface of the form and becoming the form itself? [*An Exagmination,* p. 14]

What Beckett likes is a language that refers to nothing beyond itself, a language that is not contingent, is not a system of arrows and index fingers pointing to things in the world of experience, but a language that has attained the dignity of *being*. Words will themselves blush, expos-tulate, drool, instead of representing a man who blushes, expostulates, drools; words will grow a nervous system, a brain, secrete around themselves the skin of form. In some of his early work Beckett uses Joyce's technique, tries to embody in language shapes and textures, the whole economy of things; for instance, Murphy's rocking chair challenges the narrator to provide a rocking rhythm: "Most things under the moon got slower and slower and then stopped, a rock got faster and faster and then stopped" (p. 9). But in Beckett's later work we see language articulating itself into little pseudopersons like the Unnamable, whose countless cries of "Now I'll talk about me" or "I've been talking about me all along" can be interpreted as language's own insistence on its sealed, self-referential nature, on what is called its "autosymbolism" in the Proust essay (p. 60). Both in the Joyce essay and in the "Three Dialogues," language is shown in competition with the world of experience. If language is a zone of being and does not express or represent, then the engrossed reader is suspended in outer space, has somehow entered a state of awareness that has nothing to do with the author or himself or the world he knows; well may Malone imagine himself to be on the moon, "To be dead, before her, on her, with her, and turn, dead on dead, about poor mankind" (p. 264), for language is in every sense extraterrestrial. The fictions art provides are self-consciously eerie, shining in Malone's "earthlight" yet partaking not at all of the earth. This attitude, like many of Beckett's, is derived from nineteenth-century symbolism—Nabokov has said quite aptly that Beckett's plays derive from Maeterlinck (*Strong Opinions*, p. 172)—and, as we have seen, even a little of symbolism's claim of the superiority of the world of art persists in Beckett, as well as its claim of transcendental strangeness. In Yeats's "Rosa Alchemica," a story Joyce knew well and admired, Michael Robartes tells the narrator:

> There is Lear, his head still wet with the thunderstorm,
> and he laughs because you thought yourself an existence
> who are but a shadow, and him a shadow who is an
> eternal god. [*Mythologies*, p. 275]

This is one of Yeats's favorite ideas, that the imagination can discover creatures who exist more amply, more vividly, are more *real* than the imaginer himself. It is possible that Joyce's two great characters, Stephen Dedalus and Leopold Bloom, are developed deliberately as rivals to actual men, fictions of such pertinacity, such richness, such obstinacy, that our own acquaintances seem impoverished and shadowy next to them. In such a way a book may compete with life. If Joyce wishes to be Pygmalion, to create an image that aspires to be no longer a representation of a man but a genuine human being, then Beckett wishes to be Frankenstein, the demonic Pygmalion, who creates an image that fails to be either a man or a suitable representation of a man. Beckett forces his monsters to display the sheep's shoulder, the iron hipbone, the gangrene, all the inhumanity, the feverish deadness of the parts that have gone into their construction. Words have feelings and sensations, become sullen or drunken, writhe on the page, but they manifest no man, no thing.

Where have we heard before that form and content ought to be identical? Pater says so.

> *All art constantly aspires towards the condition of music.*
> For while in all other kinds of art it is possible to distinguish the matter from the form, and the understanding can always make this distinction, yet it is the constant effort of art to obliterate it. [*Renaissance,* p. 95]

I believe that a better case can be made for *The Unnamable* than for *Finnegans Wake,* that here at last the novel has approached the condition of music. In *The Unnamable* there are four elaborate fictions: the frame, with the fixed and seated Unnamable encircled by orbiting old men; the first Mahood story, the world traveler who returns home and steps in his parents' gore; the second Mahood story, the celebrated amputee sitting in his urn, advertising a restaurant; and the tableau of Worm in his walled arena, tempted to be human. These are extended episodes of a somewhat "novelistic" character, but the rest of the novel is a welter of brief, rigid images that dissolve, that disappear as soon as they are stated, images scarcely distinguishable from the commentary that connects them, images that are found inadequate as quickly as they are configured. Of course, if language is nonreferential, there is nothing for them to be adequate to; but the narrator of *The Unnamable* seems not quite so convinced of the excellent uselessness of language as is the Beckett of the "Three Dialogues"—indeed, seems driven, compelled, to rummage in his imagination until a true expression of his predicament can be found. Except for this vain hope he is in a state of extreme imaginative liberation. Joyce must pretend that the long description of a beach scene refers, page after page, to a single solid construction, a construction at once verbal and independent of, prior to, the words that embody it, a palpable contradiction according to Beckett's doctrine. The passage in *Portrait* is like a filmstrip in which frame follows frame with only minute variations, producing the visual illusion of a single image slowly altering. This artificial constraint is largely abolished in *The Unnamable:* it is like a filmstrip in which each frame shows a different picture, so that the eye can seize nothing coherent. The Unnamable describes himself with such a ceaseless abundance of images—a talking ball, a hairless wedgehead, a skull made of solid bone, a tympanum, a red-mouthed half-wit—that no single image is held longer than an instant; each image drives out the image before it, as if the imagination's perfection consisted not in creating images but in extinguishing them. Beckett's characters sometimes flog themselves for being unimaginative (pp. 131, 114), but Beckett's imagination is dead only in that it is oblivious to its products, not interested in grasping any particular image; otherwise it is abnormally alive, febrile, engrossed in the rapidity of its own operations. It is this quality of disengagement, of teeming contentlessness, that makes Beckett's work seem musical—the biolgist Lewis Thomas has written that Bach's *Saint Matthew Passion* is about the act of thinking itself, not about any particular thought, and the same might be said of *The Unnamable*—and Beckett in his best periods is astonishingly fluent, prodigal, full of ornaments, the Mozart of unhappiness.

Beckett felt compelled to correct those who tried to read his works as the transcripts of a patient's monologue to his psychoanalyst, especially when his own psychoanalyst made this error (Bair, p. 457); but it is easy to see how one might be misled. Few authors have written novels so saturated with the feeling of autobiography, a feeling that puzzles the reader because, despite all the "I . . . my . . . mine . . . me" discourse, he seems to learn nothing about the author. The novels seem to hover at the edge of autobiography, but some evasion, some slipperiness, always seems to prevent the imminent revelation; the protagonists themselves seem disappointed by this central infirmity. A Freudian would explain this swerving away from self-expression as a psychic defense, an avoidance mechanism; but, as the "Three Dialogues" shows, there is a technical reason for this self-engorged style in the absence of a fixed hypostasis of self. The great achievement of Beckett's mature novels is to apply the method of the "Three Dialogues" not, as van Velde is said to do, to pictorial representation, but to autobiography. The aliment is Samuel Beckett, and the dispatch consists of Molloy, Malone, the Unnamable; the novels are faithful to the utter failure of likeness between them. This unresemblance and the extreme discomfort of the stance it necessitates are further embodied by the relations of Moran to Molloy, Malone to Sapo and Macmann, the Unnamable to Mahood and Worm, each little group consisting of an aliment and its dispatch, a teller and a told, though it is not always easy to tell which is which.

Every autobiography posits an I that is conscious and a self of which it is conscious. The I is essentially nominative, plastic, characterless, a maker of decisions, a naked intelligence and volition, a chooser of styles and modes of being, existing only in the present, wise without memory. The self is essentially accusative, determined, a congeries of character traits, historical, involuntary, an accretion of all the choices the I has chosen, the choices that have left weary traces, scars on the self's resilient flesh. For some autobiographers the relation of self to I is like that of the delicate spiral shell of the chambered nautilus, every section golden, to the little cephalopod, an invisible bit of tentacled goo, that secreted it. Other autobiographies see the self not as achieved, freely chosen, but as imposed from without—my father, or capitalist society, made me what I am—and the relation of I to self is like the hermit crab's more-or-less aching fit into its random shell. W. H. Auden had a subtle sense of this autobiographical drama:

> Every autobiography is concerned with two characters, a Don Quixote, the Ego, and a Sancho Panza, the Self. In one kind of autobiography the Self occupies the stage and narrates, like a Greek messenger, what the Ego is doing off stage. In another kind it is the Ego who is narrator and the Self who is described without being able to answer back. If the same person were to write his autobiography twice, first in one mode and then in another, the two accounts would be so different that it would be hard to believe that they referred to the same person. In one he would appear as an obsessed creature, a passionate Knight forever serenading Faith or Beauty, humorless and over-life-size: in the other as coolly detached, full of humor and self-mockery, lacking in a capacity for affection, easily bored and smaller than life-size. As Don Quixote seen by Sancho Panza, he never prays; as Sancho Panza seen by Don Quixote, he never giggles.
>
> An honest self-portrait is extremely rare because a man who has reached the degree of self-consciousness presupposed by the desire to paint his own portrait has almost always also developed an ego-consciousness which paints himself painting himself, and introduces artificial highlights and dramatic shadows. [*The Dyer's Hand,* p. 96]

The self is the earthly component of man, lax and blasé, the old Adam, fully come to terms with the natural, fallen world, never able to comprehend the ego's striving, its will to alter or ameliorate. The theological aspects of Auden's categories are not relevant to Beckett; but I am struck by how well Auden's description of the whole genre of autobiography fits a novel like *Malone Dies,* which sometimes seems like a ghastly competition between I and self, vying over which of these twin phantoms will take precedence, as if Don Quixote and Sancho Panza came to blows in the struggle for a pen. Malone also suffers from the "ego consciousness" that requires him to paint himself painting himself, sadly aware of the artificiality of this pose, of the fact that "Malone" is as much a construction, a lie, as the ostensible lies he tells himself about Sapo. If, as the "Three Dialogues" declares, the I is inexpressible, without the slightest hope of expression, then the I is a slug without any possibility of creating or discovering a shell. At one point the Unnamable hopes that "my monster's carapace will rot off me" (p. 325); but he never had a carapace, he only pretended to. The slug studies a pretty assortment of shells, from the "luminous oyster-grey" (p. 181) of the padded cells in *Murphy* (1934–37), the cells that are a metaphor for the insane, self-contained mind that Murphy hopes will be his in which to bask, to the jar in which Mahood, a quadruple amputee, rests in *The Unnamable*. But none of them can be the right shell; the "adhesion" (p. 314) will always be incomplete, imaginary.

It is, however, difficult to reconcile oneself to the universal failure of images to constitute themselves, and easy to forget, to hope that life's meaning will cohere, become focused on a satisfying image. If telling oneself stories about oneself can be calming, as Malone alleges, the sudden lack of stories, images, can be hell, as Murphy discovers just before his death by asphyxiation:

> When he was naked he lay down in a tuft of soaking tuffets and tried to get a picture of Celia. In vain. Of his mother. In vain. Of his father (for he was not illegiti-mate). In vain. It was usual for him to fail with his mother; and usual, though less usual, for him to fail with a woman. But never before had he failed with his father. He saw the clenched fists and rigid upturned face of the Child in a Giovanni Bellini Circumcision, waiting to feel the knife. He saw eyeballs being scraped, first any eyeballs, then Mr. Endon's. He tried again with his father, his mother, Celia, Wylie, Neary, Cooper, Miss Dew, Miss Carridge, Nelly, the sheep, the chandlers, even Bom and Co., even Bim, even Ticklepenny and Miss Counihan, even Mr. Quigley. He tried with the men, women, children and ani-mals that belong to even worse stories than this. In vain in all cases. He could not get a picture in his mind of any creature he had met, animal or human. Scraps of bodies, of landscapes, hands, eyes, lines and colours evoking no-thing, rose and climbed out of sight before him, as though reeled upward off a spool level with his throat. [*Murphy*, pp. 251–52]

Murphy is now closer than ever before to the ground of things, to the authentic figurelessness; and yet this proximity to a state in which there is neither self nor world, in which every gestalt has vanished, is not as pleasant an insanity as he had expected. This is a common pattern in Beckett's work: the hero seeks perfect detachment from the "howling fiasco" of the outer world, perfect self-containment, immured in foot-thick walls, but he discovers that there are no walls, nothing to be immured from, no one to immure. The whole fable disassembles, scat-ters itself, just as the kite at the end of *Murphy* snaps its string, flies out of sight, out of earth's orbit, a parody of the soul's escape, just as the cremated Murphy himself turns into charcoal, the barest residue of the organic, disperses into dust, gas, chaos. The image of the self as gas, "not free, but a mote in the dark of absolute freedom" (p. 112), is the least inadequate vision of one's being that the I can attain. But it is hard to remember, when talking about oneself, that any description of oneself other than as a plume of smoke is a falsification, that even this description, ex hypothesi, must somehow be a falsification.

Beckett, like many writers of the nineteenth and twentieth centuries, seems to be searching for an aesthetic refuge. The world of art, according to the "Three Dialogues," is ideally irrelevant to the world of experience, and therefore a perfect refuge. To a man obsessed, as Beckett seems to be, with the felicity of irrelation, with escape from a violent, vehement, clamoring world, the construction of a shelter by means of literary action must necessarily seem attractive. In such early works as "Assumption," and perhaps *Murphy*, the protagonist, in the act of dying, seems to attain that devastating self-expression in which everything is uttered, nothing held back; and I believe that in Beckett's writing there is a remnant of a certain magical attitude toward literature, that the writer may, with a superhuman effort, translate himself into the written, attain the security of art. The Unnamable complains that he cannot adequately talk about himself, cannot identify himself with any of his characters, and therefore cannot die; it is as if he were frustrated by his inability to pass into his own stories, resolve himself into their artifice, to name himself to death. The I would like nothing more than to find the one right august self, to surrender to its absolute lord, to merge into it, to circumvent the prohibitions against self-expression. But instead one only thrashes about, entangled in a network of predications, predications known to be incorrect but impossible to shake free of nonetheless. Every decaying husk—Sapo, Macmann, Mahood—is at once a vehicle through which the I tries to state itself finally, definitively, and a foreign corpse chained and rotting under one's nose, at once an answered prayer and a deprecation. The last, most poignant hope is that the impossibility of narration will itself become a pretext for silence, abandonment.

The episodes in *Molloy, Malone Dies,* and *The Unnamable* are little experiments in narration, as the title characters practice telling "easy" stories in anticipation of telling the one important story, the story of the self, the dying into the work. But even the easy stories present horrendous difficulties. At the beginning of *Molloy* (1947–48), Beckett's first experiment with sustained self-characterizing narrative, the protagonist decides to tell himself a little vignette about two men called A and C; they are walking on an open country road, A going toward the town, C away from it. Molloy has a certain amount of narrative skill, is capable of a degree of close observation and rational guesswork about the motives of his two wanderers; what is troublesome is the difficulty of defining his own relation to them:

> I watched him recede, overtaken (myself) by his anxiety, at least by an anxiety which was not necessarily his, but of which as it were he partook. Who knows if it wasn't my own anxiety overtaking him. He hadn't seen me. I was perched higher than the road's highest point and flattened what is more against a rock the same colour as myself, that is grey. The rock he probably saw. He gazed around as if to engrave the landmarks on his memory and must have seen the rock in the shadow of which I crouched like Belaqua, or Sordello, I forget. But a man, a fortiori myself, isn't exactly a landmark, because. I mean if by some strange chance he were to pass that way again, after a long lapse of time, vanquished, or to look for some lost thing, or to destoy something, his eyes would search out the rock, not the haphazard in its shadow of that unstable fugitive thing, still living flesh. [pp. 10–11]

The emotion evoked by C in his outward trek, anxiety, is oddly detached, free-floating, not clearly attributable either to C or to Molloy; Molloy cannot keep the teller separated from the tale, despite his manifest desire to be an obliging, proper sort of raconteur. He aspires to be an omniscient narrator but cannot quite understand how this convention operates; instead of simply taking it for granted that the narrator has privileged information about his story, Molloy has to imagine an actual vantage point from which he could observe the events described, high enough to behold A and C from a great distance. In this manner Molloy seems to manufacture his point of view as his story proceeds; he must rationalize his narrative stance, present himself physically in the described scene, just a little higher than the highest part of the road; but if the teller is a palpable part of his tale, why cannot he be seen by A and C? Is he not in danger of interfering with his little story? This consideration impels him to hide, crouch in the rock's shadow, efface himself as best he can; and so, as C recedes until he is a speck on the point of vanishing, Molloy skulks, shrinks into invisibility; instead of a casual anecdote about a small but choice, resonant event, we now have a condition in which the tale and the teller are on different planets, dead to each other. The story of A shows an equal inability to maintain proper narrative distance; as A approaches the town he looms larger and larger until Molloy can clearly see the cigar, the bare head, the orange Pomeranian. But Molloy is avid for still more information, imagines himself hobbling on his crutches after A, hailing him, interrogating him, discovering the exact nature of every detail of his life and person. Now the narrator is too greatly intimate with the object of his narration; the distance between them has collapsed. It remains only for Molloy's eye to slip inside A's body, like Kinbote in Nabokov's *Pale Fire*, who can see the colors, tell the churning, of Gradus's lungs and intestines. In the case of neither A nor C can the pretense of narration be maintained; the inexpressibility of things quickly asserts itself.

Molloy is no more competent to tell stories about himself than to tell them about A and C; when he looks at his own life he is confused by an absurdity, the incommensurability of his mind and the world of experience, the fact that in the "little night" (p. 28) of his mind there is no moon, no earth:

> And it came back also to my mind, as sleep stole over it again, that my nights were moonless and the moon foreign, to my nights, so that I had never seen, drifting past the window, carrying me back to other nights, other moons, this moon I had just seen, I had forgotten who I was (excusably) and spoken of myself as I would have of another, if I had been compelled to speak of another. Yes it sometimes happens and will sometimes happen again that I forget who I am and strut before my eyes, like a stranger. [*Molloy*, p. 42]

To imagine a Molloy who takes part in the world of experience, a Molloy who can see the moon, ride a bicycle, meet an old lady, crawl through a forest, is to imagine someone who is not Molloy-as-he-understands-himself-to-be; every attribution of self is a falsehood. The incidents of the novel, the stories Molloy tells about himself, are every bit as rickety, ludicrous, abject in narrative stance as the stories Molloy tells about A and C. The self keeps drifting away from the I; neither can imagine how it could be *related* to the other, no matter how furiously, how intimately the story is told. This essential foreignness is emblematized by Molloy's inability to imagine how he got where he is, lying on a bed in his mother's former room. He has "memories" of approaching this room from afar, of being unable to find it, of turning away from it, of approaching again, but his stories of his "former life" contain an unbridgeable gap; it is impossible that the Molloy who crawls through the forest, ever more slowly, every faculty failing, could attain the distant town in which his mother lived. He can say nothing about himself that will help to define himself; everything he says about Molloy is a further estrangement from his present condition. Though he struggles to closer and closer approximations, uses the story of Lousse to rationalize his bedriddenness, the story of the forest to rationalize his debilitation, these approximations only make his disappointment keener when they fail to connect. In the Joyce essay, Beckett rejects all analogies in favor of point-blank identity, the story that is not about something but *is* something. The vicarious narrators in Beckett's novels are all trying to write autobiographical descriptions that *are*, that fully constitute themselves, but they discover that instead they have offered dim analogies, metaphors, approximations of their plight, mere representations that fall asunder in the collapse of representation. "Molloy" is an irrelevant character in Molloy's narration.

The great *coup de théâtre* of *Molloy*, of course, is the introduction, just when the novel seems at a point where further narration is impossible, of a new narrator, Moran, a detective with the unpleasant assignment of tracking down Molloy. When the messenger Gaber tenders him this assignment, he feels, incomprehensibly, that Molloy is "no stranger to me," though he knows "nothing of the circumstances in which I had learnt of his existence" (pp. 111–12); the presence of Molloy is panting, palpable, emerging inside him:

> He panted. He had only to rise up within me for me to be filled with panting.
>
> Even in open country he seemed to be crashing through jungle. He did not so much walk as charge. In spite of this he advanced but slowly. He swayed, to and fro, like a bear.
>
> He rolled his head, uttering incomprehensible words.
>
> He was massive and hulking, to the point of misshapenness. And, without being black, of a dark color.
>
> He was forever on the move. I had never seen him rest. Occasionally he stopped and glared furiously about him.
>
> This was how he came to me, at long intervals. Then I was nothing but uproar, bulk, rage, suffocation, effort unceasing, frenzied and vain. Just the opposite of myself, in fact. [*Molloy*, p. 113]

In many ways this is the most vivid description of Molloy in the novel, a Molloy distilled and essentialized; here Proustian techniques are adapted to give an impression of the extratemporal Molloy, the ideal real. It seems that by introducing a superior narrator (Moran) the inferior narrator (Molloy) is at last narrated, captured, defined, the I given an adequate verbal embodiment, a self. But congratulations are not yet in order. Moran must turn out to be a narrator every bit as incompetent as Molloy, no more able than he to find the right narrative stance; just as Molloy found himself either slipping away from C or engulfed by A, so Moran finds that he is simultaneously chasing an unattainable figment, Molloy, and being engulfed by him. Instead of providing a clarifying overview of the situation, he only complicates it more; Molloys multiply dizzyingly in his presence:

> Between the Molloy I stalked within me thus and the true Molloy, after whom I was so soon to be in full cry, over hill and dale, the resemblance cannot have been great.
>
> I was annexing perhaps already, without my knowing it, to my private Molloy, elements of the Molloy described by Gaber.
>
> The fact was there were three, no four Molloys. He that inhabited me, my caricature of same, Gaber's and the man of flesh and blood somewhere awaiting me. To these I would add Youdi's were it not for Gaber's corpse fidelity to the letter of his messages. Bad reasoning. For could it seriously be supposed that Youdi had confided to Gaber all he knew, or thought he knew (all one to Youdi) about his protégé? Assuredly not. He had only revealed what he deemed of relevance for the prompt and proper execution of his orders. I will therefore add a fifth Molloy, that of Youdi. But would not this fifth Molloy necessarily coincide with the fourth, the real one as the saying is, him dogged by his shadow? I would have given a lot to know. There were others too, of course. But let us leave it at that, if you don't mind, the party is big enough. And let us not meddle either with the question as to how far these five Molloys were constant and how far subject to variation. For there was this about Youdi, that he changed his mind with great facility. [*Molloy,* p. 115]

In *Proust* Beckett speaks of the multiplicity of Albertine and of the narrator, who desires her, each altering at such speed that the possibility of fulfilled love is nonexistent—"all that is enveloped in time and space is endowed with what might be described as an abstract, ideal and absolute impermeability" (p. 41). Similarly, Molloy is impermeable, unattainable, and the multiplying of narrators will only make him more so, for every attempted bridge becomes itself a barrier. The whole passage cited above is a parody of Plato, with its hope that the divine idea will correspond to the reality of Molloy; but it is obvious that every idea about Molloy, every ascription of identity to him, merely adds another misshapen image to a useless wax museum of Molloys. Moran is an attempt to mediate between Molloy's image of himself and the real Molloy; but, in Beckett's calculus, even if an infinite regression of superior narrators were adduced, if a Third Man came along to tell Moran's story, et cetera, the sequence $\frac{1}{2} + \frac{1}{4} + \frac{1}{8} + \ldots$ would never converge upon 1. The narrating I is always secret, inviolate, unnamed; only the narrated self can be called "Molloy."

Moran does what he can to discredit himself both as a detective and as a narrator; he cannot find Molloy and he cannot tell him. The celebrated ending—"I . . . wrote, It is midnight. The rain is beating on the windows. It was not midnight. It was not raining" (p. 176)—serves to confirm the universal inenarrability of a life Moran had previously called an "inenarrable contraption" (p. 114); Moran is as impermeable as Molloy, an equal failure as an autobiographer. Moran supplies many hints that the reader should not take his story at face value:

> And it would not surprise me if I deviated, in the pages to follow, from the true and exact succession of events. But I do not think even Sisyphus is required to scratch himself, or to groan, or to rejoice, as the fashion is now, always at the same appointed places. [*Molloy*, p. 133]

Moran seems to believe that his story is not a single chronicle but a heap of related stories varied and elaborated in an infernal penance, the writer's obligation; it is as if the text of his report were a single specimen of an infinite number of Searches for Lost Molloy. Part 1 of the novel may be another specimen. An even more disquieting possibility is suggested by Moran's description of the only messenger who ever approaches him—this uniqueness may suggest Beckett's acquaintance with Kafka's "Before the Law"—Gaber:

> He used a code incomprehensible to all but himself. Each messenger, before being appointed, had to submit his code to the directorate. Gaber understood nothing about the messages he carried. Reflecting on them he arrived at the most extravagantly false conclusions. Yes, it was not enough for him to understand nothing about them, he had also to believe he understood everything about them. This was not all. His memory was so bad that his messages had no existence in his head, but only in his notebook. He had only to close his notebook to become, a moment later, perfectly innocent as to its contents. And when I say that he reflected on his messages and drew conclusions from them, it was not as we would have reflected on them, you and I, the book closed and probably the eyes too, but little by little as he read. And when he raised his head and indulged in his commentaries, it was without losing a second, for if he had lost a second he would have forgotten everything, both text and gloss. I have often wondered if the messengers were not compelled to undergo a surgical operation, to induce in them such a

degree of amnesia. But I think not. For otherwise their memory was good enough. And I have heard Gaber speak of his childhood, and of his family, in extremely plausible terms. To be undecipherable to all but oneself, dead without knowing it to the meaning of one's instructions and incapable of remembering them for more than a few seconds, these are capacities rarely united in the same individual. [*Molloy,* pp. 106–7]

The reader wonders whether what he is reading is not a detective's report but a messenger's commentary, a maundering in oblivion, a delusory understanding of something not understood, whether neither part 1 nor part 2 of *Molloy* is a text in the usual sense; instead, both parts may be the separate glosses or encryptions of some text outside the novel entirely. This sense of the uncanny remoteness of the reader from the actual speaking, from the things narrated, is another strategy Beckett uses to heighten the reader's sense of the inexpressiveness of the literary act. Amnesia is the ideal condition of the inexpressive narrator; it even permits the hypothesis that parts 1 and 2 have a single narrator, who forgets that he called himself Molloy and starts to call himself Moran instead. This hypothesis brings the narrator's identity closer to that of Samuel Beckett, the vigilant mouth behind all these apparitions, whose tongue keeps loosening in witty statements of its tongue-tiedness.

In *Malone Dies* Beckett, almost in propria persona, though of course the proper person is necessarily excluded from discourse, compares the characters he manipulates in his stories to stones in his pocket:

For this may well be my last journey, down the long familiar galleries, with my little suns and moons that I hang aloft and my pockets full of pebbles to stand for men and their seasons, my last, if I'm lucky. Then back here, to me, whatever that means, and no more leaving me, no more asking me for what I haven't got. Or perhaps we'll all come back, reunited, done with parting, done with prying on one another, back to this foul little den all dirty white and vaulted, as though hollowed out of ivory, an old rotten tooth. Or alone, back alone, as alone as when I went, but I doubt it, I can hear them from here, clamouring after me down the corridors, stumbling through the rubble, beseeching me to take them with me. [*Malone Dies,* p. 236]

This is the infernal equivalent of a favorite romantic fantasy, the writer romping in Elysium with the creatures of his imagination, a fancy powerfully expressed in the "Alternative Song" in Yeats's *The King of the Great Clock Tower.* Nabokov called the characters in his novels "galley slaves," but Beckett denies that they are human; every fictive identity, every predicated self is a stone, a dead lump of words. This suggests that the much-discussed passage in the first part of Molloy—in which Molloy arranges his sucking stones in such a manner that he will go through the entire sequence of sixteen without repetition, although the order of sucked stones is likely to change from one sequence to the next—is an emblem of the author's handling of his characters and their paraphernalia. Moran's narrative is a scrambling, a reshuffling of the elements of Molloy's narrative. If literary art is expressive of nothing, then the aesthetic pleasure of literature is not mimesis but the abstract permutation of neutral elements, elements that have no more intrinsic meaning or reference than the sounds that make up the notes of a musical scale. If Molloy's sucking stones had numbered twelve instead of sixteen, the principle of the intolerability of repetition would have made the whole passage a kind of parody of twelve-tone music; indeed, it is easy to imagine a fourth dialogue of Beckett and Duthuit, eternal antagonists resting in heaven after their debate like the Achilles and the Tortoise of Lewis Carroll's Eleatic fantasy, discussing the serial system of Schoenberg as the musical equivalent of van Velde's paintings, Beckett's novels. Murphy, in Beckett's first novel, contemplates with delight the fact that he can eat his five different biscuits in 120 different orders, if only he can conquer his preferences, his desire to eat the unpleasant anonymous biscuit first and the favored ginger biscuit last, a restriction that limits to a "paltry six" (p. 96) the number of arrays possible to the biscuit-eater seeking to avoid monotony in his lunch. Similarly, the theory of twelve-tone music states that if one note is repeated before the other eleven notes of the chromatic scale have been sounded, it will tend to create a key signature, a specific tonality, a state in which one note takes precedence over another; the twelve-tone style is an attempt to escape from this center of gravity, to treat all notes with equal dignity. Murphy's biscuits, Molloy's sucking stones, are emblems that teach the writer how to play with his material; Beckett has aspired to write a twelve-tone novel, in a sense, in which A, C, the bicycle, the hat, the dead dog, the shepherd, Molloy himself, and so on, are all equally important, are but arbitrary counters, inert and random, sucked in measured sequence. In part 2, many of the same elements reappear, the hat, the dog Zulu, Molloy, the bicycle, the rustic, C, and so forth—the retrograde inversion, so to speak, of the original tone row, though of course Beckett's transformations are not rigid. The lists between the chapters of the abandoned novel *Mercier and Camier*, which reduce the events of the chapters to terse captions, permit in places a similar analysis. This discipline of the imagination forces upon the writer the proper state of disinterestedness toward his material.

Certain writers in the generation after Beckett are as adept as he is at writing fictions that are like serial fugues or abstract paintings or mobiles, assemblages of unrecognizable elements turning in space without cause or effect, pointedly pointless, all opsis or melos with no trace of dianoia. But it is Beckett's gift to be able to write in this manner and at the same time to suggest that underneath the shifting images there is a grave world in which important things happen, a world of suffering that vitiates, renders ludicrous, the little puppet shuffle that is all his novels can offer. Later writers of nonreferential stories—I am thinking of Donald Barthelme's "Sentence" and certain of John Barth's experiments—accept the doctrine that "there is nothing to express, nothing with which to express, nothing from which to express, no power to express, no desire to express"; but they are not gripped by the necessity, the pathos, of the final phrase, "together with the obligation to express." Beckett fulfills this obligation by creating fables that confess their fabulous ineptitude, that, in the act of declaring themselves impenetrable, inexpressive, are designed to be slightly penetrated, to constitute an exceedingly oblique expression of the tacit world they cannot tell. The description of Gaber's qualifications as a messenger, which hints at an unspeakable text beneath Moran's narrative, is one such technique for providing clues about the existence of an inexpressible substrate underlying the whole fiction. Another can be found in a passage near the end of *Molloy,* in which Moran claims he is the only man on earth who knows that bees dance, "not as men dance to amuse themselves," but to impart information to the outgoing bees in the hive about the location of nectar—by tracing a variety of complicated figures in the air, by a pattern of humming, by a whole system of valid signs. Moran also considers and measures other variables of the dance that might be meaningful, such as the bees' altitude:

> I was more than ever stupefied by the complexity of this innumerable dance, involving doubtless other determinants of which I had not the slightest idea. And I said, with rapture, Here is something I can study all my life, and never understand. And all during this long journey home, when I racked my mind for a little joy in store, the thought of my bees and their dance was the nearest thing to comfort. For I was still eager for my little joy, from time to time! And I admitted with good grace the possibility that this dance was after all no better than the dances of the people of the West, frivolous and meaningless. But for me, sitting near my sun-drenched hives, it

> would always be a noble thing to contemplate, too noble
> ever to be sullied by the cogitations of a man like me,
> exiled in his manhood. [*Molloy,* p. 169]

There is a world in which things have meaning; but Moran, because he is human, is debarred from it. Moran and Molloy and Beckett's other puppets, stones, all cut their frivolous capers in a prescribed, arbitrary, meaningless sequence; yet these inane frolics bear witness to something that they can never tell, a world so densely significant, so complicatedly actual, that it surpasses any possibility of understanding, of expression. The power of reason, the faculties of the mind, so useful for exhausting the permutations of biscuits and stones, estrange us from the point-blank intelligibility of the subhuman world. Moran, far from being able to interpret the bees' symbols into vector and instruction, finds when he arrives home only the dust balls of dead bees (p. 174) crumbling in his hand, as if he infects the world around him with his own lapsing, his own obscurity. In his remarkable short story, "First Love" (1945), written not long before *Molloy* was begun, Beckett offers a hint that beauty as well as meaningfulness may be an attribute of the world from which living men are excluded:

> And my father's face, on his death-bolster, had seemed to
> hint at some form of aesthetics relevant to man. But the
> faces of the living, all grimace and flush, can they be
> described as objects? [*First Love,* p. 27]

The art of novel-writing is as ugly, futile, perfervid, as any other human activity; the true aesthetic pertains only to the dead. It is even possible that the rigor mortis of such recent prose pieces as "Imagination Dead Imagine" (1965) is an attempt to approximate the only beauty Beckett seems able to conceive, the beauty of the inanimate.

After *Molloy* Beckett tries ever subtler and more arcane methods of embodying in prose some vestige of the human nominative, the I, an entity just as remote, as incapable of elucidation, as the subsistent world in which bees make meaningful gestures. In *Malone Dies* (1948), the sequel to *Molloy,* the first-person narrator Malone, Beckett's most self-conscious literary artist, cannot make up his mind whether his stories about the child called Sapo have anything to do with his own childhood; this ambiguity, this straddling between invention and memory, allows Malone to disengage himself violently from any attribution of historical identity, from any prior life in the world outside the narrow room in which he is dwindling. Malone is the first of the line of Beckett's characters whose central cry is "Not I," who shrink from definition, who claim that any allegations about them must be false, must be about someone else. The real Malone, the quick of him, is an infinitesimal point invisible to any search, a pineal gland that recedes from all anatomy:

> All my senses are trained full on me, me. Dark and silent and stale, I am no prey for them. I am far from the sounds of blood and breath, immured. I shall not speak of my sufferings. Cowering deep down among them I feel nothing. It is there I die, unbeknown to my stupid flesh. That which is seen, that which cries and writhes, my witless remains. Somewhere in this turmoil thought struggles on, it too wide of the mark. It too seeks me, as it always has, where I am not to be found. It too cannot be quiet. On others let it wreak its dying rage, and leave me in peace. Such would seem to be my present state. [*Malone Dies*, p. 186]

Everything that one might wish to predicate to Malone—his irritable emotions, his ironical style, his intellect, his imagination, his body— Malone wishes to exclude from "Malone." His imagination is a detached, incomprehensible voice that speaks into his ear; his body, in Epictetus's phrase, is a corpse he is fastened to, doomed to inhabit, so uncannily distant, far-fetched, grotesquely swollen, that, "if my arse suddenly started to shit . . . I firmly believe the lumps would fall out in Australia" (p. 235). This negative path, this paring down to nothing of the traits and faculties that make us human, is a means for seizing the inexpressible core, the soul, the I so exclusive of every predicate than even *I am that I am* seems less a tautology than an overstatement.

Again it may be helpful to turn for comparison to Joyce's *Portrait of the Artist*. To a large measure Joyce conceives the child's development as a process of the soul's extrication from everything usually thought to be an attribute of it. When Father Dolan punishes the very young Stephen Dedalus by hitting his hands with a pandybat, he cries out in agony; but an instant later an odd detachment falls over him. He looks at his beaten, swollen hands and feels sorry for them, "as if they were not his own but someone else's that he felt sorry for" (p. 51). In such ways Stephen must grow estranged from all he beholds, must cultivate aesthetic distance, the mirror's knowledge that it is separable from the images that form on it. The pandybatting teaches him that his body and he are discrete, that his body is only another element of the world he must study. Soon he begins to become a connoisseur of his emotions as well as of his physical sensations: during Christmas homecoming, "he chronicled with patience what he saw, detaching himself from it and testing its mortifying flavour in secret" (p. 67); and after he is beaten by his schoolmates for defending Byron, his emotions become unreal to him—"as he stumbled homeward along Jones's Road he had felt that some power was divesting him of that sudden woven anger as easily as a fruit is divested of its soft ripe peel." Infancy is a great bath of sensation and emotion in which one's own limits are unclear, a condition in which concentric circles radiate from Stephen to the end of the universe; growing up is a divestiture, in which the soul grows at once more naked and more difficult to find, hidden inside all those things it once took for aspects, expressions of itself. Sometimes Stephen is alarmed by his detachment, his lunar remoteness, the fact that he seems a "foster child" (p. 98) in the midst of his own family; but every refining of his being, every isolation, is the prelude to aesthetic control, the divine impersonality of the artist who "remains within or behind or beyond or above his handiwork, invisible, refined out of existence, indifferent, paring his fingernails" (p. 215). By the last chapter of *Portrait* Stephen seems detached even from his own intellect: he seems to transcend those laws by which "all thinking must be bound" (p. 187) and at last tells Cranly that he does not wish to overcome his own doubts about Christianity (p. 239), as if some component of him were superior to any process of his intellect. Stephen's attitude toward himself and the world he dwells in is increasingly experimental, delicately manipulative; he takes little part in collegiate argument, lets Cranly, who is all head, and Davin, who is all body, express the passions he withholds. It is as if the corpus of his friends constitutes an elaborate *psychomachia* of Stephen from which the actual Stephen keeps aloof, except for the sake of defining explicitly, didactically, the doctrine of aesthetic detachment itself.

Malone's relationship to his stories about himself and his acquaintances is an extrapolation and a parody of Stephen Dedalus's. The irrevelance of body, affect, and intelligence to the artist's essential being has expanded monstrously; and, similarly, all the events of Malone's stories seem to be employed as a groping for self-expression. But here self-expression is rendered vain by the fact that the artist is so depersonalized, so far "behind or beyond or above his handiwork," that he can embody nothing about himself in the interactions, the denouements, of the characters in his tales—indeed, his fingernail parings fall somewhere in Australia. Malone is not much like a god aloof from his creations, watching the interesting follies of men made in his image; Malone's relation to his characters is almost the reverse, as a passage from *The Unnamable* suggests:

> I have assigned him eyes that implore me, offerings for me, need of succour. He does not look at me, does not know of me, wants for nothing. I alone am man and all the rest divine. [*The Unnamable*, p. 300]

185

The personages of fiction are fully defined, impassive, unreal, divine, dead; the maker of fiction is incoherent, urgent, suffering, human, dying. He pretends that his characters are just like him, tries to endow these stones with his clamorousness, his affections; but they remain ideal, still, innocuous, irrelevant, for all his desire to make them expressive. The faces of the puppets are painted with anguished grimaces, but they are wood; they feel no pain, nor can they be an outlet for another's pain, no matter how violently they are shaken.

Saposcat is the first genuine persona in Beckett's fiction, that is, the first character that a narrator employs as a foil or mask. It is true that Moran, unable to locate Molloy, starts to turn into him, to grow lame, spastic, solitary; but such processes of convergence never attain their goals, and Moran in any case does not understand Molloy to be either an invention or a memory of his. Malone's relation to Saposcat is marked by a certain horrified intimacy. Young Stephen Dedalus slowly learned to make distinctions, to learn the mysterious names of things—"cancer" is not "canker," white things are not invariably cold—while young Saposcat, an apprentice to senility, stamps over the countryside in a state of imbecile felicity:

> Sapo loved nature, took an interest in animals and plants and willingly raised his eyes to the sky, day and night. But he did not know how to look at all these things, the looks he rained upon them taught him nothing about them. He confused the birds with one another, and the trees, and could not tell one crop from another crop. He did not associate the crocus with the spring nor the chrysanthemum with Michaelmas. The sun, the moon, the planets and the stars did not fill him with wonder. He was sometimes tempted by the knowledge of these strange things, sometimes beautiful, that he would have about him all his life. But from his ignorance of them he drew a kind of joy, as from all that went to swell the murmur, You are a simpleton. [*Malone Dies*, p. 191]

There is a natural world, plentiful and orderly, in which the chrysanthemum may be distinguished from the crocus; in an ordinary novel the character who stands for the author in his adolescence will be the vehicle through which these distinctions are savored, made keen; but in *Malone Dies* Saposcat is the vehicle for rendering the world of experience unintelligible—a Poorprate of the Autist as a Young Man. Saposcat is an inferred creature, designed to provide an answer to the question, What sort of childhood would have been proper for a man who ended in Malone's predicament? Yet when we compare Saposcat's faculties with Malone's, it is clear that Malone is far more able,

competent—indeed, can make remarkable discriminations in the world
to which he attends:

> When I stop, as just now, the noises begin again,
> strangely loud, those whose turn it is. So that I seem to
> have again the hearing of my boyhood. Then in my bed,
> in the dark, on stormy nights, I could tell from one
> another, in the outcry without, the leaves, the boughs,
> the groaning trunks, even the grasses and the house that
> sheltered me. Each tree had its own cry, just as no two
> whispered alike, when the air was still. I heard afar the
> iron gates clashing and dragging at their posts and the
> wind rushing between their bars. There was nothing, not
> even the sand on the paths, that did not utter its cry.
> [*Malone Dies*, p. 206]

Malone, far from taking Saposcat's story as his own, imagines a boyhood the exact opposite of Saposcat's, in which the world bristles with
sharp cries. However, Malone's usual dull state has none of the acuity
of hearing possessed in his boyhood and at the moment:

> What I mean is possibly this, that the noises of the world,
> so various in themselves and which I used to be so clever
> at distinguishing from one another, had been dinning at
> me for so long, always the same old noises, as gradually
> to have merged into a single noise, so that all I heard was
> one vast continuous buzzing. The volume of sound per-
> ceived remained no doubt the same, I had simply lost the
> faculty of decomposing it. [*Malone Dies*, p. 207]

Saposcat is the ancestor of this obtuseness, if the child is father to the
man. Malone's concept of his "boyhood" alters with his altering conditions: if his hearing starts to improve, he improvises a new dummy
child to account in a rational, historical manner for this phenomenon.
Saposcat is notably inert, notably puzzled in his dealings with others, a
fantasy of a life in which puzzled inertia has a satisfyingly continuous
presence from cradle to grave; but when Malone feels angry or upset
this figment of tedious calm does not beguile his imagination, and he
tries to shake himself free of it. Malone explains at the beginning that
he tells himself stories in order to calm himself, and soon the soothing
presence of Saposcat leads him to say of the youngster, "I wonder if I
am not talking yet again about myself" (p. 189); but after a while the
boy's ideal phlegm becomes exasperating, and Malone reverses himself: "nothing is less like me than this patient, reasonable child" (p.
193). No persona, no predicated self, can ever resemble the instantaneous I, but Saposcat, with his inanity, his blasted intelligence,

seems so inchoate, provisional, malformed, leaky, that he might be a useful vehicle for submersion, perishing. Since he never became alert, knowledgeable, since he is in a sense already vanished, he may be an aid in vanishing:

> Live and cause to live. There is no use indicting words, they are no shoddier than what they peddle. After the fiasco, the solace, the repose, I began again, to try and live, cause to live, be another, in myself, in another. How false all this is. No time now to explain. I began again. But little by little with a different aim, no longer in order to succeed, but in order to fail. . . .
> My concern is not with me, but with another, far beneath me and whom I try to envy, of whose crass adventures I can now tell at last, I don't know how. Of myself I could never tell, anymore than live or tell of others. How could I have, who never tried? To show myself now, on the point of vanishing, at the same time as the stranger, and by the same grace, that would be no ordinary last straw. Then live, long enough to feel, behind my closed eyes, other eyes close. What an end. [*Malone Dies,* p. 195]

The familiar stranger, Saposcat-Macmann, can be construed either as a representation of Malone's inability to represent himself, his inability to build out of scraps and orts a human likeness, or as a deliberate unrepresentation, a mock persona incapable of sustaining itself, not stitched together correctly, dropping arms and legs behind it as it walks, sputtering into a heap. If the narrator can manage to implicate himself with this loose creature, its disintegration, its failure to constitute a connected image, will be an act of magic; for the persona is a voodoo doll the narrator dismembers in order to kill himself. Deirdre Bair has told us that Beckett did seem to his friends on the brink of death as he wrote the novel (p. 376). If the narrator remembers his inviolability, on the other hand, then the persona is preposterous only because expression is a preposterous desire; and Malone hopes not for literal death but for silence, for a remedy to the affliction of the imagination, for permission to stop this tinkering with images. The author shows that self-expression is chimerical by embodying a chimera, pointing out the frayed wings, the long, limp tail, the goat's swimming eye, and saying "I'm that" so absurdly that the reader knows, He's not that. The rhythm of *Malone Dies,* and *The Unnamable* too, consists of this alternate adhesion and revulsion, this tentative embrace of soiled images of oneself followed by strenuous repudiation of them. Auden has said that art must work to sabotage its own best effects, because it cannot both manifest the ideal and illustrate our distance from it except by deliberately ruining its revealed beauties. With Beckett the apparatus of sabotage has magnified amazingly, so that a whole Inquisition's worth of tongs, racks, iron maidens, beds of coals are brought forward to deject a few puppets, crumple some images of cellophane. Despite Beckett's admission that Saposcat came painfully close to autobiography (Bair, p. 376), Beckett's personality seems to be found less in the traits of his stooges than in the mechanisms used to depict them, as if the art of sabotage could itself constitute a kind of self-expression.

Saposcat, whose inability to make distinctions makes him seem more mindless than Moran's bees, may be called an embodiment of nonidentity, as if the principle of inexpressiveness were plumped out into human form. The little incidents in the stories that concern him also illustrate the same principles illustrated by Saposcat himself. Saposcat's chief amusement is to visit the farm of Big Lambert, a pig-starver and seasonal butcher, whose wife we see sorting lentils:

> She sat down, emptied out the lentils on the table and began to sort them. So that soon there were two heaps on the table, one big heap getting smaller and one small heap getting bigger. But suddenly with a furious gesture she swept the two together, annihilating thus in less than a second the work of two or three minutes. [*Malone Dies,* pp. 213–14]

This is one of several dwindling heaps on the farm, for the Lamberts are also filling in the grave of a mule; these disappearing piles of dirt or lentils are related to Malone's fancy that he and Saposcat are "two little heaps of finest sand, or dust, or ashes, of unequal size, but diminishing together as it were in ratio, if that means anything, and leaving behind them, each in its own stead, the blessedness of absence" (p. 222). It is remarkable how the imagery of Malone's little stories follows exactly the metaphors Malone uses to define himself; the little stories are only elaborations of self-conceptions, as the absent-minded, scatterbrained Saposcat becomes an emblem of that absence, that scattering, for which Malone yearns. Malone has no theme but the crumbling of the friable, the dispersing of ashes. Malone does not so much create Saposcat as unmake him, render him incredible, just as Celia in *Murphy* imagines her childhood, the events of her life, only for the pleasure of unweaving these images day after day, a backward Penelope (p. 149). Indeed Malone's relishing of Saposcat reaches sinister extremes:

> Yes, a little creature, I shall try and make a little creature,
> to hold in my arms, a little creature in my image, no

matter what I say. And seeing what a poor thing I have
made, or how like myself, I shall eat it. [*Malone Dies*,
p. 226]

Saposcat is a little man of marzipan, to be eaten, to be divided in a
ritual of self-cannibalism. We have seen before, in the case of Molloy
and A and C, how the author's distance from his subject may grow
dangerously small; here Malone swallows his homunculus, digests him,
as the representation vanishes into the representer, grows magically
one with him. This ideal convergence of I and self is attained, however,
only at the moment when the self disappears and makes the wry pretense of representation no longer. Indeed Saposcat never appears in
the novel again; he is replaced by the elderly, still more flagrantly
incompetent Macmann, another proof of the discontinuity, the arbitrariness of these personas, their irrelevance to the man who imagines
them.

Malone botches his creations for the sake of exterminating them; and
at the instant of their extinguishing they seem suddenly to become
accurate images of their creator:

> This exercise-book is my life, this child's exercise-book,
> it has taken me a long time to resign myself to that. And
> yet I shall not throw it away. For I want to put down in it,
> for the last time, those I have called to my help, but ill, so
> that they did not understand, so that they may cease with
> me. Now rest. [*Malone Dies*, p. 274]

Annulled they attain the poignance, the expressiveness, denied to them
while they were personages in a narration. In the last novel of this
sequence of three, *The Unnamable* (1949–50), Beckett's invention of
satisfying nonimages reaches its peak; the Unnamable has at the tips of
his paralyzed fingers a wealth of embodiments of vanishedness far
beyond his predecessors. However, he differs from Malone in that he is
not certain that he is an author and that Mahood and Worm are his
characters; in the story of the one-legged man who limps home while
his family glowers at him through the slits of a rotunda, "I" and "Mahood" are used almost interchangeably, "the subject matters little" (p.
351). First it seems to be the Unnamable's story about Mahood, but
such phrases as "According to Mahood I never reached them" (p. 318)
make the reverse seem true. The distinction between subject and
predicate, teller and told, has blurred; the Unnamable does not know
whether Mahood is an imagination whispering in his ear stories about
his own early life or whether Mahood is a satisfyingly ferocious image
provided by his own imagination. But, whether Mahood is teller or

told, the Unnamable wishes to repudiate him. The Unnamable's fraction of personal intelligence, personal volition, is so minute that everything he can posit about himself seems to pertain to someone else, not to him; all predication about himself instantly congeals into an alien persona, but he has so little ego-consciousness that he can never be certain that any image, no matter how farfetched or bizarre, is not an accurate reflection of himself. The indeterminancy of the nominative case reaches its maximum: the Unnamable can do nothing to resist any name foisted on him, whether he is called Mahood, Worm, a tympanum, a flying pig, Charles de Gaulle; where all description is irrelevant, any description will do. Our protagonist is a monster of distension, whose essential shapelessness is embodied by the confusing multitude of shapes he presents, just as colorlessness may be better embodied by a chameleon than by a glass fish. He is out of control, helpless in the toils of an imagination that, he feels, is not his own; each image is a temptation that cannot be resisted, cannot be succumbed to, for he has no criterion, no determined interior image of himself against which another image might be judged correct or incorrect:

> Do they believe I believe it is I who am speaking? That's theirs too. To make me believe I have an ego all my own, and can speak of it, as they of theirs. Another trap to snap me up among the living. It's how to fall into it they can't have explained to me sufficiently. They'll never get the better of my stupidity. Why do they speak to me thus? Is it possible certain things change on their passage through me, in a way they can't prevent? Do they believe I believe it is I who am asking these questions? That's theirs too, a little distorted perhaps. I don't say it's not the right method. I don't say they won't catch me in the end. [*The Unnamable,* pp. 345–46]

Even his determination to remain undefined, inexpressible, is rather weak; if crystallizing into a fixed form will help him perish, then so be it; otherwise he is content to be this contradictory stream of words, human gibberish. Malone has his moments of unearthly malleability, passivity—"the sensation is familiar of a blind and tired hand delving feebly in my particles" (p. 224)—but for the most part he is self-aware, irascible, the master of his puppets. The Unnamable, instead of eating his personages, may be eaten by them:

> like hyenas, screeching and laughing, no, no better, no matter, I've shut my doors against them, I'm not at home to anything, my doors are shut against them, perhaps that's how I'll find silence, and peace at last, by opening

> my doors and letting myself be devoured, they'll stop
> howling, they'll start eating, the maws now howling. [*The
> Unnamable,* p. 391]

Any definition may at last swallow the undefinable; but the Unnamable
does seem to maintain his purity, his sense of extrinsicality. He is not
eaten by his images, or he is eaten so often that digestion only improves
his self-effacement.

In the early essay on Joyce, Beckett recommended a kind of language that is intuitive, direct, stunning, and claimed that Joyce's syn-
thetic language, like Dante's purified Tuscan, attains something of the
concreteness, the vigor of hieroglyphics or Homer's language of the
gods. Beckett was also intrigued by Vico's concept of the primitivism
of poetry:

> Poetry, he says, was born of curiosity, daughter of igno-
> rance. The first men had to create matter by the force of
> their imagination, and "poet" means "creator". Poetry
> was the first operation of the human mind, and without it
> thought could not exist. Barbarians, incapable of analysis
> and abstraction, must use their fantasy to explain what
> their reason cannot comprehend. Before articulation
> comes song; before abstract terms, metaphors. The
> figurative character of the oldest poetry must be regarded,
> not as sophisticated confectionery, but as evidence of a
> poverty-stricken vocabulary and of a disability to achieve
> abstraction. [*An Exagmination,* p. 9]

The style of *The Unnamable* is also, in a sense, the child of ignorance;
Beckett is as sophisticated an author as one can find, but when he is
trying to convey something unarticulated, something beyond mind's
edge, beyond even the advanced categories of Beckett's thought, he
too, like the caveman, must resort to myth. The "Three Dialogues"
and *The Unnamable,* taken together, constitute the fullest statement of
that myth.

It is a myth about the unchanging isolation of the soul. Subtract
body, intellection, emotion, memory, history, imagination, learned behavior, genetic trait; something must be left over, if body, intellection,
emotion, and so forth can be considered as the attributes of a single
entity. What remains after this exhaustive process of removal is an
erased image, a hole cut in paper, which could be called the soul, not in
Aristotle's sense of the seat of affect but in some sense of blank sub-
sistence, corresponding to a man as Spinoza's god does to the universe, an empty ground of being, the *tabula* first *rasa* and then itself
dismantled. In Donne's "The Progress of the Soul" (not the "Anniver-

sary'' but the stanzaic poem), Donne imagines the soul as a neutral animating spark, flitting from apple to bird's egg to wolf to ape to man, blithely independent, not partaking in the nature of any of its avatars. A first-person poem in which this soul talked about itself, investigating its remoteness from its incarnations, fretting about its untouchability, its inexpressibility, would bear some resemblance to *The Unnamable*.

Since everything that alters—the body's assuaging of its pains with other pains, the affections' vacillation from calm to irritation to calm, the mind's little games of redisordering the disorder—has been excluded from the subject, an ideal stasis is hypothesized. ''The foetal soul is full grown,'' as Beckett notes in the addenda to *Watt* (p. 248), citing Cangiamila and Pope Benedict XIV; therefore the Unnamable cannot develop, cannot learn, can only watch from the pit of his immutability the fierce mutation of images. Everything transitory is but a failed simile; but many of these likenesses try to give some impression of the rigidity, the abstraction, the impenetrability, the unchangingness of the soul, likenesses themselves refined almost down to the ether. The Unnamable describes himself as a weeping egg, his hair, nose, and genitals all fallen away, but dismisses that image as too dramatic, still overinflected, anthropomorphic:

> I'll dry these streaming sockets too, bung them up, there, it's done, no more tears, I'm a big talking ball, talking about things that do not exist, or that exist perhaps, impossible to know, beside the point. Ah yes, quick let me change my tune. And after all why a ball, rather than something else, and why big? Why not a cylinder, a small cylinder? An egg, a medium egg? No no, that's the old nonsense, I always knew I was round, solid and round, without daring to say so, no asperities, no apertures, invisible perhaps, or as vast as Sirius in the Great Dog, these expressions mean nothing. All that matters is that I am round and hard, there must be reasons for that, for my being round and hard rather than of some irregular shape and subject to the dents and bulges incident to shock, but I have done with reasons. [*The Unnamable*, pp. 305–6]

He feels an obscure satisfaction in utter featurelessness, in being a sphere, closed but enclosing nothing, a figment of geometry; he wants to approach the limit of simplification, of stylization. He imagines himself as a Cycladic doll, a Brancusi ovoid, a bowling ball, anything sufficiently stark and inane that nothing can be said about it.

Although the Unnamable cannot develop, the novel of which he is the protagonist does develop, by the following principle: the efforts he makes to free himself from fictions generate more fictions. Every evasion of personality, every declaration of nonadherence, implicates the evader in a new personality, just as Worm, crawling away from the light, away from birth, puts himself in danger of getting born. To escape from the frame story, in which Malone, Mercier and Camier, and the rest orbit about him as if he were the sun, central and unapproachable, to which they all referred, the Unnamable attends to the story of Mahood, whose progressive loss of limbs gives a more satisfying approximation of featurelessness, of deprivation. When Mahood grows too engaging, vivid, urgent, restless, he is forsaken for Worm, the most annulled persona in Beckett's fiction. When even Worm seems too substantially animate, human, acquires the faculty of hearing, he disappears in favor of a long welter of momentary apparitions, abandoned as quickly as conceived. This series of personas is an interminable regression, a reeling backward, for each adhesion, each revulsion, creates a new adherer, a new revolter, who in turn must be repudiated:

> The third line falls plumb from the skies, it's for her majesty my soul, I'd have hooked her on it long ago if I knew where to find her. That brings us up to four, gathered together. I knew it, there might be a hundred of us and still we'd lack the hundred and first, we'll always be short of me. Worm, I nearly said Watt, Worm, what can I say of Worm, who hasn't the wit to make himself plain, what to still this gnawing of termites in my Punch and Judy box, what that might not just as well be said of the other? Perhaps it's by trying to be Worm that I'll finally succeed in being Mahood, I hadn't thought of that. Then all I'll have to do is be Worm. Which no doubt I shall achieve by trying to be Jones. Then all I'll have to do is be Jones. [*The Unnamable*, p. 339]

If Mahood and Worm are adduced as expressions, there is still a third entity unexpressed; if Mahood and Worm and Jones, a fourth; if a hundred, a hundred and first; the soul, naked and essential, the very unnamability of the Unnamable, will elude every proffered embodiment. *The Unnamable* is a long accelerando in which these figments are rejected at increasing speed and keep growing briefer, lighter, less passionate, more transparent and dreamlike, as the Unnamable drops his extended accusations of his surrogates in favor of the plasticity, incredulity, quick suppleness of the nominative.

Yet not until the end does the Unnamable relinquish his hopes for self-expression—what he calls birth. In certain of his moods he wishes to be born; not born as a human being, blatant, extensive, and perishing, but born featureless, neuter, reticent, immobile, born as an icon of the soul's abstraction from life, born unbearable. This desire for an expression of his inexpressiveness leads to his astonishing fantasy of Worm:

> One alone, then others. One alone turned towards the all-impotent, all-nescient, that haunts him, then others. Towards him whom he would nourish, he the famished one, and who, having nothing human, has nothing else, has nothing, is nothing. Come into the world unborn, abiding there unliving, with no hope of death, epicentre of joys, of griefs, of calm. Who seems the truest possession, because the most unchanging. The one outside of life we always were in the end, all our long vain life long. Who is not spared by the mad need to speak, to think, to know where one is, where one was, during the wild dream, up above, under the skies, venturing forth at night. The one ignorant of himself and silent, ignorant of his silence and silent, who could not be and gave up trying. Who crouches in their midst who see themselves in him and in their eyes stares his unchanging stare. [*The Unnamable,* pp. 346–47]

Here is the lapsed man, the constructed resident of a lapsed world, the genius of apathy, the empty slate upon which human feelings can never be inscribed, the zero man. Like Mr. Endon in *Murphy,* he embodies the felicity of unbeing, but Worm is less determined, less finished and rigid, more susceptible to corruption; he is only an infantile nothing, maintains his nothinghood weakly, dumbly, is in great danger of falling into being. The Unnamable is tempted to adhere to Worm, to declare that Worm is he; but, alas, even this minimal expression is impossible to sustain, for the conception of oneself as traitless, persona-less, is itself a persona. To venture even this far into self-expression is to provide opportunities for further definition, further deformity, further expansion. The soul that can identify itself as Worm has taken the fatal step that leads to birth, to "the blaze, the capture and the paean" (p. 366), to the vicissitudes of mortality, to the Samuel Beckett known to the international press. But the step cannot be taken, for the soul's incapacity for embodiment supersedes even the most blanched, tiny, frigid, embodiment; to the one who must remain at absolute zero, even such symbols as the sphere, the goose egg, the round 0 must falsify.

When the Unnamable imagines himself, or Worm, getting born, acquiring a body, developing human traits, he nevertheless hopes that this elaboration will constitute a birth into nonentity:

> If I speak of a head, referring to me, it's because I hear it being spoken of. But why keep on saying the same thing?

They hope things will change one day, it's natural. That one day on my windpipe, or some other section of the conduit, a nice little abscess will form, with an idea inside, point of departure for a general infection. This would enable me to jubilate like a normal person, knowing why. And in no time I'd be a network of fistulae, bubbling with the blessed pus of reason. Ah if I were flesh and blood, as they are kind enough to posit, I wouldn't say no, there might be something in their little idea. They say I suffer like true thinking flesh, but I'm sorry, I feel nothing. [*The Unnamable*, p. 353]

The noise. How long did I remain a pure ear? Up to the moment when it could go on no longer, being too good to last, compared to what was coming. These millions of different sounds, always the same, recurring without pause, are all one requires to sprout a head, a bud to begin with, finally huge, its function first to silence, then to extinguish when the eye joins in, and worse than the evil, its treasure-house. [p. 354]

Later he imagines that the embryo will grow legs to crawl away with, "fingers opening and closing to try and shut out the world" (p. 375). The body articulates itself not for the sake of deliberate action, locomotion, self-expression, but in order to prevent self-expression, to stifle; one grows a head in order to deafen the ears, to blind the eyes, a brain of thick straw to block out the clamor. The body is adduced to protect and obscure the soul, to insulate it, to tranquilize it; the soul, instead of exfoliating or organizing itself into a body, develops a system of defense that happens to require throat, head, arms, and legs. Yet once the soul has fallen into corporeality—as in the gnostic myth in which the spirit's lust for reflections, material images of itself, leaves it forever tainted, unable to extricate itself from the dirt in which it reveled—its body becomes an engine of torment instead of a bulwark of inviolability: the head, which ought to screen out sound, becomes a "transformer in which sound is turned . . . to rage and terror" (p. 356). It is the same tension we have often seen before, between the impossibility of expression and the obligation to express: every coordination of words that is supposed to reveal or embody the inexpressibility of things tends eerily to pervert itself into expressiveness. In Beckett's myth of art, the germ of the human is in the throat, the whole body sprouts from a tickling in the larynx; this irritation is the writer's obligation to express, from which shoot a thousand predicates, two arms, two legs, an entire self eager to parade itself in the fields of language; but then the strutter is denied, pronounced unreal, groundless, and after a great deal of surgery he is resolved into the inexpressive. Near the end the Unnamable urges himself to "Overcome . . . the fatal leaning towards expressiveness" (p. 390); but, despite his extreme tact, his niceness in undistinguishing himself, he feels tempted to exercise, excise, his larynx in an expressive act, a birth cry, a *vagitus*, a scream that would mark him irrevocably human:

> I alone am immortal, what can you expect, I can't get born, perhaps that's their big idea, to keep on saying the same old thing, generation after generation, till I go mad and begin to scream, then they'll say, He's mewled, he'll rattle, it's mathematical, let's get out to hell out of here, no point in waiting for that, others need us, for him it's over, his troubles will be over, he's saved, we've saved him, they're all the same, they all let themselves be saved, they all let themselves be born, he was a tough nut, he'll have a good time, a brilliant career, in fury and remorse, he'll never forgive himself. [*The Unnamable*, p. 383]

This, of course, is another version of the scream of the early story "Assumption," the cry that says everything, from which unfolds the whole man, a killing birth. It is doubtful that, by the last page, the Unnamable has succeeded in making this omnipotent scream, though he practices little expressive noises, "nyum, hoo, plop, psss, nothing but emotion, bing bang, that's blows, ugh, pooh, what else, oooh, aaah, that's love, enough, it's tiring" (p. 408), a preface to full expression. But there is a sense in which *Molloy, Malone Dies,* and *The Unnamable,* taken together, are an acceptable metaphor for that great shout by which Samuel Beckett could constitute himself verbally, could *express,* at the same time that they prove definitively that expression is impossible, as if we beheld a personality, down-stopped to blackness, grown vivid and exact in the instant of its vanishing.

As the protagonist of a story, the Unnamable is not quite unprecedented. In Dostoevski's *Notes from Underground,* for example, we also study a furious first-person narrator, so self-engrossed that he seems perpetually surprised, modified by what he writes, queasy with his own verbality. He experiments with his identity by means of his colorful predicates of degradation; indeed, his fascination with the ease of talking about himself seems to lead him to ever more fantastic fabrications. Yet one can meet Dostoevskian wretches at many cocktail parties, whereas no one, I hope, has ever been introduced to anyone reminiscent of the Unnamable.

What would the Unnamable look like? If Moran, having long ago abandoned the search for Molloy, were assigned to find the Unnamable and, by some miracle, perhaps with the aid of a microscope or an electroencephalograph, did blunder across him, what would he see? The Unnamable posits a great variety of appearances, among them Mahood, Worm, a deaf half-wit with a big blubbering red mouth (p. 390), but these unsettled descriptions all shrink away from the mind that tries to grasp them. Between the extremes of "I'm in words, made of words, others' words, what others . . . I'm the air, the walls, the walled-in one" and "I'm a wordless thing in an empty place" (p. 386)—between the extremes of being merely the text of the novel, the whole dictionary, and of being extrinsic to words, unrelated to anything that the novel alleges—there is no possibility of resting in a definite shape, the little graybeard into which Proteus settles when asleep. Either all allegations are true or none of them is; the reader is not permitted to pick his favorite incarnation and call the rest lies.

Yet I believe Beckett gives us a clue about the Unnamable's objective appearance: he would look like Mr. Knott in *Watt* (1943–45), Beckett's last novel written in English:

> With regard to the so important matter of Mr. Knott's physical appearance, Watt had unfortunately little or nothing to say. For one day Mr. Knott would be tall, fat, pale and dark, and the next thin, small, flushed and fair, and the next sturdy, middle sized, yellow and ginger, and the next small, fat, pale and fair, and the next middle sized, flushed, thin and ginger, and the next tall, yellow, dark and sturdy. [*Watt,* p. 209]

It goes on like that for two more pages—Mr. Knott is exceedingly various in appearance, with few stable, endearing traits by which one might remember him from one day to the next:

> For daily changed, as well as these, in carriage, expression, shape and size, the feet, the legs, the hands, the arms, the mouth, the nose, the eyes, the ears, to mention only the feet, the legs, the hands, the arms, the mouth, the nose, the eyes, the ears, and their carriage, expression, shape and size.
>
> For the port, the voice, the smell, the hairdress, were seldom the same, from one day to the next, to mention only the port, the voice, the smell, the hairdress.
>
> For the way of hawking, the way of spitting, were subject to daily fluctuation, to consider only the way of hawking, and of spitting. [*Watt,* p. 211]

Yet he does have one characteristic gesture:

> None of Mr. Knott's gestures could be called charac-

teristic, unless perhaps that which consisted in the simultaneous obturation of the facial cavities, the thumbs in the mouth, the forefingers in the ears, the little fingers in the nostrils, the third fingers in the eyes and the second fingers, free in a crisis to promote intellection, laid along the temples. And this was less a gesture than an attitude, sustained by Mr. Knott for long periods of time, without visible discomfort. [*Watt,* p. 212]

In that gesture of shutting every orifice of the senses, he assumes the iconic aspect of some of the Unnamable's poses, his eggheads and talking balls. And the stream of thought in Mr. Knott's mind is perhaps just such a monologue as *The Unnamable* itself; for the Unnamable's futile metamorphoses of identity are tangibly embodied in this phantasmagoria of shifting eyes, noses, body types, clothes, resident in a room full of pieces of furniture stood upright or on their sides or upside down, fed with a gruel consisting of the whole periodic table of the elements. If the Unnamable can say of himself "I'm all these words,"Mr. Knott is the man to whom any conceivable words refer; if the Unnamable can call himself a "wordless thing," Mr. Knott is the unspecifiable made flesh, for no particular verbal description can hold him for more than an instant. He keeps aberrating, exuberating beyond the range of language, and Watt, attempting to describe him to his friend Sam, is forced to an increasingly deformed, preposterous sort of speech:

> Dis yb dis, nem owt. Yad la, tin fo trap. Skin, skin, skin. Od su did ned taw? On. Taw ot klat tonk? On. Tonk ot klat taw? On. Tonk ta kool taw? On. Taw ta kool tonk? Nilb, mun, mud. Tin fo trap, yad la. Nem owt, dis yb dis. [*Watt,* p. 168]

This is English, spoken doubly backward, a retrograde inversion. It reads:

> Side by side, two men. All day, part of night. Dumb, numb, blind. Knott look at Watt? No. Watt look at Knott? No. Watt talk to Knott? No. Knott talk to Watt? No. What then did us do? Nix, nix, nix. Part of night, all day. Two men, side by side.

This rigid permutation of speech reminds us that Knott is himself a mathematical figment, an imaginary limit to the process of characterization itself, the Everyman in whom are rolled up all the characters of all possible novels, the whole spectrum of the human, from infrared to ultraviolet, assumed into white light. *Watt* indeed threatens to grow infinitely protracted in the pages that describe Knott: he is a black hole into which ascriptions fall without leaving a trace, a man who could eat the whole dictionary, the whole of Borges's Library of Babel, and still clamor for more. His odd exclamations, "Exelmans! Cavendish! Habbakuk! Ecchymose!" (p. 209) perhaps suggest this insatiable greed for vocabulary, this urge that, concerning him, nothing be left unsaid. Knott is one of Beckett's triumphs, a verbal construct that resists embodiment in words, that swallows up language.

Of course Knott seems like a god. His name suggests a divine nonentity; and Beckett uses the imagery of First Corinthians when Watt comes near him: "little by little Watt abandoned all hope, all fear, of ever seeing Mr. Knott face to face" (p. 146); "the few glimpses caught of Mr. Knott, by Watt, were not clearly caught, but as it were in a glass, not a looking-glass, a plain glass, an eastern window at morning, a western window at evening" (p. 147). The eye dazzles at Knott, evades him, refuses him; how could one look face to face at a face at once thin-lipped and thick, blue-eyed and brown, a face trembling into another face, a human oxymoron? Language also cannot confront Mr. Knott; but, as we know, neither can language confront a pencil or a stick any more effectively. The sidelong glance, bababababa, is the best that eye and mouth can offer. Mr. Knott, from whom all words deflect, stands for the general impermeability of things, the impotence of description; he is an effrontery to fiction, a novelistic outrage. In Forster's *A Passage to India* (1924), which is, like *Watt,* a novel in which traditional storytelling swerves into an initiation into metaphysical ultimates, in which language disarticulates itself in an echo's dead cry, a Hindu sage tells some Europeans, investigating the attempted rape of an Englishwoman, that, according to his philosophy, everyone is equally guilty when an evil act is done, that evil is only a condition that expresses Lord Krishna's absence. *Watt* teases the reader into thinking that he will solve the mystery of Watt's employer, Mr. Knott, but it offers only the spectacle of Mr. Knott's unspecificity, his indivisibility, his being everybody, his immanent absence. As Mr. Knott comes near, the whole apparatus of discrete personages behaving characteristically breaks down; he absorbs Watt, his other servants, minor characters like the hunchback Mr. Hackett, whom he never meets, all of whom sink into his abyss of traitlessness, a background so black with figures that no figure can be distinguished against it. As with Professor Godbole's indiscriminate, smearing love in *A Passage to India,* as with the echoes in the Marabar Caves, something happens in a narration that calls the whole narrative mode into question, renders narration impossible. But, whereas Forster fell into silence, Beckett began *Molloy,* then *Malone Dies,* experiments in which all the characters in a novel are resolved into the temporary inventions of a mind that discredits them, abuses them, cannot keep them distinct from itself, asks them to disappear.

The distant ancestor of Mr. Knott is the nineteenth-century conception of the genius, the Renaissance man, adept in the whole of the human, polymath, full of *terribilità*. Technically Mr. Knott has a good deal in common with such modern sophistications of the genius-protagonist as the Goethe of Mann's novel *Lotte in Weimar* (1939). Goethe and Mr. Knott are swollen, shapeless, so distended with predication that they are cosmos more than man. Mann and Beckett have used similar techniques for opposite ends: Mann would enhance what Beckett would diminish; yet Mann and Beckett agree in that they would construct an ultimate figure that no subsequent novel could surpass. Goethe is the proud epitome of our race; Mr. Knott illustrates the factitiousness of the devices of characterization used by novelists, embodies the inability of the imagination to discriminate one man from another, the chaos of personality that underlies the incised gingerbread men of traditional fiction. Mann wishes his reader to ignore his technique of contradictory descriptions and to feel the impression of a hero so pumped full of indiscriminate power that the stars shine from the heaven of his eyes; Beckett wishes his reader to feel the absurdity of his technique so keenly that Knott's divinity will disperse into incoherence, will reveal the replete void to which our blather about human beings refers.

I know of only one novel before *Watt* in which a character like Mr. Knott appears, not to glorify mankind but to reveal its impoverishment: Kafka's *The Castle* (1922). The protagonist of the novel, K., has received a commission to survey the lands around the castle; the order is signed illegibly, but he is assured that the signature is that of the very high official Klamm, to whom he seeks, for the rest of his life, in vain, to speak, in the hope that Klamm can deliver him from the inexplicable abuse he meets in the course of trying to fulfill his duty, to discover what his duty is. Near the beginning Klamm's ostensible mistress, Frieda, who becomes K.'s mistress, allows K. to glance through a peephole at a man said to be Klamm: K. sees an unexceptional fellow, "middle-sized, plump, and ponderous" (p. 47), with a smooth face, cheeks flabby with age, pince-nez awry on his nose, a black moustache. Later K.'s landlady—another former mistress of Klamm's—denies that he has in any sense approached Klamm and tells him, "You're not even capable of seeing Klamm as he really is...I myself am not capable of it either" (p. 64). This, of course, strains K.'s credulity, but all the villagers speak of Klamm similarly:

> his appearance is well known in the village, some people
> have seen him, everybody has heard of him, and out of
> glimpses and rumors and through various distorting fac-
> tors an image of Klamm has been constructed which is
> certainly true in fundamentals. But only in fundamentals.
> In detail it fluctuates, and yet perhaps not so much as
> Klamm's real appearance. For he's reported as having
> one appearance when he comes into the village and
> another on leaving it, after having his beer he looks dif-
> ferent from what he does before it, when he's awake he's
> different from when he's asleep, when he's alone he's
> different from when he's talking to people, and—what is
> comprehensible after all that—he's almost another per-
> son up in the Castle. And even within the village there are
> considerable differences in the accounts given of him,
> differences as to his height, his bearing, his size, and the
> cut of his beard. Fortunately there's one thing in which
> all the accounts agree: he always wears the same clothes,
> a black morning coat with long tails. Now of course all
> these differences aren't the result of magic, but can be
> easily explained; they depend on the mood of the ob-
> server, on the degree of his excitement, on the countless
> gradations of hope or despair which are possible for him
> when he sees Klamm, and besides, he can usually see
> Klamm only for a second or two. [*The Castle*, pp. 230–31]

This visual elusiveness, this incomprehensible mutability of appearance, brings us to the threshold of Mr. Knott. K.'s friend Olga cannot
decide here whether the observer's gaze is distorted by his own emotion, or whether Klamm's aspect really does alter; but in either case
Klamm hovers just beyond the range of apprehension, tantalizingly
near although no eye can focus on him and no one can approach him
"face to face." His name connotes tightness or clamping and can be
translated either by the noun *cleft* or by the adjective *clammy;* if he is
Lord Cleft, it suggests that he is the abyss into which human life falls,
an emblem of lapse, an animate rift-design; if he is Lord Clammy, it
suggests a certain insectile or froglike quality, and indeed he is in a
perpetual state of metamorphosis, a larva or tadpole that never quite
fixes its shape, a true amphibian of the spirit.

Like Mr. Knott, Klamm is a creature of contradiction. K.'s landlady
tells him that, once Klamm stopped summoning her to be his mistress,
she knew she would never see him again:

> He knew nothing about me by that time. The fact that he
> had ceased to summon me was a sign that he had forgot-
> ten me. When he stops summoning people, he forgets

them completely. I didn't want to talk of this before Frieda. And it's not mere forgetting, it's something more than that. For anybody one has forgotten can come back to one's memory again, of course. With Klamm that's impossible. Anybody that he stops summoning he has forgotten completely, not only as far as the past is concerned, but literally for the future as well. [*The Castle*, p. 108]

Klamm is the most powerful man known to the villagers, in control of all their destinies; yet his obliviousness is absolute, impenetrable. K. imagines him as an eagle, thinks of his "remoteness, of his impregnable dwelling, of his silence, broken perhaps only by cries such as K. had never yet heard, of his downward-pressing gaze, which could never be proved or disproved" (p. 151); yet Olga tells him later that Klamm can see nothing without his glasses, that his "eyes are almost shut, he generally seems to be sleeping and only polishing his glasses in a kind of dream" (pp. 234–35). Klamm's relation to the villagers is complicated; with his nearsighted eagle eyes he beholds every detail of the lives of people he has utterly forgotten.

The strangest feature of Klamm, though, is that despite his unattainability, his remoteness, many of the characters of the novel seem to express his presence, even seem to look like him. After Frieda has set up housekeeping with K., she grows haggard, less animated; K. wonders whether she is deteriorating because of Klamm's absence, whether she had seemed "so irrationally seductive" (p. 179) to him in the first place only because of her proximity to Klamm—it is as if Klamm were an abstract principle of vitality, the soul's vigor. Similarly, K.'s assistants, two annoying buffoons, seem oddly attractive to Frieda, even though she despises them; they become sexual, irresistible, because "Klamm's glance . . . sometimes runs through me from their eyes" (p. 183). Much later the assistants are called puppets who give "the impression of not being properly alive" (p. 305); and indeed all the characters in the novel are stick figures except for the animating spark of Klamm. This is clearest in a canceled passage—I mean a passage locally canceled, for the whole *Castle* is a canceled passage, consigned by Kafka to be destroyed—in which K. and Frieda kiss, slide to the floor, fumble "at each other hastily, breathlessly, anxiously, as though each were trying hide in the other, as though the pleasure they were experiencing belonged to some third person whom they were depriving of it" (p. 459). Sexual intercourse is vicarious; Klamm is the true referent of all human emotion. In this way Klamm absorbs into his amplitude Frieda, the landlady, the assistants, even K. himself, who are but debased expressions, rudimentary, haphazard, provisional, of Klamm, who remains above them, divine and ignorant. It is as if the characters of the novel must learn to overcome the illusion that they are individuals, distinct persons, must learn to subsume themselves into the great blur, the multifarious Klamm.

I doubt that *Watt* would have been possible without the example of *The Castle;* both novels illustrate the abdication of finite expressions in favor of the inexpressible, the never-to-be-approached. There is in both novels a yearning for the sublime, in a specialized sense. Charles Rosen, discussing the harmonic structure of Schoenberg's *Erwartung,* speaks of the ideal "consonance" as "chromatic saturation," the sounding of all twelve tones of the chromatic scale at once. Klamm and Mr. Knott are chromatically saturated characters: all the vocabulary that can be employed in describing human beings is sounded at the same time. Kant speaks of the mathematical sublime as that shudder we feel when contemplating the infinitude of starry space; Klamm and Mr. Knott are the personal equivalent of this, the human sublime, against whom men are simple, limited, trite, as if only the unspeakable were worth speaking.

Both Klamm and Mr. Knott are the inventions of authors who feel a certain hatred of the image, of the imagination. Nothing with a definite shape, a specific trait, can satisfy; only what has a tinge of the indeterminate, the unintelligible, will give pleasure—as Malone says, "a touch of the unimaginable . . . that would do me good" (*Malone Dies,* p. 236). This distrust of the image is by no means rare in writers beset with intuitions of the inconceivable; the Shelley who has his Demogorgon assert, "the deep truth is imageless," who employs in his "Hymn to Intellectual Beauty" such bright fleeting similes that they provide an iridescence rather than an image of Intellectual Beauty; the Lawrence who begs his wife in "Image-Making Love" to love *him* rather than an image of him, the same plea that Porphyro makes of Madeline in Keats's "Eve of St. Agnes," all use the gifts of the imagination in a deliberately tentative, suspicious manner. In *The Unnamable,* as we have seen, the faculty of making images is considered extrinsic to the man himself, a plague on him. But the fullest description I know of the operation of the imagination in both its creative and its hateful aspects is Nabokov's *Lolita.*

Lolita in no sense demands to be read as an allegory; it makes perfect sense as a realistic tale, a case history of a real pervert, his real adolescent victim, and a real but bizarre playwright with whom the pervert competes; but much of the richness of the novel springs from its allegorical undermeaning, the story of the liberation of the Image from the artist who conceived her, Galatea and Pygmalion once again, with the secondary complication of Pygmalion shooting the male muse of sculpture. At the beginning Humbert sees Lolita as a transcendental incarnation; indeed, in the first line of the novel he calls her "my soul." It is not necessary to take this description as entirely figurative, for the child of Charlotte Haze, the commonplace American teenager, becomes an almost accidental pretext for an act of creation, a neutral doll transfigured, quickened by Humbert's fantasy; after his first, chastest consummation of his desire, he says of her:

> I felt proud of myself. I had stolen the honey of a spasm without impairing the morals of a minor. Absolutely no harm done. The conjurer had poured milk, molasses, foaming champagne into a young lady's new white purse; and lo, the purse was intact. Thus had I delicately constructed my ignoble, ardent, sinful dream; and still Lolita was safe—and I was safe. What I had madly possessed was not she, but my own creation, another, fanciful Lolita—perhaps, more real than Lolita; overlapping, encasing her; floating between me and her, and having no will, no consciousness—indeed, no life of her own.
>
> The child knew nothing. I had done nothing to her. And nothing prevented me from repeating a performance that affected her as little as if she were a photographic image rippling upon a screen and I a humble hunchback abusing myself in the dark. [*Lolita*, p. 64]

She is, more than a girl, a filmed image; and through much of the novel Lolita seems to have a photographic more than a corporeal reality, capable of enlargement, tight focus—even, in the case of Humbert's fantasy of begetting upon her two or three more generations of nymphets, reprinting. This colorful specter is slowly animated, made congruent with the "real" Lolita, who is, as in similar stories of the relation of the artist to Image, such as Mann's *Tristan* and *Death in Venice*, oddly pliable, *complaisante*, though she differs from Tadzio and Frau Klöterjahn in that she retains a stubborn ordinariness, refuses to become absorbed into his fantasy. She obliges him sexually, but not with a swooning, a lapsing, only with a giggle, or a yawn, or a shiver of fear. Nevertheless, what he wants has *exactly* come to pass: the artist has taken an Image and made it real, human. Alas, she is too real, too human, an obstinate creature; but this is the price the miracle demands.

The imagination at its zenith has invented, animated, a little girl; how, then, is it to keep itself busy after its great deed? It seems to have no further useful function; having created Lolita, it can think only of depraving her, debasing its own Image. Artifice, when it intrudes on human life, grows oddly dangerous in the fables of many modern writers; one appreciates all the more the tact of Stephen Dedalus in neglecting to offer a dinner invitation to the girl on the beach. Humbert's sexual relation with Lolita coincides with the emergence of the monstrous Quilty, who seems to represent Humbert's imagination grown detached, impersonal, horrifying. Nabokov himself states in his afterword to *Lolita* that art includes "curiosity, tenderness, kindness, ecstasy" (p. 317), an ample description of what is valuable in life as well as in art; but Quilty is narrower, a pure principle of play, of combinational genius, apathetic, amoral, careless of the human. Quilty is Ariel. Humbert, contemplating Quilty's handiwork, the tissue of puns and allusions he leaves behind as a tease for Humbert in the paper-chase scene, seems to regard Quilty as a kind of alter ego:

> The clues he left did not establish his identity but they reflected his personality, or at least a certain homogeneous and striking personality; his genre, his type of humor—at its best at least—the tone of his brain, had affinities with my own. He mimed and mocked me. His allusions were definitely highbrow. [*Lolita,* p. 251]

"Homogeneous" is perhaps the wrong word; to me, Quilty, when he at last appears in person, seems a grab bag of miscellaneous affectations, a conglomeration of literary styles, inconsistent not only in his French accent but in his very being; even the prospect of his imminent murder is only another occasion for joking and posturing. He often claims that he is playwright, and at one point he even pretends he will help Humbert construct a convincing scenario for killing him. They struggle not only over the pistol, but also over which one of them will exert artistic control over the unfolding scene—clearly Quilty wishes it to be just the sort of unreal and farfetched drama he specializes in, in which cork bullets trickle slowly onto the floor, in which nothing serious, no genuine death, can happen. In all these aspects, Quilty may be seen as a personification of the imagination, for his whole demeanor is fantastical. In his final plea for his life he tempts Humbert with baroque sexual delights:

> By the way, I do not know if you care for the bizarre, but if you do, I can offer you, also gratis, as house pet, a rather exciting little freak, a young lady with three breasts, one a dandy, this is a rare and delightful marvel of nature. Now, *soyons raisonnables.* You will only wound me hideously and then rot in jail while I recuperate in a tropical setting. I promise you, Brewster, you will be happy here, with a magnificent cellar, and all the royalties from my next play—I have not much at the bank right now but I propose to borrow—you know, as the Bard said, with that

cold in his head, to borrow and to borrow and to borrow. There are other advantages. We have here a most reliable and bribable charwoman, a Mrs. Vibrissa— curious name—who comes from the village twice a week, alas not today, she has daughters, granddaughters, a thing or two I know about the chief of police makes him my slave. I am a playwright. I have been called the American Maeterlinck. Maeterlinck-Schmetterling, says I. Come on! All this is very humiliating, and I am not sure I am doing the right thing. Never use herculanita with rum. Now drop that pistol like a good fellow. I knew your dear wife slightly. You may use my wardrobe. Oh, another thing—you are going to like this. I have an absolutely unique collection of erotica upstairs. Just to mention one item: the in folio de-luxe *Bagration Island* by the explorer and psychoanalyst Melanie Weiss, a remarkable lady, a remarkable work— drop that gun—with photographs of eight hundred and something male organs she examined and measured in 1932 on Bagration, in the Barda Sea, very illuminating graphs, plotted with love under pleasant skies—drop that gun—and moreover I can arrange for you to attend executions, not everybody knows that the chair is painted yellow— [*Lolita,* pp. 303–4]

At this Humbert kills "Clare the Impredictable"—a portmanteau word that includes, as Alfred Appel points out, the meaning "impredicable." In a sense Quilty is a worthy companion of the impredicables Klamm and Mr. Knott; for Quilty, like them, has exhausted all combinations, embodies a paradox (the impotent orgiast), exists only as the locus of a nervous and jejune shifting of images. But whereas Watt founders on Mr. Knott and K. on Klamm, Humbert destroys Quilty.

The shooting of Quilty is not a renunciation of art but a defense of it. Imagination is necessarily a restless faculty; having seized upon an image, the imagination will tinker with it, deform it, stretch its neck out like that of Tenniel's Alice, cast it aside for a more novel image. This is intolerable in art as well as in human life; the artist must somehow refine, record, freeze what the imagination has given him, an activity in which the imagination will only be a distraction, a multiplier of chimeras. Therefore, just as Humbert must learn to love the actual Lolita, descended from fancy into flesh, "Ninety pounds... sixty inches" (p. 259), finally dirty and pregnant, aging, with blue, ropy veins, extraterrestrial no longer, so the artist must dismiss the imagination and its mischievousness, what Auden's Simeon calls the imagination's vain fornication with its images. The imagination, grown runaway, giddy, cacophonous, becomes for many modern writers a voice that must not be attended to with perpetual care; and silence, so estimable at times, may become simply a ground against which some cry, some finite image, may be heard. O Word, thou word that I lack; in that lament the word fails, but vibrates, grows rich in overtone, expressive from the quaver in the voice that cannot pronounce it.

Bibliographical Notes

This book is to some extent an attempt to update or revise the chapters on the twentieth century in Erich Auerbach's celebrated study of Western literature, *Mimesis*—a whole body of modern criticism has already arisen to accomplish this task—but it is also an attempt to apply the devices of recent art criticism to literature and music. Such books as Rudolf Arnheim's *Art and Visual Perception: A Psychology of the Creative Eye* (Berkeley: University of California Press, 1974) and his *Visual Thinking* (Berkeley: University of California Press, 1969) try to display the means by which images are defined, constituted, by the imagination. Arnheim presents the findings of gestalt psychology and their relations to the acts of invention of the artist; any reader interested in the processes of image formation will find much here to engage him. (Beckett, for example, began his career as a novelist with a discussion of gestalt psychology, in the opening pages of *Murphy,* where figures are always disappearing into grounds; Murphy even mentions the name of the famous gestalt investigator Herr Koffka.) Other books of art criticism I have consulted with pleasure

209

include E. H. Gombrich's *Art and Illusion: A Study in the Psychology of Pictorial Representation* (New York: Pantheon Books, 1960); his *The Sense of Order: A Study in the Psychology of Decorative Art* (Ithaca: Cornell University Press, 1979) (certain recent authors, such as Donald Barthelme, seem to construct their fictions in a fashion analogous to Gombrich's principles of decoration: framing and filling-in); and M. L. d'Otrange Mastai's *Illusion in Art: Trompe l'Oeil: A History of Pictorial Illusionism* (New York: Abaris Books, 1975).

CHAPTER 1

My citations from Kandinsky's *Concerning the Spiritual in Art* are from the Dover edition (New York: Dover Publications, 1977). Other works cited are Thomas Mann's *Doctor Faustus* (New York: Modern Library, 1966), W. H. Auden's *The Dyer's Hand* (New York: Random House, 1962), *Collected Longer Poems* (New York: Random House, 1965) and *Collected Shorter Poems* (New York: Random House, 1966), and the following works by or about Schoenberg:

Schoenberg, Arnold. *Style and Idea*. Ed. Leonard Stein, trans. Leo Block: London: Faber and Faber, 1975

———. *Letters*. Ed. Erwin Stein, trans. Eithne Wilkins and Ernst Kaiser. London and New York, 1964.

Adorno, Theodor W. *Philosophy of Modern Music*. Trans. Anne G. Mitchell and Wesley V. Blomster. New York: Seabury Press, 1973.

Reich, Willi. *Schoenberg: A Critical Biography*. London: Longman, 1971.

Rosen, Charles. *Arnold Schoenberg*. New York: Viking Press, 1975.

Steiner, George. *Language and Silence*. Harmondsworth: Penguin, 1969.

The most pleasant way to acquire the texts of Schoenberg's vocal settings is to buy records of his music. The eight volumes released by Columbia (now CBS) Records contain, for the most part, excellent performances by Robert Craft and Glenn Gould and include informative essays, many of them by Robert Craft; alas, some of these volumes are out of print. The LaSalle Quartet's recording of Schoenberg's string quartets includes a superb documentary study, edited by Ursula v. Rauchhaupt (Deutsche Grammophon 2713 006). As for *Moses und Aron*, I recommend Pierre Boulez's version (Columbia M2 33594), which includes an engaging essay by Harry Halbreich. David Atherton's recording of Schoenberg's complete chamber music contains a few rarities and provides the purchaser with a copy of the essay by Alexander Goehr cited at the beginning of my chapter (London/Decca SXLK-6660/4). Readers interested in technical discussions of Schoenberg's music may consult the various articles of Milton Babbitt, Dika Newlin, and George Perle.

CHAPTER 2

Defoe's *A Tour through the Whole Island of Great Britain* may be found conveniently in the Everyman's Library edition (London: J. M. Dent and Sons, 1962). The citations from Heidegger's *The Origin of the Work of Art* (trans. Albert Hofstadter) are from *Philosophies of Art and Beauty*, ed. Albert Hofstadter and Richard Kuhns (New York: Modern Library, 1964). The citations from George Eliot's *Adam Bede* are from the Signet Classic edition (New York: New American Library, 1961). The passage by Virginia Woolf is from *Moments of Being* (New York: Harcourt Brace Jovanovich, 1976).

In the following list of Nabokov's works cited in my text, I have chosen the editions, often paperback, most likely to be owned by a large number of readers. The dates on the left are, whenever possible, the dates of composition of the works, not the dates of publication. These principles are followed for the other chapters as well.

1925. "A Guide to Berlin." In *Details of a Sunset and Other Stories*. New York: McGraw-Hill, 1976.

1932. *Despair*. New York: Capricorn Books, 1965.

1934. *Invitation to a Beheading*. New York: Capricorn Books, 1965.

1935–37. *The Gift*. New York: Capricorn Books, 1970.

1938. *The Real Life of Sebastian Knight*. New York: New Directions, 1959.

1939–40. "Ultima Thule" and "Solus Rex." In *A Russian Beauty and Other Stories*. New York: McGraw-Hill, 1974.

1946. *Bend Sinister*. New York: McGraw-Hill, 1974.

1948. "Signs and Symbols." In *Nabokov's Dozen*. New York: Popular Library, 1958.

1949–54. *Lolita*. My citations are from *The Annotated Lolita*, ed. Alfred Appel, Jr. New York: McGraw-Hill, 1970.

1962. *Pale Fire*. New York: Berkley Medallion Books, 1968.

1966–69. *Ada*. New York: McGraw-Hill, 1969.

1972. *Transparent Things*. New York: McGraw-Hill, 1972.

1974. *Look at the Harlequins!* New York: McGraw-Hill, 1974.

Autobiography. *Speak, Memory: An Autobiography Revisited*. New York: Pyramid Books, 1968.

Interviews. *Strong Opinions*. New York: McGraw-Hill, 1973.

Biography. Andrew Field. *Nabokov: His Life in Part*. New York: Viking Press, 1977.

Criticism. Nabokov himself recommended the works of Alfred Appel, Jr., and Andrew Field.

CHAPTER 3

Kafka's works cited in the text:

1905. "Description of a Struggle" ["Beschreibung eines Kampfes"]. In *The Complete Stories*, ed. Nahum N. Glatzer. New York: Schocken Books, 1971.

1908. "Wedding Preparations in the Country" ["Hochzeitsvorbereitungen auf dem Lande"]. In *Complete Stories*.

1911–12. *The Man Who Was Never Heard from Again* [*Der Verschollene*]. Trans. Willa and Edwin Muir as *Amerika*. New York: Schocken Books, 1962. Kafka tried desultorily to complete the manuscript for a few years after 1912.

1912. *The Judgment* [*Das Urteil*]. In *The Penal Colony: Stories and Short Pieces*, trans. Willa and Edwin Muir. New York: Schocken Books, 1961.

1912. *The Metamorphosis* [*Die Verwandlung*]. In *The Penal Colony*.

1914. *In the Penal Colony [In der Strafkolonie]*. In *The Penal Colony*.

1914–15. *The Trial [Der Prozess]*. Trans. Willa and Edwin Muir. New York: Schocken Books, 1968.

1915. "Blumfeld, an Elderly Bachelor" ["Blumfeld, ein älterer Junggeselle"]. In *Complete Stories*.

1917. "The Cares of a Family Man." ["Die Sorge des Hausvaters"]. In *The Penal Colony*.

1917. "The Great Wall of China" ["Beim Bau der Chinesischen Mauer"]. In *The Great Wall of China: Stories and Reflections,* trans. Willa and Edwin Muir. New York: Schocken Books, 1970.

1917. "A Report to an Academy" ["Ein Bericht für eine Akademie"]. In *The Penal Colony*.

1917. "Reflections on Sin, Pain, Hope, and the True Way." ["Betrachtungen"] In *The Great Wall of China*.

1919. *Letter to His Father [Brief an den Vater]*. Trans. Ernst Kaiser and Eithne Wilkins. New York: Schocken Books, 1970.

1920. "He" ["Er"] (a collection of aphorisms). In *The Great Wall of China*.

1922. *The Castle [Das Schloss]*. Trans. Willa and Edwin Muir. New York: Schocken Books, 1974.

1922. "A Hunger Artist" ["Ein Hungerkünstler"]. In *The Penal Colony*.

1922. "Investigations of a Dog" ["Forschungen eines Hundes"]. In *The Great Wall of China*.

1923. "The Burrow" ["Der Bau"]. In *The Great Wall of China*.

1924. "Josephine the Singer, or the Mouse Folk" ["Josephine, die Sängerin, oder Das Volk der Mäuse"]. In *The Penal Colony*.

Miscellaneous writings. *Dearest Father: Stories and Other Writings*. Trans. Ernst Kaiser and Eithne Wilkins. New York: Schocken Books, 1954.

Diaries. *The Diaries of Franz Kafka: 1910–1913*. Ed. Max Brod, trans. Joseph Kresh. New York: Schocken Books, 1974.
   The Diaries of Franz Kafka: 1914–1923. Ed. Max Brod, trans. Martin Greenberg, with the cooperation of Hannah Arendt. New York: Schocken Books, 1974.

Letters. *Letters to Milena*. Ed. Willi Haas, trans. Tania and James Stern. New York: Schocken Books, 1970.
   Letters to Felice. Ed. Erich Heller and Jürgen Born, trans. James Stern and Elizabeth Duckworth. New York: Schocken Books, 1973.

Biography. Max Brod. *Franz Kafka: A Biography*. Trans. G. Humphreys Roberts and Richard Winston. New York: Schocken Books, 1960.

Memoir. Gustav Janouch. *Conversations with Kafka: Notes and Reminiscences*. Trans. Goronwy Rees. New York: New Directions, 1971.

Criticism. Two well-known, brilliant studies of Kafka are Erich Heller's *Franz Kafka* (New York: Viking Press, 1974) and Walter Sokel's *Franz Kafka* (New York: Columbia University Press, 1966). These succinct guides introduce Kafka well. I also recommend Ronald Gray's *Franz Kafka* (Cambridge: Cambridge University Press, 1973), a sober, straightforward account, and James Rolleston's *Kafka's Narrative Theater* (University Park: Pennsylvania State

University Press, 1974), a book that treats Kafka in the tradition of literary criticism to which American readers are accustomed. Wilhelm Emrich's *Franz Kafka: A Critical Study of His Writings,* trans. Sheema Zeben Buehne (New York: Fredrick Ungar, 1968), is a Teutonic, often labored, sometimes bizarre book, but one that addresses itself to important matters that do not seem to be discussed elsewhere. I do not recommend the psychoanalytic studies of Kafka that I have seen.

CHAPTER 4

The citations from Joyce's *A Portrait of the Artist as a Young Man* are from the usual edition (New York: Viking Press, 1963). The passage by Pater is from *The Renaissance,* Mentor edition (New York: New American Library, 1959). Beckett's works cited in the text:

1929. "Dante ... Bruno. Vico .. Joyce." In *James Joyce/Finnegans Wake: A Symposium.* New York: New Directions, 1972.

1929. "Assumption." *Transition* (Paris) 16–17 (June 1929):268–71.

1930. *Proust.* New York: Grove Press, 1931.

1933. *More Pricks Than Kicks.* New York: Grove Press, 1972.

1935–37. *Murphy.* New York: Grove Press, 1957.

1943–45. *Watt.* New York: Grove Press, 1959.

1945. "La peinture des van Velde; ou, Le monde et le pantalon." *Cahiers d'Art,* 1945–46, pp. 349–56.

1946. *Mercier and Camier [Mercier et Camier].* New York: Grove Press, 1974.

1946. "First Love" ["Premier Amour"]. In *First Love and Other Shorts.* New York: Grove Press, 1974.

1947–48. *Molloy.* In *Three Novels.* New York: Grove Press, 1965.

1948. *Malone Dies [Malone meurt].* In *Three Novels.*

1949. "Three Dialogues" (with Georges Duthuit). In *Samuel Beckett: A Collection of Critical Essays,* ed. Martin Esslin. Englewood Cliffs, N.J.: Prentice-Hall, 1965. The original source is *Transition Forty-nine,* no. 5 (1949).

1949–50. *The Unnamable [L'Innommable].* In *Three Novels.*

1952. *Texts for Nothing [Textes pour rien].* In *Stories and Texts for Nothing.* New York: Grove Press, 1967.

1959–60. *How It Is [Comment c'est].* New York: Grove Press, 1964.

1965. *Imagination Dead Imagine [Imagination morte imaginez].* In *First Love.*

1966–70. *The Lost Ones [Le Dépeupleur].* New York: Grove Press, 1972.

1969. *Lessness [Sans].* In *New Statesman,* 1 May 1970, p. 635.

Poems. *Collected Poems in English and French.* New York: Grove Press, 1977.

Biography. Deirdre Bair. *Samuel Beckett: A Biography.* New York: Harcourt Brace Jovanovich, 1978.

Criticism. There is a wide variety of attractive books on Beckett. A few of them are:

Abbott, H. Porter. *The Fiction of Samuel Beckett: Form and Effect.* Berkeley: University of California Press, 1973.

Cohn, Ruby. *Back to Beckett*. Princeton: Princeton University Press, 1974.

————. *Samuel Beckett: The Comic Gamut*. New Brunswick, N.J.: Rutgers University Press, 1962.

Federman, Raymond. *Journey to Chaos: Samuel Beckett's Early Fiction*. Berkeley: University of California Press, 1965.

Fletcher, John. *The Novels of Samuel Beckett*. London: Chatto and Windus, 1964.

Harvey, Lawrence E. *Samuel Beckett: Poet and Critic*. Princeton: Princeton University Press, 1970.

Kenner, Hugh. *A Reader's Guide to Samuel Beckett*. New York: Farrar, Straus and Giroux, 1973.

————. *Samuel Beckett: A Critical Study*. New York: Grove Press, 1968.

A fine study of the origin of Beckett's ideas about the lack of efficacy of language (and therefore the lack of efficacy of verbal images) can be found in an article by Linda Ben-Zvi, "Samuel Beckett, Fritz Mauthner, and the Limits of Language," *PMLA* 95, no. 2 (March 1980): 183–200. The best comparison I know of the works of Beckett and Kafka—very little has been done on the relation of Nabokov to either author—is by Ruby Cohn: "Watt in Light of *The Castle*," in *Comparative Literature*, vol. 8 (Eugene: University of Oregon Press, 1961).

Index

Adorno, Theodor, 19, 23, 25, 30, 35, 37, 45; *Philosophy of Modern Music*, 16; "Schoenberg and Progress," 19
Aesthetic novel (nineteenth century), 129
Aesthetic refuge: Beckett haunted by, 156; in figurelessness, 172–75; its impossibility, 174–75; *l'azur* as, 156
Allegory, in *Lolita*, 204–7
America: in *Amerika*, 108, 111; in European literature, 108
Amis, Kingsley, 75
Amphion, 156
Appell, Alfred, 207
Aristotle, 192
Arnold, Matthew, *1853 Preface*, 160
Art, 148–49; to Beckett, 162; Beckett's myth of, 196; its danger, in *Lolita*, 207; its defense, in *Lolita*, 207; as destruction of art, 148; as distortion of expression, 127; gap between conception and execution of, 145–46; its odd gracelessness, 145; as idolatry, 7; its incapacity to represent, 164; Kafka's parable about the nature of, 165; modern, 162; abolishes meaning, 154; as more than reality, 30; as self-cancellation of the artist, 125, 147, 148; as self-contradiction of the artist, 125–26; as self-effacement of the artist, 143–44; self-expression in, as death, 155; as transpersonal, 146
Artaud, Antonin, 147
Artist: as alchemist, to Schoenberg, 26–27; depersonalized in *Malone Dies*, 185; the Heideggerian artist, 81; Malone as,

215

159–60, 185; his strange stance toward objects, in Beckett, 157; Schoenberg's parable of, 21; secret glorification of in "Three Dialogues," 167–68

Auden, W. H., 68–69, 135, 188–89; on Christian art, 48; *For the Time Being,* 139, 207; "The I without a Self," 112–13, 171–74; "The Quest," 99; *The Sea and the Mirror,* 49–51, 69, 70, 74, 78, 83, 105–6, 145; "Words," 100

Autobiography, 9; Beckett's fiction as, 171–72, 180, 188–89; impossibility of Beckett's narrators constructing, 176–77, 195; Kafka's fiction as, 108, 116

Babel, 107, 113–15, 200–201

Bach, Johann Sebastian, 5, 49; *Saint Matthew Passion,* 171

Bair, Deirdre, 166, 188, 189

Balzac, Honoré de, *Le chef-d'oeuvre inconnu,* 1, 2, 4–5, 6

Barth, John, 182

Barthelme, Donald: "Sentence," 182; "At the Tolstoy Museum," 66

Beckett, Samuel, 5–7, 8, 74, 121, 150–214
    his aesthetic: art as excrement, 162; art as failure of expression, 156, 193–97; artist's stance toward objects, 157; beauty of inanimate, 183, 187; self-expression as death, 155, 160 (*see also* "Three Dialogues")
    compared to Kafka, 136
    comparison of self with Schoenberg, 6
    detachment in, 173–74
    on Image (*see* Image)
    on Joyce, 2, 5, 177 (*see also* "Dante … Bruno. Vico.. Joyce")
    "Assumption," 154–56, 162, 174, 197
    "Dante … Bruno. Vico.. Joyce," 168, 177, 192
    "First Love," 164, 183
    How It Is, 166
    "Imagination Dead Imagine," 183
    "Lessness," 10
    Malone Dies, 6, 9, 10, 156, 157–60, 163–64, 165, 166–67, 169, 171, 172, 173, 174, 180, 183–90, 191, 194, 197, 200, 204
    Mercier and Camier, 157, 181–82, 194
    Molloy, 59, 156, 160, 171, 174–83, 186, 197, 200

Murphy, 162, 168, 173–74, 181, 189, 195
    "Not I," 183
    "Proust," 166–67, 169, 177, 178
    "Three Dialogues," 160–62, 166–67, 169, 170, 171, 172, 174, 192
    The Unnamable, 7, 157, 160, 165–66, 169, 170, 171, 173, 174, 185–86, 188, 190–98, 199
    Watt, 164, 193, 199–204, 207

Beethoven, Ludwig van, 15, 38, 45

Berg, Alban, *Lulu,* 19

Bergson, Henri, 166

Bettelheim, Bruno, *The Empty Fortress,* 137–38

Bioy-Casares, Adolfo, 3

Blaue Reiter, Der, 25, 28

Borges, Jorge Luis, 56; *Chronicles of Bustos Domecq,* 3; *Labyrinths,* 135; "Library of Babel," 200; "On Rigor in Science," 3; *Tlön, Uqbar, Orbis Tertius,* 3

Botticelli, Sandro, 153

Brancusi, Constantin, 193

Brecht, Bertolt, *The Three Penny Opera,* 68

Brod, Max, 111–12, 149

Browning, Robert, "Andrea del Sarto," 69, 168

Calvino, Italo, 135

Cangiamila, 193

Carroll, Lewis, 181; *Alice in Wonderland,* 133, 207

Cézanne, Paul, 6, 13, 160, 162

Chalfant, J. D., 14

Chateaubriand, François René (Vicomte de), 108

Chromatic saturation, theory of, 18–19, 33–34

Cinema, 143, 170

Conrad, Joseph, 66

Corinthians, 200

Craft, Robert, on *Erwartung,* 18

Criticism, Beckett vitiates, 162

Daedalus, 151

Dante Alighieri, 49, 100, 164, 192

Da Vinci, Leonardo, 57

Debussy, Claude, 29, 133

Defoe, Daniel, 167; on Stonehenge, 53–54

Dickens, Charles: *Amerika* as imitation

of, 108; *Bleak House,* 54–55

Donizetti, Gaetano, 38; *Lucia di Lammermoor,* 17, 33

Donne, John, "The Progress of the Soul," 192–93

Dostoevski, Fyodor, *Notes from Underground,* 197

Dumas, Alexandre (père), 152

Duthuit, Georges, "Three Dialogues," 160, 181

Eidlitz, Walter, 41

Eliot, George, 54, 55, 66; *Adam Bede,* 56–58, 62; *Middlemarch,* 54

Eliot, T. S., 14, 166; "Burnt Norton," 76; "East Coker," 46; "Little Gidding," 46; "Tradition and the Individual Talent," 160

Epictetus, 184

Escher, M. C., 14

Everyman, 199

Expressionism, 20; abstract, 13, 15

Fantasy, heroic and evasive, 85–86, 91–94; rules for distinguishing, 86–91. *See also* Nabokov

Faust, 2

Fiction: danger of, in Kafka, 132; generates fiction, 193; Kafka's last preoccupation, 143; self-dispelling of, in Beckett, 164; illusion of wholeness in traditional fiction, 165

Flaubert, Gustave, 58; *Madame Bovary,* 56

Forester, E. M., 55; *A Passage to India,* 200

Frankenstein, Beckett as, 169

Freud, Sigmund, 81, 117–18; Beckett's parody of, 162

George, Stefan, 26

Goehr, Alexander, 16, 25

Goethe, Johann Wolfgang, 26, 201

Golden calf, 40, 42, 44, 46

Gruen, John, 6

Heidegger, Martin: Heideggerian artist, 81; "The Origin of the Work of Art," 70–71, 78, 79, 82, 93. *See also* Rift

Helen, 152

Heller, Erich, 135

Herbert, George, 49

Hölderlin, Friedrich, 71

Huysmans, J. K., *A Rebours,* 129

Hyperrealism, 5; in painting, 12

Ictinus, 71

Image: Beckett's lack of, 154, 156–57, 162–64, 166–67; in Beckett's fiction, 171, 173, 189, 190, 199–200; Beckett and Schoenberg disgusted with, 6; false images in Kafka, 8–9, 138; and genius of imagination, 150–53; and imagination, 7; making and unmaking of, 10; as mediator, 151, 155; modern artists' calculated dispelling of, 9; in modern literature, 150–54, 159; parodied by Joyce, 153; Pynchon's treatment of, 153

Imagination, 129, 137–38, 139, 140, 141–42, 207–8; Beckett as realist of, 165; corruption of, 6–7; as corrupt, 153; not dead, 170–71; as destroyer, 7; and discipline of nonrepetition, 181–82; disinterested in images, 171; in *How It Is,* 166; and image, 7; in modern literature, 150

Inspiration: demonic, 20, 21; divine, 23–24; to Schoenberg, 20, 23–24; as seizure, to Beckett, 166

Inversion, 95, 123–26, 199

Jackdaw, Kafka as, 108, 136

James, Henry, 55

Janouch, Gustav, *Conversations with Kafka,* 102, 108, 110, 118, 126, 138, 140, 141, 143

Jarrell, Randall, 5

Jesenská, Milena, 117, 127

Joyce, James, 169; epiphanies in, 80, 81; Nabokov on, 93; *Finnegans Wake* (also mentioned as *Work in Progress*), 3, 5, 168, 170; *Portrait of the Artist as a Young Man,* 150–54, 155, 159, 170, 184–85, 186, 205–6; *Ulysses,* 55, 56, 153, 169

Kafka, Franz, 95–149
  abstraction in: abstract characters, 109–10; in "The Penal Colony," 124; Samsa's into silence, 120; the soul's abstracting, 138
  Babel in, 106–7, 113–15
  comedy in, 110, 118, 123; dark, 119;

high, of the spirit, 119; in *The Trial*, 127–28

and compulsion of the imagination, 8

gnostic tendency in, 97

images in: false, in *The Trial*, 129, 131; of spiritual truth, 140–41

inversion in, 95, 123–26

jackdaw, Kafka as, 108, 136

justice in, 124–26, 129–32, 133

lightness in: heaviness of world and word, 134; heaviness as measure of distance from the spirit, 97; protagonist becomes airy, 143–44; in relation to Kafka's tuberculosis, 134; world without gravity, 97–98, 122

maze in, 115; in "The Burrow," 137–38; in *The Trial*, 127, 128, 133

parable about nature of art, 165

on photography, 141–43

picaresque novel, subverted in, 111

playfulness in, 133

on Prague, 140–41

relation: in Kafka's fiction, 117–18, 120; of subordinate entities to protagonist (psychomachia), 116; protagonist as emblem of relation, 116

silence in: in "Investigations of a Dog," 145; in "Josephine the Singer, or the Mouse Folk," 144–48, 154; Kafka's own, 148; in *The Metamorphosis*, 120; in *The Trial*, 127–29

spectacle: theatrical, 118, 119–21, 124–25, 132; in his own life, 126, 147

spirit and the spiritual, 117, 141, 144; imperishable, 148; Paradise as imageless truth, 135; unrepresentable, 131, 141; in the vanishing, 141–43; world as its antechamber, 132

Amerika, 9, 108–15, 116, 118–19, 120, 126, 142; American characters in, 111

"Blumfeld, an Elderly Bachelor," 97–98

"The Bucket Rider," 96–97, 104, 133

"The Burrow," 114, 136–40

"The Cares of a Family Man," 101–3, 133

The Castle, 8, 97, 98, 108, 111, 114, 134–36, 201–4, 207

A Country Doctor, 133

"A Country Doctor," 133

Dearest Father, 96, 117

"Description of a Struggle," 103–7, 108, 109, 110, 115, 121, 133

Diaries I, 8, 100, 117, 136, 139, 143

Diaries II, 9, 22, 108

"Eleven Songs," 133

"First Sorrow," 99, 119

"The Great Wall of China," 103, 134

"He," 99–100, 108, 112, 138–39

"A Hunger Artist," 143–44, 148, 154

"Investigations of a Dog," 99, 115, 145

"Josephine the Singer, or the Mouse Folk," 144–48, 154

"The Judgment," 116–19, 143, 144; comedy in, 118, 120; Georg Bendemann as emblem of relation, 116

Letter to His Father, 119, 125–26, 128, 143

The Metamorphosis, 9, 119–24, 133, 143

"In the Penal Colony," 124–26, 127, 129; spectacle in, 119

"Reflections on Sin, Pain, Hope, and the True Way," 111, 141, 148; quoted, 95, 96, 97, 103, 107, 115, 123, 125

"The Refusal," 107

"Report to an Academy," 120, 123; spectacle in, 119

"The Top," 98–99

The Trial, 8, 127–33, 135; "Before the Law," 127, 131, 179; compared to aesthetic novels, 129–30; its theme of distortion of expression, 127; sex in, 128

"Unhappiness," 155

"The Warden of the Tomb," 107

"Wedding Preparations in the Country," disembodiment in, 121

Kandinsky, Wassily: on abstract design in art, 13; as apologist for abstract art, 7; compared to Beckett, by Beckett, 6; plea for nonrepresentational art, 160, 162; and Schoenberg, 25–27; on self-expression, 26; his tables of the emotional effects of colors, to Beckett, 6; on Cézanne, 13; on repetition of a word, 29; *Concerning the Spiritual in Art*, 25, 27

Kant, Immanuel, 11

Keats, John, 44, 204

Laing, R. D., 90

Language, 96, 207–8; as being or object, 168–69; as nonreferential, 170, 200

Lawrence, D. H., "Image-Making Love," 204
Leda, 152, 153
Lescaut, Manon (character in story by Abbé Prévost), 108
Lévi-Strauss, Claude, *The Savage Mind*, 13, 49
Levin, David, 40
Ligeti, Györgi, *Clocks and Clouds*, 15
Locke, John, 12, 61

Maeterlinck, Maurice, 169
Mahler, Gustav, 44, 52; "The World without Gravity," 96. *See also* Schoenberg, "Mahler"
Mallarmé, Stéphane, 156–57; "Les Fenêtres," 156
Mann, Thomas: on *The Castle*, 135; on subjectivity, 45; *Death in Venice*, 205; *Doctor Faustus*, 19–20, 45; Leverkühn, 30, 34, 36–37, 45–46; "Felix Krull," compared to *Amerika*, 110; "The Holy Sinner," 122–23; *Lotte in Weimar*, 201; *Tonio Kröger*, 110, 152; *Tristan*, 205
Masson, André, 162
Merleau-Ponty, Maurice, 10
Messiaen, Olivier, 52
Michelangelo Buonarroti, 65; his Moses, 41, 46
Milton, John, *Paradise Lost*, 2
Mimesis, 11–14, 68–69; antimimetic theme, 48–49; paradox of, 12–13, 166
Mondrian, Piet Cornelis, 160
Monet, Claude, 52
Monteverdi, Claudio, 15; madrigal passions, 37
Moses, 41, 46, 107
Mozart, Wolfgang Amadeus, 171; *La Betulia Liberata*, 11; *Zaïde*, 38
Munch, Edvard, "The Shriek," 19, 155, *See also* Scream
Music, twelve-tone, 6, 28, 33, 34–35, 37, 199, 204; Beckett's parody of, 181–82; Schoenberg's, to Beckett, 6
Myth, *The Unnamable* as, 192–93, 196

Nabokov, Vladimir, 119
   and diseases of the imagination, 6
   Ada, 68, 75–78, 81–82
   Bend Sinister, 94
   The Gift, 7, 64, 82, 85; Fyodor, 7, 58, 67, 89, 91, 92
   "A Guide to Berlin," 65, 90
   Invitation to a Beheading, 4, 69
   Lolita, 204–7; Quilty, 65
   Pale Fire, 7, 64, 75, 78, 82–86, 87–93, 176
   The Real Life of Sebastian Knight, 66, 93
   "Signs and Symbols," 93
   "Solus Rex," 86, 87
   Speak, Memory, 78–80, 81, 88
   Strong Opinions, 63, 64, 93, 169, 181
   Transparent Things, 10, 60–70, 74, 159
   "Ultima Thule," 86, 90
Narcissus, 9
Newman, Ernest, 15
Newton, Isaac, 36
Nietzsche, Friedrich, 155
Novel, aesthetic (nineteenth century), 129–30; picaresque, subverted, 111

Odyssey, The, 2
Old Testament, 124
Orpheus, 155
Ovid, 122

Pappenheim, Marie, 17
Paradise Lost, 2
Paradox of mimesis, 12–13, 166
Pasquini, Bernardo, 52
Pater, Walter: on form and content, 170; his Mona Lisa, 152, 153
Pencil, 60–71, 97, 157–60, 163, 164, 166–67
Plato, 15; Beckett's parody of, 178; Nabokov's reverse of, 68
Platonism, 99
Plotinus, 96
Poe, Edgar Allan, "The Fall of the House of Usher," 133
Pollock, Jackson, 13, 14, 15, 36
Popper, Sir Karl, 15
Pound, Ezra, *Cantos*, 2, 3, 5
Prévost, Abbé, 108
Proust, Marcel, 80, 166–67, 169
Prudentius, *Psychomachia*, 108
Psychomachia, 103–7, 110, 116–19, 127–33, 136–40, 143, 185. *See also* Prudentius
Pygmalion, 2, 6, 153, 169, 204
Pynchon, Thomas, *V.*, 153

Raphael (Raffaello Sanzio), 168

Realism, 141–49; in art, 2; Beckett as realist of the imagination, 165, 181–82; Beckett as realist of wordlessness, 165; Kafka's 95–96, 143; of *Lolita*, 204; as a vanishing from representation, 142–43. *See also* Hyperrealism

Reference, unavoidable, 14

Referent, Beckett strips language from its, 162, 165–66

Reich, Willi, *Schoenberg: A Critical Biography*, 22, 36

Relation: Beckett removes from readers' experience, 163; lack of, 172–73, 177; objects without, 164. *See also* Kafka, relation

Representation, 2–3; art's inescapable nonrepresentationality, in Beckett, 160–65, 177; danger of, to Kafka, 99–103, 105–7; dubiousness of, in *The Trial*, 130; always incorrect, 127, 129, 145–46; incorrect, as sign of lofty vision, 169; of light, 148–49; of unrepresentable spirit, 131; vanishes into representer, 189; vanishing as retreat from, 119–20. *See also* Kafka, lightness in

Rift (*Riss*), 73–74, 79; rift-design, 79, 81, 115, 125, 134; rift-experience, 80; of Kafka's fiction, 103; rift-line, 73–74

Robbe-Grillet, Alain, 58

Rosen, Charles, on harmonic structure of *Erwartung*, 18, 204

Sade, Donatien Alphonse (Marquis de), 129, 135

Saint Anne, 152, 153

Saint Anthony, 167

Saint Paul, 167

Salome, 154. *See also* Wilde, Oscar

Savonarola, Fra Girolamo, 153

Schoenberg, Arnold, 5–7, 11–51
  hatred of material, 26–27
  light in his music, 23–35
  and self-expression, 27–28, 44–45
  Book of the Hanging Gardens, 21
  "Composition with Twelve Tones" (essay), 34–35
  Der Glückliche Hand, 20–21, 22, 23, 24, 28, 31–32
  Die Jacobsleiter, 33
  Erwartung, 16–20, 21, 22, 29–31, 32, 33, 37, 155, 204

  Four Orchestral Songs, 33
  Gurre-Lieder, 21
  Harmonielehre (*Theory of Music*), 18, 33
  Kol Nidre, 24, 46
  Letters, 39, 41
  "Mahler" (essay), 37, 44
  Modern Psalm, 46–47
  Moses und Aron, 6, 21–22, 37–44, 45, 46, 47, 48, 51, 145–46
  "New Music" (essay), 31
  "Opinion or Insight?" (essay), 44
  Pierrot Lunaire, 22
  Quartets (string); First, 21; Second, 21; Third, 22–23; Fourth, 21
  "The Relationship to the Text" (essay), 23, 28, 29, 44
  Six Little Piano Pieces, 33, 34
  Six Pieces for Male Chorus, 40, 41
  Suite for Piano, 21
  A Survivor from Warsaw, 46
  "This Is My Fault" (essay), 27
  Verklärte Nacht. 21
  Von Heute auf Morgen (opera), 37

Schoenberg, Gertrude, 37

Schubert, Franz Peter, 26

Scott, Sir Walter, *Heart of Midlothian*, 2

Scream, 165, 197; in "Assumption," 155, 156, 162, 197; language comes to approximate, 165; in twentieth-century music, 19

Semiotics, 81

Seurat, Georges, 13

Shattuck, Roger, 147

Shelly, Percy Bysshe, 204

Silence: in Beckett, 154, 174, 200, 204, 208; in Kafka, 96, 120, 127–29, 144–49

Singer, Isaac Bashevis, 47

Sontag, Susan, 134

Spenser, Edmund, House of Alma, 108

Spinoza, Benedict (Baruch) de, 192

Steiner, George, "Language and Silence," 38

Sterne, Laurence, *Tristram Shandy*, 56

Stevens, Wallace, "The Idea of Order at Key West," 81

Stick, 157, 162–63

Strauss, Richard, 11, 31; *Der Rosenkavalier*, 15; *Intermezzo*, 37; *Salome*, 31; *Symphonia Domestica*, 15

Stream of consciousness, 11, 165

Sublime mockery of, 154–55, 156, 204

Swoon, 117
Symbolism (nineteenth century), 169
Symbolist poetry, 157
Synge, John M., *The Playboy of the Western World*, 118

Tenniel, Sir John, 207
Thomas, Lewis, 171
Tinguely, Jean, 125
Tolstoy, Leo, 164
Trompe-l'oeil painting, 14, 69, 82–83

Unmaking, 148–49. *See also* Art, cancellation and self-cancellation; Kafka, lightness in
Updike, John 55

Valéry, Paul, 135
Vampire, 152, 153
Van Gogh, Vincent, 70, 71, 73, 74, 82
Van Velde, Bram, 160, 162, 167, 171
Villiers de l'Isle-Adam, Auguste, 152

Wagner, Richard, 29; *Parsifal*, 111; *Ring des Nibelungen*, 15
Webern, Anton, 33; on twelve-tone music, 35–36
Wilde, Oscar: *Dorian Gray*, 9, 48, 152; *Salome*, 153
Williams, William Carlos, 5
Wittgenstein, Ludwig, 44, 162–63
Woolf, Virginia: *To the Lighthouse*, 152; *Orlando*, 59; *A Sketch of the Past*, 80–81
Wordsworth, William, 66

Yeats, William Butler, 165; on Pound, 2, 5; "The Circus Animals' Desertion," 162; *The King of the Great Clock Tower*, 180–81; "Rosa Alchemica," 169; *A Vision*, 2, 3, 5

Zeno's paradoxes, 135, 181
Zeuxis, 160

DO NOT REMOVE
SLIP FROM POCKET

DEMCO